The Trumpet

Its Practice and Performance

A Guide for Students

Howard Snell

Rakeway Music

First published in September 1997
(reprinted 1998)
Rakeway Music
The Red Barn Hollington Staffordshire

A Catalogue record for this book
is available from the British Library.

ISBN 0 9511 961 2 X

Printers and Sole Distribution Agents

Kirklees Music
609 Bradford Road
Bailiff Bridge
Brighouse
West Yorkshire HD6 4DN
Tel/Fax: 01484 722855

Dedication

To my wife, Angela.

Acknowledgements

Firstly, my thanks
to all the wonderful musicians with whom I have worked over the years,
and to my students, on whom I have practised.

Secondly,
for his defining ideas, I must mention
Dr. Keith Davids
from the Sports Science Department of Manchester Metropolitan University.

Thirdly,
I cannot thank **Margaret Veal** *and* **Jo Whiterod** *enough*
for their unstinting help, advice and criticism with everything, from
thousands of commas to the validity of ideas.

All quotations are acknowledged in the text; everything else is my responsibility.

Finally, my profoundest thanks go to my wife,
Angela,
for those everyday encouragements
and endless readings and re-readings of these pages.

The Trumpet - Howard Snell

'Howard has written the New Testament of Trumpet Playing. I urge every trumpet player to read this excellent book. All the fundamental Old Testament values are there, but the fog of ages is demystified in language and structures we can all understand.
Howard has laid bare the essentials for success. I have already started to use it as the basis for my own playing and teaching.'

John Wallace
Trumpet Soloist and Artistic Director of Brass at the
Royal Academy of Music, London

'Howard Snell draws upon his wide experience and uses his penetrating intellect to give young trumpeters a book which covers the essential areas of study which are more often inferred than expressed. His advice, some philosophical, some psychological, all practical, is of tremendous value to students and young professionals.
It has also to be said that Mr Snell's advice could be applied equally to any young musician.'

Denis Wick
Principal Trombone, London Symphony Orchestra (1957-1988)

'This book is a triumph and will be seen for years to come as 'the thinking man's Arban.'

Rod Franks
Principal Trumpet, London Symphony Orchestra

'I remember (Howard Snell) as a dominant hugely courageous player in the London Symphony Orchestra. He was also the most intelligent of players possessed of an enquiring analytical mind .... becoming an artist of real distinction, supreme accuracy in performance being allied to a fierce tenacity of purpose and the ability to concentrate, which is the hall-mark of the top professional. His new book - 'The Trumpet' - is the most remarkable of its type I have ever read.

For young aspiring professionals it is a fount of wisdom and observation for which he will be thanked every day of their working lives; for the professional even at the top of the trade, it contains reminders of the basic golden rules of positive thought and correct mental approach .... It is a book not just for trumpeters or brass players but for all performers. For the trumpeter it presents a pedagogy as complete as I have seen in print.

If it had existed forty years ago I would have been its first reader and disciple - it would have saved me several years of irritating frustration - but the book had to wait for Snell to live the experience, to formulate it, and here memorably to find the words.'

Elgar Howarth
Conductor, Composer and formerly
Principal Trumpet with the Royal Philharmonic Orchestra and the
Philip Jones Brass Ensemble

FOREWORD

1

This book is directed towards students of the trumpet from the time they decide to study it seriously until they are launched on professional careers. The initial decision is usually taken between the ages of fourteen and seventeen and is accompanied by the resolve to enter music college in order to make a career in music.

For many years I auditioned potential students for music college and was consistently concerned by the almost total lack of knowledge displayed by these candidates about life as a musician. This was quite apart from the knowledge of both trumpet playing and musical standards needed.

For the young trumpet player, still at school, and looking forward to a college career before becoming a professional, the glamour and excitement of being a musician must be supplemented by information about the day-to-day reality. At best, careers guidance on this subject is limited, while at worst it doesn't exist. This is not surprising or the fault of career guidance specialists, because the world of performing music in Britain is structured very informally, and has few clear paths of career progression. Only those who work in music discover the tracks through the jungle. In performance, for example, many of our finest performers have no academic credentials whatsoever, while many with good credentials are mediocre performers.

I set out my view of the key elements necessary to ensure the development of brass players in general, and trumpet players in particular, of whatever talent. In matters of actual playing I go as far as possible with general principles, but stop before the point of direct teaching. Even though I include exercises and routines for problem solving, the book is not in any way a tutor or method. Much that I have included may be of interest to student performers of all instruments.

This book is practical rather than academic and is centred around my playing and teaching experience. Its tutorial element, together with the music examples, are intended both to underline the basics of playing and to encourage creativity and realism in practising and performing.

I offer three main kinds of help in this book.

- The first helps the student to form a picture of what a trumpet playing career in music is like.

- The second offers exercises and routines. Some of these give immediate results, as long as the player is within realistic range of the solution. Others are for the longer term.

- The third sets out a background to which the student can relate his or her ideas of how to improve. To perform well, a player must prepare well, must learn how to ease off before performance, and then know how to play freely in a performance.

From the practical point of view, my ideas are based on observation of what the finest players do when they play and how I have assessed them at work during forty years as a professional musician. The main aim of the book is to show that significant improvement comes with the adoption of good habits over a long period.

From the theoretical point of view, good playing requires a network of skills. Networking activity between different parts of the brain amounts to 40% of its work. Every body-action is the result of a thought and its communication to the body; therefore the quality of an individual's thinking is vital. Patience, persistence and boldness rather than impatience, wavering, and fear are the qualities needed to bring about long term progress.

Awareness is the key to good performance of any kind. Within our awareness we must be able to focus attention on our chosen activity. When attention is at its strongest we call it concentration. The success or failure of the way we deal with these three states of mind - awareness, attention and concentration - determines whether or not our talents flourish.

I have always followed a wide range of interests, finding that they throw light on each other. Sports and games, for example, share a great deal of territory with the performing arts. In spite of superficial differences, all fields of human activity match up in a way which is fascinating and fruitful.

Human activities are rooted in the same sense of play by which all animals learn their skills. Performance *is* play, and should always be seen that way.

2

The Lay-Out of this Book

- The reader can use this book as

    1. A *Reference Book* for immediate help on single topics, not meant to be read through front to back.

    2. A *Practice Workbook.*

3. A **Set of Ideas** against which to measure their own.

4. A **Starting Point** for further research.

- The book is organised into general **Subjects**, divided into **Chapters** in alphabetical order. Each **Chapter** begins with a key sentence. Then follows the **Discussion** of the subject, with **Headings** placed in the text to allow the reader to find any topic at once. The **Subjects** are listed in the **Contents.**

- While **Chapters**, *and* **Headings**, can be read in isolation, all parts of the book hang together as a whole. It is only to help understanding that we make distinctions and focus closely on particular points of interest. The complete picture is the only thing that matters. **Each of these subjects is a different doorway into the same space.**

- The referential nature of the book means that there are deliberate duplications of points, ideas and wordings throughout. This occurs in order that each subject is presented reasonably complete in itself. **Cross References** are frequent should the reader wish to link to related Chapters. They are bracketed with the initials CR. These cross references underline the basic premise of the book: that music performance is a unified process and not a series of artificially assembled parts.

- I have included a little historical and theoretical information, together with personal views, some of which are not directly relevant to becoming a master player. My hope is that they will give leads which some readers will want to follow.

- The **Recapitulation** is placed at the end of the book and is its most concentrated reading. It summarises my views globally.

The Background to my Work as Musician and Teacher

My professional career began after training at the Royal Academy of Music in London, where I studied the trumpet with George Eskdale. He was at that time Principal Trumpet of the London Symphony Orchestra. The major part of my playing career was at the LSO, between 1960 and 1976, where I rose to the position of Principal Trumpet. For a period of five years I was also Chairman of the Board of Directors. As a concerto soloist, I recorded both in the studio and appeared twice on BBC television whilst also being active in contemporary chamber music and the commercial studios.

The second phase of my career started when I left the LSO in order to conduct. The life of an orchestral and studio musician had ceased to be stimulating. I founded the Wren Orchestra which linked up with London's Capital Radio to give hundreds of concerts and recordings over several years. During this time I also conducted and recorded with the Royal Philharmonic Orchestra, the Philharmonia, and the LSO and Philip Jones Brass Ensembles. Recently, as Musical Director of the English Haydn Festival for two years, I had the opportunity to focus on a composer whose music interests me particularly. I continue to be active as an occasional orchestral conductor with, among others, the London Mozart Players and the City of London Sinfonia.

After leaving the LSO I returned to an interest in brass bands, where I had played as a child. Since then I have conducted and developed a number of bands from moderate levels up into the highest rank in banding, including Desford Colliery, Britannia Building Society, CWS (Glasgow), and Eikanger Bjørsvik from Norway. Alongside my conducting I have arranged, composed and published a wide range of music for brass and brass band. Many of these works have now become part of the standard brass repertoire.

As a teacher I first taught privately in London, but latterly I have been associated with the Royal Northern College of Music. My former students are to be found in almost all of Britain's orchestras, and in many abroad.

CONTENTS

Section 5: Careers and Situations

Section 6: Attitudes, Strategy and Tactics

Section 7: Recapitulation

SECTION ONE

MIND SKILLS

INTRODUCTION

This group of chapters includes the mind skills which are not specific to the trumpet or to any other single instrument. They are interior mental skills, only able to be judged from the outside by the quality of the performer's work.

The chapter entitled 'Time and Rhythm' could arguably be placed in the Performance Section, but such is its closeness to 'Listening' that I decided to keep them together. The principles of 'Melody Playing and Phrasing' being similarly (surprisingly) close to 'Time and Rhythm' suggested also that these chapters should be together.

LEARNING MUSIC

The learning of music has two aspects. Firstly how to learn quickly, and secondly how to learn thoroughly. Both can be mastered easily.

Learning Defined

Learning is the acquisition of knowledge more or less permanently. The knowledge of a piece of music is created through a number of different learning processes, some physical, some intellectual. In practical performance terms, a well learnt work can be refreshed after a long break and then be performed within a matter of hours.

Speed Learning

Imagine the following scenario: you are a young player who has been asked to perform an unknown concerto at one week's notice. Excitement competes with uncertainty. Can you do it? The piece is difficult but not impossible, and the fee is not good. Forget the fee. Do it!

1. Establish a calm attitude to the task. (CR Anxiety control) Immediately the picture will become clearer and the outline of what has to be done will emerge.

2. Glance through the piece, and establish the whole picture. (CR Interpretation)

3. Expect to read fast. The professional expects, and is expected, to read fast, accurately and to play in the appropriate style within a couple of read-throughs at most. This expectation starts up the reading process with the right amount of urgency. (CR Reading Music)

4. Recognise the composer's patterns of writing. Unless it is a radical new work there will not be a great deal in an unknown piece that you will not have seen before. This is where your general knowledge, experience and previous study of repertoire will be invaluable.

5. While the player in the recording studio is reading-playing-and-forgetting in a short term situation, learning quickly but thoroughly needs the application of other skills. First impressions as to how to shape the music must become firm without delay. Check the section

on Interpretation. Use of the simple techniques suggested there will speed up effective learning.

6. Underlying all of this is the ability to memorise fast and recall accurately. Planned and timed memorisation sessions can concertina all of the necessary work. (CR Memory)

7. As soon as possible play through the music without interruption, in complete sections. Much of it will fall into place quickly, thus isolating the passages of critical difficulty. The inefficient learner fiddles with details while Rome burns.

8. In terms of detailed practice, do not waste time playing passages which are well within your grasp; focus on the difficult moments and mobilise all the most efficient practice techniques. In the section of exercises there are enough practice routines to solve most problems. Be imaginative about creating new ones if necessary.

9. If, on the brink of the performance there are still one or two problems left as yet unsolved, there are two courses open.

> Firstly, can the passage be bluffed and bullied through just by will power? All players have an unexplored frontier to their playing beyond which they would like to go. They know that to improve they have to go through it, and these are the right times to find that extra gear. Like sportspeople who occasionally perform beyond the limit of their previous ability, can you find the extra under pressure of the event?

> The big, unforgettable performances take place in unexplored territory. These are the opportunities which lift players, take them up onto the next level, and for which players should look out. Trust yourself to find something inside yourself that you didn't know you had!

> Secondly, as a fallback position, the player should also prepare possible (slight) changes to the 'impossible' moments. These opt-outs are there to be used should the player decide. A small change of note in a fast, very awkward passage, a note left out in a hidden corner - these are the tactics with which most professionals are familiar.

10. Finally the player must remember that it is a performance, not a play-through. The audience will have paid its money, and will expect high quality. Whatever misgivings and insecurities lie under the surface, the performer must carry off the event with panache and seeming confidence. The swan may be paddling furiously under the water, but the onlooker must see only the calm gliding effect. (CR Performance)

Thorough Long Term Learning

In the first stages always expect to learn a piece of music quickly. Two weeks for the preparatory stages of any standard work of major proportions is ample. If this is not possible the work should be put away till the player is nearer the work's level.

My preferred strategy is simple, whether for concert or audition pieces and excerpts. Work on it for a while, then rest it for a while. Come back to it, then rest it again .... and so on until the piece is totally secure. The rest periods are essential, as they allow the sub-conscious mind to sort and absorb the material which has been practised.

During my work as Principal Trumpet with the London Symphony Orchestra, I would look at the schedule some six months ahead, noting the pieces which I didn't know or hadn't played for some years. If necessary I would put in a few days' work on the most difficult passages, and then forget them until the concert rehearsals. What I had learned was that my sub-conscious mind would have absorbed the material and organised it ready for performance.

Since that time, particularly in my conducting work with brass bands, I have used this technique to prepare difficult works, or works in an unfamiliar idiom. Ensembles can be all at sea with a piece, only to find that on re-reading months later it has somehow fallen into place. This merely utilises the mind's ability, when left to itself, to absorb and order unfamiliar material. When the conscious mind worries about something, learning and improvement will not take place. The player becomes excellent at worrying! (CR Memorisation)

Learning: some Comments

Methods of learning are rarely taught in the education system at any point. How to learn should be the first subject on any curriculum. The fact that it is not points to the inadequacy of approach of most schools and educational establishments.

We learn well when we are interested. The flow of excitement which starts a child on musical activity can disappear very quickly. At this point it is necessary to impose a pattern of work on a talented child because of the need to develop patience, a skill which most of us have to learn.

On entry into the higher levels of education, the student is largely left alone. It is assumed that the student is competent, having got this far. This is a massively mistaken assumption. 'How-to-learn', the key skill for any student, is never covered. Somehow it is assumed that the school student and the college student will just 'learn'.

A commitment to learning is the best strategy for enjoyment of one's life and work. (CR Careers) The basis for learning is memory, both conscious and unconscious. Effective use of memory enables any person to achieve fulfilment: the better it works, the deeper the fulfilment. You will find many references to memory, to learning and to different kinds of thinking throughout the book, with repetition of information. The reason for this is that the mind's activity is a seamless thread which runs unbroken through all our interests and concerns, for an average of nearly eighty years! Is that important? (CR Memory)

As outlined in the section on Auralisation, for the fastest and most effective learning of music, firstly study the text without playing it. There are many benefits which follow from this practice.

1. The performer can be imaginative and adventurous with ideas of how to play the piece and not be hampered by playing the instrument at the same time. Most performers get to know a piece of music only while playing it. This means that during the early stages of learning, they are trying to take in what the composer is saying musically, whilst at the same time trying to play the instrument. This divides the player's attention.

2. It may be said that this is the normal way of learning a piece. I would reply that learning a piece without the hindrance of simultaneously playing it is far better. The player then knows exactly what to do when it comes to performing it. The actions taken to play will be wholly confident because the mind will have a strong, clear image of how the music should sound.

3. It is my contention that great players achieve musical mastery by thinking masterful musical thoughts. The player is wrong who thinks that when technical competence has been achieved expressive playing will follow. That particular type of player will never be more than competent, because that has been his or her goal. The players who play more expressively, or faster, or higher, or whatever, do it only because they think 'do it!' Wynton Marsalis improvises at such phenomenal speed because he is thinking that fast. He is not playing gibberish, or just rattling the valves and reading the shape; he means what he plays, and plays what he means. He intends it; he is thinking it. (CR Reading)

4. Auralisation (CR), the musical equivalent of visualisation (CR), can be carried out, with or without music, at any time, in any place. Such use of otherwise waste time, using situations where playing is not convenient, makes extra time for the busy player. I frequently ask my students to prepare a study or a piece for their next lesson, with the proviso that the first time it is to be played is at the lesson. The results are generally extraordinary for a first effort, and on some

occasions they could stand as a formal public performance. Before conducting I do all my preparation in my mind, running critical passages through time and time again after I have memorised them.

5. Auralisation will ensure success in performance. Unclear understanding of a difficult passage will almost certainly lead to inaccurate performance. One detail needs to be outlined here; when rehearsing silently, do not physically finger the passage, with or without the instrument, as this hinders learning. Think the fingering, but do not do it.

The nineteenth century pianist Paderewski, active in the more leisurely days of trains and boat travel, would often learn and memorise a new encore for the next concert, without playing it before the actual performance.

LISTENING

If there is one key skill necessary for musicians it is listening, the main controller of musical performance.

The Nature of Listening

Normal Listening

An audience listens to music as a whole experience. Musicians also listen to music in the same way, but have to learn how the experience is created. By this means a musician becomes a good performer.

Analytical Listening

Musicians must learn to hear the detail of music very precisely; by this means, the musician becomes a good technician. The exercises, loops and routines given in Practice: 2, 3, and in the Time Patterns at the end of the chapter on Time and Rhythm, achieve their results by forcing the player's attention to become as concentrated as possible. As soon as effective listening and understanding takes place, the body makes the right adjustments to solve almost all playing problems.

The Expert Player

There are two types of musical listening. Firstly, while practising, the expert player listens to his or her own work, compares it to the ideal present in the mind and then responds, altering it to bring it closer to the ideal. Other musicians' performances allow us to build up a musical picture of what is possible and so we develop better ideals ourselves.

Secondly, in performance, listening is the prime ensemble skill above all others. Musicians who listen to the other players in an ensemble as much as to themselves respond automatically to what they hear. The creation of musical rapport is instant. The will to listen brings its own instant reward.

All human performance is variable, which means that it can be better or worse than previously. Challenge, response, co-operation, question and answer all result from the interplay of awareness among a group of musicians. Any orchestra's quality of ensemble depends largely on the musicians' ability to listen to each other.

The quality of ensemble which results from good listening is entirely superior to that which results from visual clues such as time beats from the conductor's baton, or rehearsal instructions about tuning, etc. (CR Intonation) Feeling the music together gives an ensemble's playing a sensitivity far beyond that which can be initiated by a conductor talking, unless he or she is skilled with words. The expression of the music is then at its most natural and unforced. Players' body movements, very restrained but sympathetic to the music, can also help to create a shared approach.

To an expert orchestra or other ensemble, a conductor's time beating is largely an irrelevance. Good players rarely pay close attention to that aspect of the conductor's work. Setting tempi, handling changes of tempi and the use of gesture to indicate feeling and the progress of the music, these are the only occasional signs that expert players need in order to supplement *their* listening. The good conductor creates a stimulating framework for the players' listening and playing. He or she does not make any sound except by proxy through the players.

The Need to Develop Creative Listening

The need for today's player to develop very sharp listening and response skills is obvious, because the range of styles required of the modern player is wider than ever before. These can only be learnt by listening expertly and absorbing. Listen and listen again.

It is easy to imagine the difference between focusing the vision on a precise spot, and letting it become peripheral. (CR Anxiety Control) The same is true of the ear. It can be precisely targeted or it can be generalised. The expert musician develops wide-screen listening, within which his or her precise attention is constantly on the move, checking all points of reference.

While playing, the soloist must be listened to, followed and matched in expression. In other contexts he or she should expect to listen and fit with another instrument's solo. There will be contexts and repertoire where the ensemble perspective is constantly renegotiated, bar by bar. Much Renaissance and Baroque music springs to mind in this regard, for example, the Gabrielis' Canzonas.

The Inexpert Player

Without being able to listen and respond while playing, it is not possible to rise above a very moderate level of performance. Players who only have ears for themselves, and are unaware of all but the crudest traffic signals from the conductor, will be useless to their fellow players. Until they open up their awareness and attention to the whole ensemble they will remain forever imprisoned in the dullest musical mediocrity. Poor players all resemble each other in their unawareness of ensemble, intonation, and tone quality. (CR Awareness)

MELODY PLAYING AND PHRASING

Good melody playing is one of the basics of performance. In concerto and solo performance, or in chamber music, a high level of melodic skill is desirable. In orchestral playing it is less important for trumpet players: solo melodic writing for the trumpet is rarely extended beyond a few bars.

Some performers have a natural ability to play melodies well, while others have to develop it. It is achieved through a feeling for, and an understanding of, lyrical phrasing.

Warning

The arts of melody playing and phrasing are totally elusive to verbal description. What follows are some arrows and pointers to a territory beyond orchestral playing, which many trumpet players are reluctant to visit, as if it were somehow improper to be there and be caught playing beautifully.

My predecessor as Principal Trumpet at the London Symphony Orchestra, Willy Lang, was possessed of the most gorgeous trumpet sound that I have been privileged to hear in person, added to which was a touch for phrasing that turned base metal into gold.

Another giant, Harry Dilley, not particularly well known because he spent most of his career in the Royal Opera House Orchestra, had a wonderful talent for the long phrase which was only one part of his impregnable capability and musicianship.

If all this sounds too much like 'long ago and far away', unfortunately most of the finest exponents of melody playing and phrasing are just that. Today's players have other priorities. Recordings however return them to us if we wish. I can only recommend the young player to listen and listen again to as wide a range of performers as possible. My own preferences are for cellists and female singers.

The Note - *This first paragraph -The Note - is reproduced at the start of Time and Rhythm because of its equal relevance.*

A note has three parts, the relationships of which are infinitely variable

1. **The start of the note.** This is important both for its timing - the when-to-play-it factor - and for its kind of articulation - the how-to-play-it factor.

2. **The body of the note** is concerned with sound quality, and, when long enough, changes in dynamic.

3. **The ending of the note.** Like the start of the note, this is important for the when-to-stop and the how-to-stop.

Good players vary the relationships of these three parts in the same natural way that we shape and phrase our speech in normal conversation. Poor, anxious players sound wooden and stiff because they mishandle these relationships. In the same way, our speech is affected when we are nervous; we may speak in a monotone instead of freely and we may even forget or mispronounce words.

In a melodic passage, the body of the note is the most important part, the start and the ending normally being less prominent. On the other hand, in a short note in a rhythmic passage, the start of the note is the critical element. In rhythmic music, the longer the note, the more important the timing and character of its release becomes. In the brass music of John McCabe, for instance, the ends of long notes are notated with a short tied note defining the exact moment to stop. The release of the note, in both its timing and character, is as important as its start.

The relative prominence of one part of a note above the other two does not mean that the others should ever be neglected. In high quality playing these elements are all present, being continually ordered and re-ordered, note by note, by the musicianship of the player, in continuous response to the music.

Phrasing

Phrasing is the act of shaping a melody or melodic line both overall and in detail. It is achieved by varying time and volume in amounts too small to be notated. By subtly pushing and pulling both tempo and volume, we are able to show an individual expressive response to the music. A melody's full expressive value can only be revealed by effective phrasing.

Musicianly phrasing can make even a moderate melody seem better than it really is. When playing routine melodic studies such as those by Concone, the student should treat them as if they were by the greatest of composers. In the last analysis, the quality of phrasing in any kind of music can only be determined by its appeal to the listener's deepest feelings.

A Melody

A melody is a sequence of pitches with a beginning, a continuation and an ending, with a single musical character. Most people's idea of a melody is this complete-in-itself, enclosed shape. Expressive legato usually predominates over the rhythmic and staccato feeling.

A melody will have a number of phrases, each with its own phrase point, usually at the main cadence. The phrase point is the note or notes towards which the phrase naturally aims. Each phrase may or may not have a number of minor phrasing points. A good basic rule in playing traditional types of melodies is to minimise phrasing points within a smooth legato line, without emphasising them unduly. This gives a sense of continuity or wholeness to a melody, whereas strongly pointed, interrupted phrasing suggests the opposite.

Most melodies are made up of phrases which suggest the shape of a single curve up towards the phrase point. However where a melody or line is punctuated by minor phrasing points, the curve upwards can be also thought of as a series of smaller gestures leading up to the ultimate phrase point.

Final phrase points are most often long notes which fall away a little in volume and presence. Occasionally there will be a small group of notes leading away and downwards in feeling.

A Melodic Line

A melodic line has the characteristics of a melody but not necessarily with a beginning or an end. It may be picked up from one instrument and handed on to another. It can be as little as two notes or very long indeed, and unlike an enclosed melody its character can change dramatically as it proceeds.

A Theme

A theme can be either a melody, or a melodic line long enough to develop a clear character. It is usually of primary importance to the piece of music, providing material for development.

Many instrumental lines and themes can be angular in the extreme, particularly in modern music. Even in this situation the player must try to maintain a sense of continuity in the music.

A Motif

A motif is usually a fragment of a melodic line or a very short theme. Its chief characteristic is that it has a very obvious identity whenever used.

While the theme is regarded by academics as the most important element of symphonic writing, it is arguable that the motif has been even more important during Western music history. Much Renaissance, Baroque and Twentieth Century music is obviously motivic rather than thematic. It is also arguable that in Classical (and increasingly in Romantic) music, themes were just the carriers of motifs. For brass players, the name of Richard Wagner comes to mind most readily in this regard. His consistent use of motifs, many of which were conceived in brass sound, made him one of the two major forces to propel the brass to prominence in the orchestra. The other composer was Hector Berlioz, whose use of brass was equally compelling and revolutionary, but in an entirely different musical manner.

Good Melodic Playing

The main characteristic of good melody playing is a smooth sostenuto line. (See the section on Phrasing above.) Create the sound and its feeling in the inner ear during the instant before playing. Once the sound has been produced, carry it through each successive note rather than making a new sound on each note, grading it towards the phrase point, and then away, if necessary. This allows the quality of the performer's sound to be heard at its best, as a single uninterrupted line. (CR Practice)

The performer must use his or her imagination to find the character of the melody or line in order to show it to its best advantage. Any melody should be played as if the performer thoroughly loves it. A poor melody needs all the skill a performer can lavish on it. It is the height of professionalism to be able to make a moderate piece of music seem good. It is my view that the stronger the player's musical input, the less any technical blemishes will occur or matter.

Rubato must be within the natural boundaries of the tempo, as must any inflexions of the dynamics; any vibrato used must fit the character of the melody and not be used indiscriminately, note by note. (CR Time and Rhythm, and Vibrato)

Some Practical Points

- Take care to choose a breathing place which does not damage the composer's melodic line by breaking it when it should be sustained. If a breath has to be taken mid-phrase, do not soften or weaken the tone before the breath, but keep it full in order to create a bridge to the note after the breath. The listener's attention must be carried across the gap.

- When taking over a melodic line, it is essential that the incoming player is (1) aware of continuing in the same style as the outgoing player, maintaining the expressive style and detail for the sake of coherence (and musical good manners), and (2) ensures that the line is still alive and open when handed on to the incoming player. The parallel with a relay race is obvious.

- Smaller notes must never be neglected. In slower melodies, keep the small notes broad in tonal value if not length; they carry the melodic flow as much as the more obvious longer notes. In quicker music they must be clear.

- When working to find the character of a melody, play it through in different transpositions, as if looking at an object from different angles in order to really know it.

- Talented players will always invent new and interesting phrasings. The master player is always trying fresh ideas and musical sensations. When I first heard Timofey Dokshutzer play I was almost alarmed by the extravagance of the phrasing and the vibrato. I soon realised, however, that he had created a completely new world of expression for the trumpet.

- Do not confuse slurring marks with phrasing. Slurs signify an un-articulated legato.

- It should also be remembered that tenuto lines under a slur denote legato tonguing, and that staccato marks under a slur denote mezzo-staccato.

- Although it is not an exact parallel with a musical phrase, a simple sentence shows how phrasing can change meaning. Move the emphasis along the following sentence, word by word, finally add a question mark, then watch the meaning change constantly. 'The cat sat on the mat'. These changes of emphasis have the same effect as moving the underlying phrase points of a melody; they change the shape and musical 'meaning'.

- Good rhythm is vital to any melody, even when the mood is quiet and gentle. The progressions of groups of notes *towards* strong beats and minor phrase points are often neglected, because insecure performers tend to count *from* the previous strong beat or barline. This latter habit leads to dragging. Except when relaxing from the main phrase point, always try to *play towards* the next main beat or phrase point. The examples of music progressing *from* a beat are many less than those which progress *to* a beat, because the climax point of most phrases occurs at or about their end.

- When playing softer melodies, using the open, raised bell gives the audience the sound's full quality. Full beauty of tone is masked by the bell which is hidden behind the stand.

A Simple Exercise for Melody Shaping

The following phrase contains two minor, and two major emphasis points. Playing the phrase on one pitch, as in the first version, guides the player's attention to the shaping of the notes towards these points. The second version uses an adjacent note to bring in slurring. The third gives the actual phrase. This exercise is akin to miming - a dumb melody!

Example 1

MEMORISATION

Playing from memory brings many benefits to the performer and to the audience. All that is needed is the will and the patience to do it.

Making the Choice

Without memory we can do nothing. Most of our daily actions have been learned during childhood, deposited in memory ready to be recalled whenever needed. Everyday memory for routine subjects is casual and relatively easy. This applies whether it is physical memory such as for walking, or intellectual memory such as for arithmetic.

For specialist use in music performance memory must be developed much more methodically.

Facts about Memorisation

- Initially, spend short periods memorising, say ten minutes.

- Take a ten minute break.

- Revise the memorised material.

- Take an hour's break.

- Make a final review of the material.

- The next day do a similar review, by which time you should be almost there.

This initial short period can then be increased as the memory's power increases.

Types of Memory

For the musician there are, in practice, three types of memory:

1. The very short *see-and-forget memory* used for short term playing assignments. There is also a very valuable even shorter version of this which I call *snapshot memory*, discussed later.

2. The **working memory** of learned but un-memorised repertoire, which is effectively prompted by the music page.

3. Total and **permanent memorisation**, needing only the occasional refresher.

The First Stage in Memorisation: Inputting

Learning a piece of music so that it is known well enough to be read with ease involves passing it through short-term memory enough times for it to be firmly held in medium-term, or working memory. This is the type of memory used by orchestral players who know their orchestral excerpts reasonably well. The process can be speeded up if the musician makes a deliberate effort to remember while reading, as one does travelling along unfamiliar roads. (CR Learning) At this stage excerpts cannot be played safely without the copy as a prompt.

- As soon as a piece is thoroughly known, testing should begin to find out what has been memorised so far. Most players who have never tried to play from memory are surprised by the amount that they are able to recall, but in the first stages are also discouraged by the passages which have not stuck automatically.

- Conscious memorisation of those passages should then take place (see Facts about Memorising above). Focused, concentrated repetition is often enough, but can be backed up by taking a snapshot of the passage as a picture, which can be visualised, then read. This latter ability varies from person to person, but develops with regular use, as do all faculties!

- When a student stumbles during a first attempt to play from memory, I then ask to hear the passage sung or vocalised. This always results in a near perfect performance, to the renewed confidence of the student. Complete performance soon follows.

- Accompaniment during rests should be memorised. As a back-up in passages which are confusing, remember the bars' rest as a sequence of numbers. Identifying and remembering special cues is a further help.

- Every player naturally builds up his or her own mixture of techniques. All that is needed is the will to take the first steps, and not be discouraged by a few initial failures.

The Second Stage in Memorisation: Retaining

Most fully memorised material remains intact in the mind, needing only the occasional refresher.

In my experience material held in the working memory (2 above) needs more revision than that which is held in full performing memory. The student in the process of learning the orchestral repertoire must constantly revise the important excerpts.

The Third Stage in Memorisation: Recalling

The recall of memorised music can be strengthened by repeatedly running the music through in the mind, only taking care not to memorise in any errors. (CR Auralisation) Not only does this process allow the player to consolidate the memory of a piece of music without the instrument, but it gives opportunities for the player to try out different approaches, tempi, nuances, and other details.

If a player can imagine the National Anthem played through, then the Haydn Concerto will present no problem. The latter simply needs more work than the former.

Snapshots in Ensemble Performance

The habit of taking snapshots (short-term visual memorisations of awkward moments) is very valuable in ensemble performance of all kinds. Awkward rhythms, ensemble interlocking, rallentandi, accelerandi and changes of tempi are the moments when being aware of everybody around, including the conductor, is essential.

The Memory in Solo Performance

The value of solo performances played from memory cannot be overstated. Apart from the deeper knowledge of the music which it demands, and the eye-contact and interaction with the audience which it allows, by freeing the eyes the performer's mind is freed. The removal of the page as the main focus allows the performer to attend unhindered to the real business in hand: expressing the music to the listener. When the performer plays from the music it is inevitably a barrier to the audience. It is as if the performer is only allowing the audience to overhear a private read-through.

Playing from memory frees more than just the attention. It gives a general confidence which spreads to both the expressive and technical qualities of the playing. Would an actor appear on stage to play Hamlet with the script in hand? Tightness of breathing which naturally comes with close reading under pressure is removed. The opposite option then becomes available to the performer: to be able to look around the concert hall while playing, releasing the posture, the breathing and the vision.

Getting More from your Memory: Help It Along

Remembering to use memory may seem like a joke, but failing to remember is the primary reason for most performers' poor practising habits. In this case, write the practice schedules down! Inefficient practising leads to slow or stalled progress not just on memory playing, but on all fronts. In the chapter Practice: 1 (CR), I lay out a timetable for the use of time and the consistent coverage of all aspects of work-in-progress. This reduces the potential damage which poor memory can inflict on the student's efforts to improve.

READING MUSIC

Every student musician's reading skills should be continuously improved by regular practice.

Reading Defined

Reading is a learned skill in which the eye sees and the brain then recognises and interprets a wide range of symbols. As with all skills, repetition speeds up the process to a certain degree.

Exceptional speed is secured only by conscious effort. This is like word reading, where we progress to a reasonable degree without effort. To improve beyond the comfort zone, however, deliberate techniques must be adopted in order to achieve even greater speed and comprehension.

Sight reading, which takes place with unseen material, is dealt with later in this section, together with advice on practice methods.

Assessing the Standard

When I encounter a student whose reading is slow and inaccurate, I ask the question, 'Can you read music as easily as you read a newspaper?' If not, 'Why not? Do you seriously want to become a professional musician? That is the standard for quality professionals, every day of their lives. In the studio each title is read through once, and then recorded. In the concert hall there is a little more time but not much.'

The ability to read music instantly is one of the benchmarks of professionalism. To be the slowest reader in any ensemble is to have an unwelcome spotlight placed on you. (CR Professionalism, Careers)

Playing Improvement Linked to Reading Improvement

Reading the music is the prelude to playing, even though it takes place only a brief moment before. If that brief moment of reading is confused and uncertain, the act of playing will be badly affected by it. If it is incapable of recognising and sorting the written information quickly and accurately, the brain will be unable to send confident and positive instructions to the body as to what and how to play.

Therefore upgrading the speed and accuracy of reading skills will have a significantly beneficial effect on the performer's playing skills. Certainty in reading allows an immediate, comfortable technical relationship with the instrument.

The best sportspersons seem comfortable, sure, and unhurried. They are 'reading' their game with mental time to spare, therefore their physical movements are to the point, economical in effort, and precise in output. They are very intelligent in terms of their game, whatever one might think of some of them outside their sport.

The poor reader of music is always fumbling for the next solution, deaf to ensemble matters, intonation etc., in the desperate hurry to select the next note before nemesis. The poor sportsman is all arms and legs, uncoordinated, late and slow with responses and moves. Speed and certainty are an essential in any competent physical action, whether it is playing or walking. Speed playing forces the eye and mind to work faster. It will be obvious, therefore, that inadequate reading skill is one of the main barriers to playing progress. (CR Speed Playing and Recapitulation)

Achieving the Standard

At the highest level of professional playing, the daily combination of reading activity, together with the shortage-of-time discipline in professional music sessions, sharpen up reading to a great degree. The player with ambition must therefore have top quality reading ready for those few opportunities which occur. It is not good enough to wait until the chances appear and then learn to read well thereafter.

Most students (on all instruments) wake up to this matter very late in their time at college, usually after some embarrassment or other. The conversation with the teacher usually runs as follows, 'What can I do about my sight-reading, it's terrible!' 'Have you followed my advice and practiced sight-reading?' 'Er, no!'

A Sight Reading Crash Course for the Desperate Student

Every day set aside as many periods as possible (minimum four) of, say, fifteen minutes each. During those periods, read through previously unseen or unknown material, with the metronome set at the correct speeds.

- *The absolute priority is to read the rhythms correctly. The pitches will largely look after themselves.* (CR Practice and Practical Steps 3:2 below)

- *Do not stop in the course of a passage for any reason whatsoever, except a death in the family.*

- *Don't think or interfere, just do it!*

- *Expect to read well; there will be nothing on the page you haven't seen before.*

- *The reading material can be anything. Tidiness and quality of performance are of no importance whatsoever.*

- *The sole priority is to make the eye and the brain work faster. Treat the lazy eye/brain as muscles to be exercised vigorously. You will feel very tired after the exercise. (Brain work uses more energy than physical work.)*

- *Look back after a week and you will see an enormous difference. Continue the routine until you feel thoroughly in charge. (CR Progress)*

The only players whose reading will not dramatically improve with this treatment are those with eyesight problems of a medical nature, and those very few with musical dyslexia. I experienced an example of this latter condition with a player possessed of a fine sound and excellent musicality, but who could only play the note at which he was looking. The result was that while he was effective in slower music, faster tempi destroyed his playing in a devastating manner. This went together with a further problem, that he was unable to retain the patterns of scales and arpeggios other than the commonest. In some non-musical areas (for example, computers) his intelligence was very well developed indeed, but a career in music was not possible for him.

Further Reading Improvement

For further improvement, a more consciously considered course of action becomes necessary, based on a little knowledge.

The eye moves in stops and starts, not smoothly as most people imagine. Normally it can make up to four stops or fixations per second. At each stop, the eye focuses and takes in a small chunk of information, which is passed to the brain. Because of the time lapse involved between the sending and the processing of the information, the eye is able to move on to the next chunk. Control of seeing must be deliberately improved like all the senses.

Practical Steps for Reading Improvement

The eye receives the music symbols in chunks.

- The poor reader takes in one or two symbols at a time whereas the good reader takes in chunks or groups of notes. To improve, consciously take in larger and larger chunks. Quality, in terms of the effective scanning of detail, will also improve.

Control the speed and type of eye movement.

- Avoid the temptation to check back on material already passed and the speed of reading will improve.

- Use a slightly slower, smoother eye movement.

- 'Sweep' the page with more open (peripheral) vision. Avoid peering, and leaning forward anxiously.

- The habit of reading music without playing has untold benefits, not only for reading improvement, but also for making musical decisions, and developing interpretative ability. (CR)

Musical material consists of relatively few patterns.

- The instant recognition of rhythmic patterns is the key to all good reading. (CR Time Patterns) Almost all music is constructed from a very few symbols and patterns. These are then combined for the composer's purposes to be turned into sound.

- Consciously develop this ability in order that a *change in pattern, which is a main difficulty in reading music,* will happen without delay or hindrance. Again, read without playing. Set different patterns against each other in a wide variety of speeds. When a player knows these patterns perfectly and can recall them instantly at any tempo, then he or she is a good reader, and will almost certainly play well.

Use snapshot memorisation of short passages.

- Make a habit of snapshot memorisation of passages such as (1) the start of pieces, (2) new tempi, (3) difficult accelerandi and ritardandi, and (4) corners where full attention is needed for the performance. This habit, which is hard to start only for reasons of fear, leads to a significant improvement in performance.

- Avoid tunnel-vision reading, the unawareness which blots out the listening process. In normal reading, we can only play if the music is briefly memorised, while the next chunk is being processed. After being played it quickly vanishes without trace. Ask most orchestral players to play a substantial tutti passage from a repertoire work without the music, and unless he or she has made a deliberate memorisation of it, it is unlikely that they will be able to do it. The usual process of ensemble music reading is actually just sight-reading of familiar, as opposed to unseen, material.

The process of reading while playing is immensely complex. The linking together of different senses and parts of the brain is complication enough. Adding the act of playing to this process can only make one wonder at the miracle of the mind's capabilities when extended.

Linkage between the Senses

In common with all activity which needs co-operation between different senses, the separate parts must be made to function well in isolation, and then combined. Sight is our prime sense for the intake of information, and must be fully linked to the ear if musical skills are to be satisfactorily developed. (CR Auralisation and Visualisation)

The eye learns to hear and the ear learns to see.

STYLE AND STYLES

Individual players develop a style in accordance with their personality, and by which their playing is recognised. This is then varied by detailed changes (styles) to take account of the specific requirements of composers and historical contexts.

Choosing a Style

Players are led by their musical tastes and feelings towards certain repertoires and styles of playing. These determine their future field of performing. Whether a player's interest is in orchestral music, early music, chamber music, popular music, or a mixture, one of these categories will naturally predominate, and that is where the student must concentrate. A few players have a wide and successful crossover in their early years, but most will follow one main path and pursue it on an exclusive basis.

Each musical field has a different form of musical dialect. Musicality in one dialect may be very unmusical in another. For example the articulation required for Baroque playing is quite different to big band performance, as is the sound. The New Orleans jazzman would hardly sound well in the setting of modernist experimental jazz. Traditional brass band sound and articulation are quite different to modern band style, not to mention orchestral.

Specialisation is increasing as more fields of music become distinct and separate. It is almost as if boundaries are being drawn to divide up musical territories. Symphony orchestras now very rarely play Bach, because of the advances of authentic performance (although pianists have started to re-colonise Bach's keyboard music). Going the other way, period orchestras have now invaded Brahms, Wagner and the early twentieth century with original instruments, if not period style of performance.

Very few musicians have the capability to be successful across several fields. In contemporary trumpet playing, Wynton Marsalis is convincing in whatever he does. At the moment, at his level, he probably stands alone. As a role model he is ideal: serious yet with a light personal touch, intellectual yet common-sensical and natural.

Choosing Styles

Within each field there are differing styles appropriate to different periods and composers. In the orchestral repertoire Mozart demands a wholly different approach to dynamics and articulation than does Mahler - who in turn requires a very wide expressive range, much more so than, say, Stravinsky. Take every opportunity to listen carefully to experienced musicians. Very early in my career I had the good fortune to sit next to the horn player Alan Civil for a series of recordings of late Mozart symphonies. A master performer and master musician, Alan displayed a wonderful range of rhythmic and tonal nuances for the brass parts, discussing what to do and when to do it.

The Young Player's Choice

Student players at music college are now given experience in all kinds of ensembles and types of music. A warning, however! This wide range of opportunity does have its drawbacks. Apart from the dangers of over-playing and under-practising, the young student with symphonic ambitions may well enjoy a regular gallop in the big band. Unless the player is already mature in breathing, articulation and embouchure, big band playing can create musical habits which have no place in symphonic playing.

Listening habits create playing habits. The extrovert style of big band articulation and attack is not good preparation for the kind of playing which the orchestral trumpeter is required to deliver. Today's young player has a short period in which to make a mark. Taking the wrong playing track for even a short time may mean being left behind in the race to establish a name. (CR Time and Rhythm)

TALENT and PERSONALITY

What is talent? Everyone asks themselves 'How much have I got? Is it enough for me to realise my ambitions? Am I being realistic?'

How Do We Recognise It?

Talent is immediately recognisable in all areas of skill, even in those of which we have no personal experience. Its presence is signalled by ease and smoothness of operation, especially when facing extreme tests. It is flexible and inventive in the face of difficult challenges. It rarely hurries or stumbles but can operate at high and low speeds when needed.

Where Does It Come From?

Along with almost all forms of ability, musical talent is shaped during the first years of life. Research suggests that the various faculties of rhythm, pitch, and sensitivity to types of sound are stimulated and shaped in the years well before puberty. A baby banging drums and other objects, then singing tunelessly, are as much part of mental development as any of the other skills it learns.

With time and experience, this awareness evolves into a more precise appreciation of rhythm and pitch. If for any reason the development of these abilities is incomplete then the musical talent is also incomplete. The child then starts to manipulate the materials of music by imitating what it hears. This is usually the point when, through instruction, contact with an instrument begins.

These are the building blocks of a complete musical personality, which interlock with the aid of good teaching. The two main skills are (1) gaining awareness and control of the parts of the body which play the chosen instrument, and (2) reading music.

In order that these intellectual and physical skills are smoothly linked together as soon as possible, it is essential that the skill of reading music is taught quickly and thoroughly. (CR Reading)

The more stimulating and challenging the child's environment, the more likely are its latent talents to emerge. I am always amazed at the quality and quantity of talents most people have and how few of those talents are developed.

Testing and Realising our Talents

Only by entering more and more demanding situations can the young player test his or her talent to find out how far it will go. These situations need not be as orchestral principals or soloists. To be a top flight Second Trumpet is as much of a challenge as any other. While appreciation for this role may not be as public as that for the Principal, it is professionally almost as highly judged and valued. After each challenge has been surmounted, it is up to the player to assess the result and decide on the next one.

For players who feel that their talent is good but not of the finest quality, it is my experience that patient, totally determined students can, more often than not, make up for the shortfall. A strong personality is essential if musical talent is to be released and realised. Only strong personalities have the will to develop and bring together the many diverse abilities needed to perform well. Will-power enables a player to be bold when scared, to work patiently when exasperated at a lack of progress, and to be persistent when all seems lost. Personality is the platform on which talent operates.

I have former students who were not regarded as high fliers, but are now in a number of top quality orchestral positions. Determination and intelligence saw them through where flashier talents petered out.

Talent, Personality and Interest

1. Research has shown that performing ability in some children can develop to a high level of facility without them having any real interest in either music or playing. This phenomenon of facility without interest can be hard for parents to understand.

2. With the growth in the number of educational places available for studying music, only the best colleges exercise a strict entry standard.

3. On the other hand there are many players who desperately desire to be fine performers, but simply do not have enough ability. For young people to go down the wrong road, realising too late that a mistake has been made, often has tragic consequences.

4. The student with a moderate performing achievement at the age of college entry, but who is academically gifted, should enter university and take part in its performing life. If the player is a late developer then postgraduate study can be undertaken after the main degree. (CR Careers)

Coda

A love for, interest in and enjoyment of performing music should not be mistaken for a talent capable of being developed to professional standards. For many professional performers, including some of the finest, music is simply the material they play. It is not an interest in itself. Their interest remains solely in those areas relevant to their instrument and does not extend beyond those boundaries. In itself this is a perfectly rational attitude.

While this is perfectly understandable, it is my view that the fullest development of talent is achieved on a foundation of wide-ranging musical interest. Many great players have stopped short of their highest potential because they are enclosed a little too tightly in their own particular musical world, and content to listen to music only when it is for their own instrument or ensemble.

TIME and RHYTHM

The ability to time the start of notes accurately is not only the basis for good rhythm, but is the main co-ordinator of the physical actions of playing. Rhythm is created by the way the notes are played.

Warning

We musicians talk about time and rhythm in very sloppy ways indeed, often using the key words interchangeably. Unfortunately the core concepts must be separated and understood before they can be related to each other.

This is probably the book's most difficult chapter and may strain the more delicate brains, but in order to write usefully about the subject I must clear the ground a little. The subject is definitely one of the most pivotal in the book, so stick to it!

If some of the meanings don't penetrate too easily the first few times, don't worry. Let the easier paragraphs soak in first, before returning to the others.

The Note

A note has three parts, the relationships of which are infinitely variable

1. ***The start of the note.*** This is important both for its timing - the when-to-play-it factor - and for its kind of articulation - the how-to-play-it factor.

2. ***The body of the note*** is concerned with sound quality, and, when long enough, changes in dynamic.

3. ***The ending of the note.*** Like the start of the note, this is important for the when-to-stop and the how-to-stop.

Good players vary the relationships of these three parts in the same natural way that we shape and phrase our speech in normal conversation. Poor, anxious players sound wooden and stiff because they mishandle these relationships. In the same way, our speech is affected when we are nervous; we may speak in a monotone instead of freely and we may even forget or mispronounce words.

In a melodic passage, the body of the note is the most important part, the start and the ending normally being less prominent. On the other hand, in a short note in a rhythmic passage, the start of the note is the critical element. In rhythmic music, the longer the note, the more important the timing and character of its release becomes. In the brass music of John McCabe, for instance, the ends of long notes are notated with a short tied note defining the exact moment to stop. The release of the note, in both its timing and character, is as important as its start.

The relative prominence of one part of a note above the other two does not mean that the others should ever be neglected. In high quality playing these elements are all present, being continually ordered and re-ordered, note by note, by the musicianship of the player, in continuous response to the music. (CR Melody Playing, where this Heading is reproduced in its entirety because of its equal relevance.)

Time and Timing

The ability to place notes exactly where the player wants them is an essential musical skill. Without it no-one can reach professional competence.

For the technical development of trumpet players in particular and brass players in general, the timing of the starts of notes is the most important control element in developing technique.

- Playing the trumpet requires the co-ordination of breathing, throat, tongue, embouchure and fingers. These faculties **must** work together at the **same chosen instant,** in spite of the fact that each of these elements has its own different speed of response. The certainty and precision of this co-operation determines whether 'technique' is secure or not.

- Without precision in choosing these moments to play, our physical actions are unsure. The aim of the routines given in the chapters on Practice is to create certainty by the development of high quality listening. Effective listening then insists that these faculties work together and issues orders which the body will try to obey. (I understand that this may be an unusual way of describing the best way to technical improvement, but my view is that listening (plus boldness) creates technique - and in that order.)

The Placing of Notes in Time

The importance of the correct placement of notes in time varies with different kinds and periods of music. Music of the Baroque generally proceeds with regular pulse and barring and an absence of tempo changes within movements. Its normally contrapuntal texture and interlocking rhythms mean that equal importance attaches to great and small time values alike. Contemporary minimalist music interlocks in the same way, but much more mechanically, because of the nature of the melodic and harmonic material. In much of this latter kind of music, metronomic time is the main priority. Exactness of beat is pre-eminent, and rhythm, which I define as the expressive phrasing of time, is virtually redundant. (See below: Some Practical Advice)

Rhythm

Rhythm is created by the way the notes are accented and varied dynamically, i.e. phrased. The most important notes, those on the pulse, are very slightly accented to give them precedence. Other notes fall away from, or go towards, those important notes.

In the following examples, the time value of a crotchet (a quarter note) is divided into three semiquavers (sixteenths) and a semiquaver rest. This group, which occurs very often indeed in music, is given in four examples to illustrate how different rhythmic contexts are created by varying the application of accents.

The first bar is given unmarked. The second is given with the added detail necessary for a performance in which the listener knows exactly what is happening. In the fourth example added dynamics would be mistaken, as the beat is on the silence; the notes should therefore be played as evenly as possible in order not to suggest a pulse-note.

Example 1

Example 2

Example 3

Example 4

Time and Rhythm in Orchestral and Ensemble Playing

In order to give unanimity and style to ensemble playing, the performers in any ensemble must each have the same feeling for time and for rhythm. This is one of the most important points considered by orchestral sections when filling a vacant position. The potential candidate must 'feel' the relationships between notes in the same way as the section does.

Related Matters

1: Rubato

Originally rubato (robbed time) required that the basic pulse of the accompaniment remain unaltered, inflexible even, while the solo line dragged or hurried according to taste. In the twentieth century, the practice of solo line rubato against strict tempo accompaniment has disappeared.

Today the term is used to mean an expressive variation of the main tempo. All parts, whether leading or following, stay together. The only practical consideration for the performer is that the listener must not lose the pulse or the barline because of any distortion.

True original rubato is now a lost skill, except among jazz and popular music artists, the best of whom are especially brilliant at both leaning back into the time, or temporarily leaving it behind. These tensions among the different lines of music open up unique sensations now lost to serious music. Listen to Dizzy Gillespie in slower, rhythmic numbers; if he doesn't make you smile with pleasure you are a lost soul!

2: Tempo (and Pulse)

The word 'tempo' denotes the speed of a passage of music, whether a complete piece or not. All tempi vary slightly as they proceed, for different reasons, including both the emotion of the music and the demands of performing it. This natural variation of tempo is linked to the idea of 'pulse' with its human meaning of varied regularity.

Tempo, whether it sometimes relaxes or tightens, is the backcloth against which all rhythms are felt. A useful performing rule is that, special exceptions excluded, fast tempi should be inherently steady, while slow tempi must always flow. Against this background the rhythms will remain coherent.

The most common fault of the inexperienced student is to set a tempo, then find that it varies badly because his or her attention has wandered away to other playing matters. Players who let a tempo slacken to a dull comfortable jog, to what I call the slowest common denominator, are common. Players who hurry anxiously, usually with their eyes on the next problem, are equally so. When this happens players have not considered and weighed up the music to a professional level. It is simply being run through without the musical thought being in charge.

Variations of tempo, such as an ***accelerando*** or a ***rallentando***, make their best effect left late in the passage. The inexperienced player bolts at the first sight of an 'accel,' and brakes fiercely at the mention of a 'rall' or a 'rit!' Crescendi and diminuendi should be treated in the same way.

3: Beat

Today this word usually denotes metronomic time as heard in rock music. Machines are increasingly being used for the drumming part of popular music because they are better at being machines than are humans!

While the 'beat' in jazz is much more exact than 'tempo' in serious music, time in jazz still maintains its own human feeling and flexibility, because of its essentially human, creative and improvisatory nature. This concept of time has been turned to wonderful musical use by the sheer personality and fabulous invention of a century of jazz musicians. In jazz the beat has been manipulated, decorated, transformed, and given a life never dreamed of by serious musicians, to whom variable pulse is the natural medium. Throughout its history serious music has always been attracted towards popular music by its sheer animal vitality, before moving away again, as if alarmed by its unashamedly extrovert spirit.

Some Practical Points

- In most music that can be characterised as 'rhythmic', as opposed to 'melodic', the ends of notes the length of a crotchet (quarter-note) and above, and especially before a rest, can be released rhythmically. The body of the note has to be be well sustained to allow this to happen. (CR The Note paragraph above.)

Example 5

Example 6

- Rhythmic groupings of notes can be put into a loop to achieve accuracy. The routine is laid out in Practice: 2, Routine 2.

- It is surprisingly common to hear good quality student players time their first notes very inaccurately indeed. These players stop listening before the entry, as all their attention is centred on the anxiety of the first note. I am not even referring to difficult entries, but to entries on, for example, the first and third beats of a 4/4 bar.

- Off the beat entries, for example, should be auralised accurately, so that the player knows what is required musically. (CR Auralisation) Uncertainty often leads to an explosive accent on the wrong note, which then 'throws' the ensemble out of rhythmic true. A useful rule is as follows: start early and then relax. See Example 4 above for an off the beat rhythm which can be awkward to perform at speed, if the player is unclear about the time-placement of the notes.

- The playing of quick off-beats is a skill of the same type. The first example presents no problem to the player. The second example, which is identical except for its placement in the bar, can cause instability and often a certain amount of grunting as the player desperately tries to hold on to the pulse. (CR Body Movement for an exercise to improve this weakness.)

- Apart from consideration of small rhythmic groupings, it should be remembered that rhythm must be phrased over the wider context as is Melody. (CR Melody) Rhythm always goes to, or from, some point or other, in a way which may not be convenient for the player. Well known examples where rhythmic (and melodic) phrasing is often wrongly played, because awkward for breathing, are as follows:

Example 7 - Tschaikowsky: Symphony No 4. (1st Mvmt.)

Andante sostenuto

- In the same way, the last movement of Sibelius' Second Symphony contains a melody which phrases right up to the barline. This contradicts the obvious place to breathe, which, in the 4th bar of letter Q is before the final minim (half-note).

- The inexperienced player is always likely to be thrown by any distinct alteration of context. Changes of tempi, ritardandi, rallentandi and accelerandi, dynamics, range and changes of sequence, all cause trouble for the unwary. (Good composers always stop a sequence before it becomes predictable, unlike bad composers!)

- Many players lose track of the pulse inside bars while worrying about details and difficulties ahead. (See third point in this paragraph) Even good players can lose the pulse in trills and ornaments due to anxiety about fitting them in. (CR Ornaments) All performers have tendencies to rush or to drag in certain contexts. It is important that each one recognises where this is likely to happen to them and to guard against it.

- The student player must learn how to handle both interlocking, and competing, timings and rhythms. Three against two is the simplest interlocking rhythm, but even this is not handled well by a majority of student players. At a time when more and more complex divisions of time are becoming common, this is an unsatisfactory state of affairs. See the Time Patterns which follow this Chapter.

A Personal View on The Everpresent Beat

The rhythmic differences between modern popular music and serious music are rooted in the opposition of beat and pulse. The use of percussion to emphasise 'the beat', *from the outside*, has always been common in dance music of all kinds and times. However, in the twentieth century the *exterior application of mechanical time* has come to dominate popular music to an extraordinary degree. Layers of rhythm, which plug directly into the nervous system of the listener, are now what most popular music is about.

In both the serious and the vernacular music of the Western World, the *pulse is felt internally, in the mind.* It is not imposed from outside the music; it comes from within the music. Against the background of a tempo, the pull and push of varied time values is what creates the music's energy, its forward motion.

The listening diet of most young people is now dominated by pop music. There is a substantial imbalance in favour of music where the components of time and rhythm are mechanical and explicit, as opposed to music where time and rhythm are human and implicit.

The presence of muzak everywhere, at random, and without a choice being possible, is helping the unvarying 'beat' of commercial music to drive out the expressive, flexible 'pulse', of that I am sure. The 'beat' is drip-fed everywhere now, in almost all public places, a kind of chewing gum for the ears. The everpresence of commercial popular music, first dulls, then kills the internal pulse in many of the impressionable young, whether future players or audience. Today I hear a lot of boring and uninteresting playing by otherwise brilliant young technicians. My view is that most have been musically brainwashed and their talents pasteurised.

Among the generality of younger student players, without any doubt, rhythmic and melodic subtlety and awareness have diminished and are continuing to diminish. When a student's listening habits are moulded by such massive over-exposure to a musical language foreign to the one they are supposed to be mastering, at this formative age the damage is likely to be permanent. The language of European music, of all kinds, has evolved without a break, up to the middle of the twentieth century. It is now in danger of becoming the second (musical) language for the young.

The lesson is surely that the young serious musician must be very selective about his or her diet of listening.

TIME PATTERNS

These exercises, used a little but often, will have a significant effect on security, reading and performance. Accurate time and rhythm are important for three reasons.

1. The purposeful timing of notes co-ordinates all parts of the playing system, directing them to work together, with the same reactions.

2. An ability to play time and rhythm accurately and instantly, in any tempo, is the basis of professional level sight reading.

3. Professional ensemble work requires the highest quality (a) of timing, i.e. the metronomically accurate placing of notes, (b) of rhythm, i.e. the shaping of groups of notes in the bar-context, and (3) of equality of articulation and sound. All players in an ensemble must feel these elements in the same way for there to be coherent ensemble.

Even though the first bars look easy, even for the beginner, very few students will be able to play them with the accuracy which professional work requires. The development of discerning listening (CR) is not served by the casual playing-through.

These time patterns can be played by two players, or by one player using a metronome to set the time.

• The players should play different pitches, which then can be frequently varied into all ranges.

• Play each bar many times, listening intently for every detail.

• Once competence has improved, string several bars together.

• Constantly vary the tempi and the dynamics, as both affect time and rhythm. Also play them accelerando and rallentando. Use them on scales and arpeggios for another dimension. Exercise the imagination!

• If the result sounds acceptable, listen again, even more intently. Almost certainly there is always more to be heard.

Trumpet 1

Trumpet 2

SECTION TWO

PLAYING SKILLS

INTRODUCTION

This Section includes chapters whose subject matter is almost totally exclusive to the trumpet and the brass family of instruments. There are however many parallels with the playing of other instrumental families.

ARTICULATION

The act of articulation must provide a musically appropriate and technically secure start to the note. It is one of the skills essential for good trumpet playing.

The Act of Articulation

As with all playing skills, the first requirement is a clear musical idea. Whether hard, soft, espressivo or sforzato, the right articulation will vary from situation to situation, but it is vital that the player knows what he or she wants to do.

For many players the anxiety of achieving a safe first note to any passage blocks out the musical feeling. This attitude of 'once I am started everything will be fine' is a very serious failing. In many cases it leads to a stuttering inability to start any articulation at all, except with a conductor's beat from a third person. Imagining the note before playing (auralisation) and singing the note with the type of articulation required (vocalisation) offers the best way forward for these players. Imagination of what is wanted must push out the fear.

It may seem strange to say so, but often the player is so anxious about starting, that he or she does not have any idea of what they want. If necessary, the player should sing or vocalise the first note to find out what he or she wants! Careful listening then matches the playing result to the musical idea. The resulting feedback enables the gap between the two to be closed. (CR Auralisation and Vocalisation)

Physical Memory

In the chapter entitled Practice: 2, Improvement Routines, I give exercises for the purpose of helping players find their best articulation. As I have described elsewhere (CR Teaching) the natural constraints of the exercises make students adopt their own best tongue position without any verbal explanation being needed. With these exercises there is no need to discuss how-and-where-to-tongue. Students can simply note what they do when playing the exercises, and then remember it as a physical act in exactly the same way as they remember how to throw a ball at a target, for example.

Articulation: Key Points

1: The contact point at which the act of tonguing takes place

The standard wisdom is that, in most circumstances, the contact point of the tongue is approximately behind the upper teeth, or on the gum-line. Beyond that, descriptions of the use of the tongue become very personal. I have listened to descriptions of tongue positions of all types and variations, particularly in the matter of range. Like the human body, mouths and tongues come in all shapes and sizes. These exercises identify each player's best articulation point.

With one or two exceptions, most master players make tongue contact behind the upper teeth. The exceptions include one of the finest orchestral trumpeters that I ever heard. Gordon Webb, Principal Trumpet of the London Philharmonic Orchestra in the late sixties and early seventies, tongued between the teeth. He enjoyed a faultless technique, articulation, range and overall capability.

2: The Act of 'tonguing'. (Articulation)

The act of articulation is the controlled release of the airstream. The air in the lungs is propelled out at the same time as the tongue is removed from its contact point. The musical effect is the opposite. It is one of articulation or attack, in which the note seems to be started as a positive action. The words traditionally used for this aspect of playing are contradictory and confusing: 'attack', 'soft/hard tonguing', and so on. The latter phrase would be more accurate as 'slow/fast tongue withdrawal'.

3: The shape, and positioning of the tongue in the mouth

The tongue shapes itself according to the demands of range. Whether in low, high or middle range, if relaxed the tongue changes shape quite naturally. However, most players have ranges in which their tongue shapes work perfectly and others where they need care and attention. The on-off routine given at the end of the chapter on Range quickly makes clear what is needed in all cases. (CR Range)

4: The tongue as it passes through the soft palate (pharynx) down to the voice-box

The tongue is a much larger muscle than is normally imagined, stretching all the way from the teeth down to the voice box. Warming up the tongue is as important as warming up the embouchure, especially after a day of hard blowing. Relaxing it after playing, with some warming down exercises, is equally important. Not only does the tongue make each articulation, it constantly changes shape to modify the airstream in the production of pitch. (CR Sound)

A Warning

I must stress that the reader should not think that parts of the body can be dealt with as separate items. The working of the body is indivisible. The tongue and throat are wholly unified with the embouchure (CR Embouchure) and the upper body musculature (CR Posture). One part cannot be dealt with unrelated to the whole. A change in one part causes adjustment in all.

Types of Articulations in brief

I have identified four main physical types of note-starts, as follows:

1. The normal first- and/or separate-note articulation.

2. The normal legato-articulation, for continuation notes, i.e. the tongued slur.

3. The air note, with no articulation of the airstream.

4. The air note, the airstream articulated at the cough position, or with a 'k'.

Types of Articulation in Greater Detail

1: The First-Note Articulation

For the standard first note articulation the tongue is placed in the chosen contact position. The air stream can be used as follows:

- It can be held up in the throat at the cough position, with the throat surfaces closed. The tongue is then withdrawn from its contact position in co-ordination with the release of the air from the throat.

- The throat can be held open, and the articulation made into a moving airstream.

The degree of 'hard' or 'soft' attack depends on the speed with which these linked actions are carried out. The 'hard' attack is the result of fast release of tongue and air, while the 'soft' attack is created by a slow release. As mentioned earlier, the words 'fast' and 'slow' are more accurate in describing the tongue release than are 'hard' and 'soft.'

The type of articulation for any particular context must be decided by the musical idea of what is right. The musical idea drives the physical action. Experience and memory combine, and the body responds to the musical wish. (See the first paragraph)

The letter 'd' is very valuable for a certain shaping of shorter notes. It always delivers clarity of production because of the controlled explosion it produces. It is possible to feel the positive breath follow-through from the diaphragm which supports that articulation.

Even softer consonants such as 'l' can help the unarticulated note into life. The key is experimentation; all players are different, with differing imaginations and ideas.

Fear of the First-Note

Fear of the first note afflicts many players, and is the result of anxiety caused by the anticipation of failure and the resulting shame. (CR Anxiety) Consultation with an experienced teacher is important, but the main point to bear in mind is that contained in the very first section of this chapter.

2: The Legato Continuation Articulation

The legato articulation can also be called the tongued slur. This technique is usually for continuation playing, i.e. after the passage has begun, from the second note onwards until a break occurs. The tone is created on the first note and then carried forwards. The sound is not recreated at each note.

The contact position is the same as in (1a). To achieve a first class legato tongued slur, the airstream must flow continuously. It must not be squeezed thinner as the tongue moves towards its contact position for the next articulation. Therefore the tongue must move in as late and fast as possible, without interfering with the breadth of the tone/air flow. It then moves back out of the way as fast as possible. The sound is similarly unaffected when the tongue withdraws quickly.

When the tongue action is sluggish, the 'twaah' effect is created, which is so damaging to legato and disfiguring to cantabile. This fault can be heard in other musicians, for example in singers at word or syllable changes, and with string players at bow changes. (CR Slurring)

Most split notes within a legato passage are caused by poor continuation tonguing.

Processes of improvement

Three processes can be used to improve legato.

1. Most importantly, I insist that the student uses the musical imagination to hear a smooth musical line in the mind. As described above, the actual playing result is then matched to the ideal. (CR Auralisation) This can be backed up by listening to examples of the best legati from all types of musical instruments, especially the voice, the violin and the cello. The pure uninterrupted flow of sound must be paramount.

2. Secondly there is the use of the image. Linking a phrase or a piece to a picture or a feeling is a very long-standing method of improving or altering playing quality. It can improve technique, as in legato playing, but it can also change the expressive character of a passage. Used systematically it can upgrade the whole nature of a performer's technique and personality. The student's own images tap directly into his or her's deepest feelings, and therefore evoke a direct and clear response. The character of the articulation must be part of this musical image.

   The student can proceed as follows: for example, to produce smooth playing, call up a favourite image of smoothness. It can be the feel of silk, the pouring of oil, or the sensation of eating a particular kind of chocolate! Whatever it is, match your playing to it. Check the result, then do it again. The effect is always an improvement of musical and technical performance. (CR Teaching, where I underline that analytical explanation is only ever useful as a backup to the musical process.)

3. Use the first routine given in the chapter entitled Practice: 2.

3: The Air "Attack" without Tongue

In this (non) articulation, the airstream is set in motion without a discernible start. The note appears when the wavelength of the airstream and the position of the embouchure are well attuned. The result is a vibration heard through the instrument. Expert players will (silently) help the air-note to appear by a push on the airstream at the right moment, or by a tongue action so slow as to be without discernible contact and therefore inaudible.

As mentioned above there are master players, who play 'on the airstream', by activating the airstream before starting to play, and articulating the first note into it. This is not to be recommended as a basic technique in orchestral playing. It does however have a lot to recommend it in freer and more extrovert types of playing, in jazz and popular music.

Practising on the Airstream, 'Breathing Notes In'

This process is an extremely valuable method of practice. It exactly matches up the airstream tension and embouchure. Practice should be without the use of air pushes or the slow tongue. This produces precise embouchure shape, the tongue shape, the soft palate and the pharynx (the lower throat). Most valuable of all is practising crescendi and diminuendi, from inaudible to just-audible and back again, from nothing to a shadow subtone. This gives the kind of control which is invaluable in soft playing.

This type of practice focuses the airstream exactly. It is directed straight through the throat, mouth and embouchure, and actually benefits all volumes and ranges of playing.

4: The Air "Attack" Articulated in the Throat

This technique, using the stop at the cough position, gives the air-stream articulation an added certainty without an identifiable start. The air is held by the closed throat and released in a positive even flow. The start of the note can be calmly placed and is controllable without effort. This is most useful in soft playing, particularly in high soft entries, above the stave.

The 'k' articulation I have also found excellent in all ranges, especially for repeat notes in a high range legato context.

The soft entries on high B in the first trumpet part of Sibelius' Second Symphony (slow movement) come to mind, as does the second trumpet's wicked, cold-entry, high Bb (concert pitch) found just before Variation 3 in Richard Strauss' Don Quixote.

While I found these throat articulations utterly reliable under all conditions, I know some fine players who are unable to do them.

Variation in Articulation (and Sound)

Like a fingerprint, each individual physique is unique. Similarly the sounds we produce are totally personal. A player's musicality is the main factor affecting articulation as it is in most areas of performance. Compared to the human voice instruments in general have only limited variations of sound available, yet they can be made very personal and distinct. Trumpeters in jazz and popular music show what can be done with sound; consider the sounds of Miles Davis, Harry James, Dizzy Gillespie, Roy Eldridge and countless others.

Trumpet pedagogy from the time of Arban has used the letter 't' to denote the normal articulation. English speakers must be careful to use a clean 't', without the natural hiss before the actual sound explodes.

The softer version of the 't is the letter 'd', which requires the throat to be shut at the cough position, therefore adding a controlled but positive breath push at the moment of articulation. The 'd' can be softened until it reaches something like the letter 'l', after which it disappears totally. (See 1a above)

A further type of secondary articulation exists when the initial 't' is followed quickly by a 'd' on the rebound, giving a hard/soft pairing. This two note group, 't-d', is often used for repetitions such as the following:

Example 1

Allegro

Care must be taken not to use it lazily, either in larger note values when it takes on sloppy character, or when the composer tries to guard against it by writing staccato marks on shorter notes. It is, however, exactly the right tonguing pattern to use when accents are placed on the smallest notes in order to achieve a special effect, as in Don Juan by Richard Strauss. Here is the rhythm of a typical passage.

Example 2

Allegro (♩)

Essential in a different way, the letter 'k' is a ricochet (rebound) tonguing, and needs much more care and attention than most students give to it. The 'k' is a much cruder consonant than the 't' or 'd' and needs exact listening to control it. It is a consonant which tends to open the throat wide and therefore lets through much larger quantities of air. This is why the 't' and 'd' find it an awkward companion. The softer version of 'k' is 'g', a very useful soft articulation in its own right for isolated notes.

Proceeding from low to high, on a sliding scale, the vowel syllables 'uh, oo, aah, eh, ee' are the normal inner mouth shapes adopted. These are capable of endless variety, although the constraint of the trumpet itself prevents the use of as much subtlety as the human voice. We are told that English has five vowels. In fact twelve vowels have been identified, with more available that are not used in English. Think of the sounds of Russian, for example.

Some Points for Control of the "K" Articulation

- Singing a long steady note, place a hand on the larynx, observing the stillness of the larynx. Then with the hand on the larynx, sing legato double and triple tonguing through the long note. While maintaining the same stillness of the larynx, play double and triple tonguing normally on the trumpet. Observe the difference. Being aware of the good effect which a still larynx can have on tonguings which use 'k', will go a long way towards controlling both evenness of timing and the note lengths. This routine also creates awareness of the evenness of the airstream.

- If mastery is to be achieved then patient slow practice of double and triple tonguing, a little and often, cannot be avoided.

- Flexibility of usage of these compound tonguings can be gained by playing on a single pitch, say middle G. Start off with the articulation 'dahgah-dahgah' completely legato, graduating to the shortest possible dry (joke) staccato 'tiki-tiki' before returning to 'dahgah' to finish. This creates awareness of what happens during the process of tonguing. Interestingly, a good staccato double tongue is only a minute fraction longer than the joke one. Repeat for triple tongue.

In triple tonguing, two standard patterns exist; 't-t-k' and 't-k-t'. The first is naturally legato in character, suitable for stretches of tonguing as found in the older style of variation solo. The second is much clearer and defined in effect, being very successful in fanfare triplets which need to be heard but not especially loudly, as in the recapitualtion near the end of The Mastersingers Overture by Wagner. Even more usefully this pattern is ideal where the third note of a triplet is higher than the other two. The following example from La Mer by Debussy illustrates this latter point.

Example 3

Mixed Tonguing

Many situations exist when time and pitch combinations are awkward, or when orchestral excerpts require preparation at both faster and slower tempi. Becoming fluent with single and compound tonguings is therefore commonsense, and in my experience, very valuable indeed. The following example gives a typical rhythm from part of the trumpet solo near the start of Maurice Ravel's Piano Concerto.

Example 4

Allegro

Mixing compound tonguings, such as triple and double alternating through six-note groups, is illustrated at the end of the Time Pattern Exercises. An example of some possible combinations can be seen with this excerpt from the last part of Rimsky-Korsakov's Scheherezade.

Example 5

Vivo

Trumpet in A

BODY MOVEMENT

Extrovert body movement while playing is becoming more and more common. There are rights and wrongs of which to be aware.

Body Movement: the Positive Case

By its very nature, music presents feeling as sound; therefore it is natural that our bodies should respond with a display of matching movements and gestures. The practice of extrovert gesture and movement is becoming more widespread, to the point where it seems to be pursued as an end in itself.

Each case has to be looked at on its merits. Generally today's players are less inhibited than their predecessors, when compared with some of the world's finest performers of the past who used the minimum physical movement necessary.

Whether movement is visible or not is irrelevant. What is important is the quality of the movement. If the player feels free, the body can be still.

The Negative Case

I have seen players on all instruments exhibit a great deal of movement, and yet not be free: players who appear to be engaged in a fight to the death with the instrument. Everyone has seen conductors who appear to be wrestling with an invisible opponent. Large movements do not necessarily mean freedom.

Equally we have all seen players rigid and tight in their posture, the muscles of their bodies stiffly locked together. This is perhaps the worst situation in which to be. (CR Posture) Breathing will be restricted and shallow, the upper chest, throat and face will be without flexibility, and the player will experience a general sense of helplessness however hard he or she tries.

Either way energy is being wasted by the wrong kinds of tension and effort. Smooth co-operation among the body's muscles is the state needed for productive use of energy, whether the player has a quiet or an extrovert presence. (CR Posture)

Types of Movement

1. Response to the Mood of the Music

This response is less important to the orchestral brass player than to pianists or string players, who are active externally while performing. While some movement can be natural in a brass player's solo performance when standing, in the orchestra too much is obtrusive. I am leaving to one side the question of raising the bell as an option in varying the sound, whether voluntarily or as required in, say, a Mahler Symphony.

Among brass players the obvious exceptions in this matter are the virtuoso jazz trumpeters whose exuberance and theatricality carry them naturally towards extrovert performance. In the solo performance of much contemporary music, body movement can often illustrate the music's progress. (CR Contemporary Music)

2. Response to the Phrase

This type of response shows the musical shape of the phrase. More often than not the phrase point or points coincide with the highs or lows of the pitch. Body movement of this kind, if used well, helps to shape the phrasing for the performer and for the listener, who is of course also a watcher.

Response to the phrase must be used with great discretion. Repeated excessively, it can be extremely annoying to watch. Many phrase points occur at the highest pitches of a phrase, so that if the bell is always high for high notes, and low for low notes, this can be an irritation because it becomes so predictable. Young woodwind players, keen to show their musicality, are currently waving their instruments about to the most alarming degree. Rarely does it improve the musical result.

3. Response to Phrase Points and Barlines

When all main beats or barlines are marked by a gesture, regardless of the phrasing, the player is exposing a weak sense of rhythm. He or she beats time like this in order to give a false sense of security. The result will be an over-accented style of playing, in which the music will lurch from bar to bar. Tempi will drag and split notes will occur because of the physical instability created at the embouchure. (CR Anxiety, Reading Music)

4. Movement with the Breath

There are players who quite unconsciously adopt head and neck movements with the taking of breath or with the upbeat. On a brass instrument, these movements cause instability at the moment of first articulation. It is important that, at the first note, the instrument is as still in the hands as possible, so that the embouchure is settled and steady.

General Freedom Of Movement

The use of the word 'play' in connection with music is common in many languages. The freedom and enjoyment which the word suggests can easily disappear beneath the drive and concentration which musicians apply in order to improve their performance. The same applies to sportspeople's sense of play. In both music and sport, the ability to produce the 'unexpected', whether it is 'revelation' or 'fun', is one of the most prized attributes of the performer.

Music's relationship with sport as another form of play is revealing. Sport, like music, is play structured by time and space. Also like music, a variety of physical skills is needed by the master sportsperson to use in his or her particular arena of time and space. The musician, like the sportsperson, needs to feel free in response to the instrument and the music.

Constantly sitting to play, as most orchestral musicians do, hinders this freedom to respond. To counter this tendency to immobility and stiffness, the occasional exercise should be used to freshen up the body. Mahler's frequent instructions in his symphonies for the trumpets to play with 'bells up' still cause difficulty to some players!

A Simple Thirty-Second Loosening Exercise for the Body

- In either a standing or sitting position and while playing a middle register long note, smoothly lower the bell until it points at the floor, 90 degrees from the horizontal. Then raise it to the ceiling, also 90 degrees, then back to the horizontal. Similarly move in as wide a circle as possible. After a few trials this exercise will free the body from being too rigid and static.

- Follow the same routine while strolling around.

A Simple Loosening Exercise for the Brain

This little exercise disengages the natural physical response to awkward off-the-beat notes, which, in faster tempi, often choke the young player.

1. With the metronome set to crotchet (quarter) 160 or above, play the first bar. Remember the tongue speed and the feeling of breathing smoothly.

2. Now play the second bar, which is exactly the same, except that the notes are off the beat. Keep the breathing smooth, as if playing on the beat. If it doesn't fit, don't respond by tightening up - some players grunt internally on the beat - simply play faster or slower until it fits, as if casually ignoring the problem. Gradually your mind's response will loosen up and free itself from your body's control.

Example 1

BREATHING

1: THE PROCESS

Effective breathing is the foundation of all good playing. It also controls the levels of many of our responses.

Posture, Breathing, and Sound

It is my view that when a player's posture is good, the body's normal breathing is perfectly adequate as a basis for playing. The activity of playing a brass instrument (if carried out sensibly) will strengthen the breathing process to the level necessary for all aspects of playing. No distortions, straining, or undue instructions are necessary, and should be avoided. Improving and strengthening the breathing should simply follow the body's natural system.

Good posture, a clear concept of sound and a general musicality, are the bases from which I teach. Undue emphasis (i.e. interference) on particular physical processes of the body may produce a momentary effect of improvement, but will certainly not be of lasting benefit. The effect will be to add extra tension to the player. Interference through seemingly precise verbal instructions - to do this or that with this or that - is both unnecessary and potentially harmful. (CR Posture, Sound, and Anxiety)

All teachers have to deal with the subject of breathing for playing. Many students with excellent natural breathing feel uneasy if the subject is not discussed, just because players universally recognise it as a central matter. Therefore most teachers try to describe this extra breathing used in playing.

This is where problems start. Even if teachers were all skilled in the use of language, the same words mean different things to different people. My view is that it is better to proceed as follows:

- Check and correct the basic posture, which can be done visually.

- Activate the student's musicality, particularly the sense of sound quality and the ability to listen well, then let the body do the rest. The unconscious mind knows best in these matters.

BREATHING

2: THE AIRSTREAM

Once it has been started, the airstream is then altered and manipulated according to the needs of the musical moment. In addition to providing the energy to be turned into sound, the well developed airstream provides vital support for the embouchure.

The Starting Breath

The starting breath must allow the player to begin comfortably, and achieve an effective first articulation. The sound of the breath as it is taken in is a good clue to its quality. If the intake of breath scrapes like an asthmatic person's or a heavy smoker's, then the breath is only filling the upper part, and not the whole of the lungs. This will lead to the limitation of air quantity, shortage of oxygen, and subsequent tightness and strain in the body. This restriction suggests a need for the player's posture to be checked and corrected.

If the breath is taken as soundlessly as possible, with a relaxed open throat, it will smoothly fill the lungs from the bottom, as water fills the cup. The overall sensation will be of comfortable expansion, downwards, sideways and backwards.

As with all physical habits, this openness can be overdone. I have had students come to me straining with effort to fill up with air through grotesquely over-stretched throats. Once again, overdone effort produces only strain. My simple advice is to breathe normally, plus a little bit extra. (CR Anxiety)

In situations where a large amount of breath is needed for the next entry, and if there is time, breathe in for as much as two bars before. This will result in a much fuller intake than normal, but without any strain.

The Continuation Breath and Topping Up

The continuation breath is usually taken perfectly easily and freely, in the manner of the first breath. Sometimes, however, composers are quite unhelpful in this matter, making no allowances for the need to breathe.

The player should not wait until the breath is almost exhausted before looking for a breathing space. Apart from the staggering of breathing slots within the orchestral section (CR Orchestral Playing: section work), when air quantity is important the player should keep the lungs topped up, with small rather than complete breaths, using convenient points before the breath supply is at zero.

Example 1: Hummel Trumpet Concerto (2nd mvt.)

The Continuation Breath under Stress

One of the most important techniques necessary to all advanced players is to be able to take a breath while in the high range or under stress. The inexpert player will always breathe as if taking a first breath. The mouth and throat will open wide, and the embouchure will lose its shape before trying to snap back into place.

In order to achieve stability at high-risk moments, the expert player will take the necessary breath with the following safeguards:

- Keep the shape of the external embouchure.

- Keep the shape of the inside of the mouth and the throat position.

- Keep the position of the tongue in its high range position while breathing in.

- Maintain the breath support at its high range position.

Example 2: Haydn Trumpet Concerto (1st mvt.)

Taking Too Much Breath

Anxiety will often cause the inexperienced player to take in an unnecessarily large quantity of breath. This creates discomfort, and an excess oxygen intake. (CR Anxiety) An additional physical problem is then created; mouth and embouchure are likely to become overloaded with air, with resulting inefficiency in note-production. The general feeling the player will have is of being distended with air. For short passages take only the amount of breath needed.

The Breath 'in tempo'

Taking a breath 'in tempo' is sensible only when the tempo is moderate or slow. A quick breath taken in response to a fast tempo will result in a shallow restricted breath. The player will often feel flustered and rushed, and yet will continue to repeat the same process time and time again.

This habit is frequently linked to unnecessary head and arm movements, as if to emphasise the beat and to help the player to stay with the tempo. These redundant movements and excess tensions ensure that the opposite to what the player actually intended occurs. Tempi drag and breath supply is inadequate. (CR Body Movement)

The Snatched Breath

Players of the larger brass instruments are forced to become adept at fast, open throated, snatched breaths. The capacities of these instruments demand them. Large mouthpieces make this easier than on the trumpet, but there is a lot to be learned from these players. Watch a good tubist play Wagner's Ride of the Valkyries and you will see snatch breathing at its best.

THE EMBOUCHURE, THE MOUTH AND THE THROAT

Of all the parts of the playing system, the embouchure attracts the most attention from the player. This attention is very often unbalanced, misguided and harmful.

The Airstream

As it passes from the lungs, through the throat, the mouth, and the embouchure, the airstream is modified by each in turn. The airstream's interaction with the instrument, through the mouthpiece, creates the sound. The airstream must support the embouchure at the mouthpiece.

The Throat

This general designation covers the area beyond the mouth as far as the voice-box. Its official name is the pharynx. It is only necessary to say that the pharynx is the 'yawn' area down as far as the voice-box. In common with all body channels the throat has the ability to expand, contract and stretch, although to a limited extent. The glottis, just below the voice-box, is able to shut off air supply at will.

The normal functions of the throat respond automatically to the passage of air, food and drink. Equally, the well-taught player will have little cause to interfere in the throat's working, because the right musical habits tap into the throat's actions without conscious thought.

Problems arise for players who mistakenly interfere with the musical process and try to play safe. They unknowingly chew and filter the notes with excess throat movement and stiffening, resulting in the well-known 'twaa' effect. This is due to poor listening habits and a continuing inability to distinguish the qualities of good sound and legato. (CR Sound, Breathing)

As the airstream passes through the throat, the pharynx must be normally open for a good sound to result. This openness can be set by good relaxed first-breath preparation, a procedure that is now well recognised in brass teaching. However, with the standard human weakness of over-doing things, some players make ridiculously huge efforts to be wide open for the first breath. Breathe naturally!

The Mouth

The roof of the mouth behind the teeth is hard and is named the hard palate. Farther back it becomes softer and is named the soft palate. The bottom of the mouth is dominated by the tongue, which is much larger than we are generally aware, to all intents and purposes stretching back and down as far as the larynx.

Warning. At this point I must make it clear that, in dealing with the mouth and the embouchure, I have a different view of their relative importance to that of most of my colleagues.

In my view, range and pitching on the trumpet are controlled by the modification of the airstream as it passes through the mouth. If the mouth passage through which the air passes is narrowed, the pitch of the note rises, and vice-versa.

This change in frequency is the prime factor in range control, high and low. Most players are aware of this through the vowel effect, ee-ah-uh, high to low. The shaping of the embouchure is complementary and secondary to the shaping of the inside of the mouth.

The tongue is therefore the most important agent of alteration to pitch. As it also articulates the notes, these two functions are mixed together, which sometimes creates problems. When anxiety exists in a player, these competing functions can begin to conflict with each other. Single tonguing speed may be slowed down badly, and the highest notes of the range cannot be accurately tongued. A sense of being tongue-tied is felt. (CR Articulation)

The Embouchure

As I wrote in the previous paragraph, I view the external embouchure as complementary to the inside of the mouth, the internal embouchure as I call it. The muscles of the face respond to the shaping of the inside of the mouth as it creates different vowel sounds for speech. I hold the view that the process is much the same in playing; embouchure shape responds to the interior mouth shape, and is therefore secondary, not primary.

In other words, if the actions of the throat and mouth are effective up to the point of the lips - in creating the necessary tension in the airstream for the desired note - the embouchure will work well without interference. (I am excluding faces with structural problems, or where the player has been very badly taught as a beginner.)

Many problems are blamed on the embouchure for which it is neither guilty nor responsible. It is blamed because it is the most visible part of the playing system. Though the embouchure interaction with the mouthpiece is partially visible, the varying muscle and bone structures of faces are so variable as to make some players appear very facially active, while others seem to do almost nothing. I argue that the embouchure is not pro-active, but re-active, and should be given attention only when noticeably out-of-sorts.

The Summary

My view is that this inconceivably complex series of connections must be controlled primarily by attention to, and awareness of, the musical effect required by the player. The body, with over 750 muscles and 100 joints, is far too complicated for detailed conscious control. Any attempt to interfere at one point will always result in an unwanted, probably harmful, change elsewhere.

The Teacher's Role in Changing Embouchures

This topic is always spoken of in a manner similar to that of a severe illness. The finest exponent of this craft that I have ever met is John Dickinson, formerly Principal Trumpet of the Hallé Orchestra, and currently in charge of wind and brass at Cheethams School in Manchester. His ability to make physical changes that then lead the player back to full musical health is remarkable, even changing downstream embouchures to upstream.

In matters of mature players' embouchures, the teacher with the ability to adjust or change them successfully is very rare indeed. It is a process to be undertaken with the greatest care, and only on a person to person basis.

FINGERING and HAND POSITIONS

Fingering skills vary widely, but the majority of the best players use approximately the same set-up.

Simplicity Itself?

The simplicity of manipulating three valves (pistons) with three fingers causes many players to ignore how it should or should not be done. If the correct valve combination is used at the right time what else is there to consider?

As one of the physical actions of playing, it comes at the bottom of the list of priorities. If something goes wrong with a passage the fingers are blamed only if the combination is awkward. The quality of the fingering is rarely considered. It is one of the first points I notice when listening to and watching a new student, because it reveals a great deal about tension in the arms and shoulders.

The Preferred Fingering Method

The finger presses the valve down, then the valve should push the finger up when the pressure is relaxed. Allowing the valve to push the finger up gives the hand muscles a very brief rest before the next action downwards takes place. The finger movement downwards must be quick and clean, but without a noticeable bump at the bottom of the travel.

Common Faults

The player should not lift the fingers off the valves. If he or she does, the back of the hand will tighten. This tightness, created by lifting the fingers, hinders the next push-down. If the player feels the fingering working downwards from the main knuckles, there will be no back-of-the-hand tension created.

This tension also spreads up the arms to the neck and shoulders, but because we use our hands and arms so much we are often insensitive to how we use them. Tightness in the arms links into a slight curving of the upper back and the complementary depression of the upper chest, thereby creating tension and restricting the breathing. How many people suffer stiffness and aching in the shoulders and neck and have no idea where it comes from? (CR Posture)

Back-of-the-hand tension hinders the speed and accuracy of response in faster passages. It can also blur the co-ordinations of tongue and finger, especially where awkward combinations are needed. The embouchure or the articulation are often blamed when it is the fingering which is at fault.

This hand tension (of which many players are unaware), causes them to squeeze the valve down slowly. The downwards movement should be fast, particularly at the start of the push, otherwise co-ordination for the next note is blurred. The squeezing habit is also associated with the 'twaa' effect, because the airstream has to be squeezed at the note-change in order to push the note through the 'gate'. Unravelling this complex mix of habits is not easy.

The fault of squeezing the valve is especially common in soft dynamics, where players often become tense. (CR Dynamics) The need to maintain an uninterrupted airstream in soft playing is paramount. If the sound is lost when playing **piano,** it is hard to regain. The squeezed valve and the accompanying throat squeezing guarantees that the legato will be lost at some point. The sense of struggle is also damaging to confidence. Easy smoothness is comforting and confidence building.

Valve squeezing and arm tension usually go together, with the elbows clamped to the ribcage.(CR Posture) Watch a player with this combination of habits going for a high note. There will be a lot of self-defeating effort used!

Observe the excess effort which many players put into their fingering action. It inhibits speed and accuracy of fingering. Fingering strain always gives the clue to other hidden tensions in the upper body and breathing. All these posture elements go together.

Speed Fingering

Speed fingering of more than a handful of notes requires minimum muscular tension and, as outlined above, no friction between muscle groups and tendons in the back of the hand.

Even Fingering

Even quality of fingering especially during fast legato passages is constantly a problem for players with faulty fingering habits. Movement between second and third finger positions is especially prone to inaccuracy. (CR Scales and Arpeggios for articulation exercises which will equalise finger actions.)

The Very Pointed Fingertip Position

My objection to this set-up is that it is almost impossible for the valves to push up the fingers. The fingers have to be lifted, thereby creating the already noted tightness in the back of the hand. This extra lifting action doubles the number of muscular movements undertaken and does not allow the fingers any rest on the valve-top.

In the case of many cornet players, the opposite situation applies, in that the finger/valve contact takes place far over on the centre finger-pad, with the fingertips touching the bell-pipe!

Ways of Improving Fingering Technique

The chapters on Scales and Arpeggios contain a great deal of material which will lead to improvement of finger work. Especially useful are the examples where the tonguing of groupings of notes is varied.

As one of the basic actions of playing, there is also a need for fingering to be exactly co-ordinated with the other basics. The routines given in the Practice chapter focus the player's attention on this by stimulating better listening and discrimination.

At the end of this chapter there are finger exercises for all the simple combinations, during which the manner and technique of fingering can be addressed.

Basic Check: To Find the Best Position for the Right Hand

Hang the arm loosely by the side, then shake out the hand and fingers into their loosest position like athletes do before a race. (They know that free finger movement relaxes the arms, shoulders and breathing.) This is the best shape for the hand/finger position. The fingers will probably be very slightly curved.

Lift the shaken out hand on to the valves, still loose. Rest the finger pads on the valves midway along the end section of the fingers. This is the optimum fingering position.

My preferred position for the thumb is with the tip placed between the first and second valve casings or close to the first. The advantage of this is that the thumb directly balances against the downward push of the valves and helps to give a relaxed stability to the instrument as it is being played. It is also harder to over-tighten the bent thumb. For stability many players splay out the thumb on the lead pipe and the fifth finger tight in the finger grip.

I prefer the fifth finger resting on top of the finger ring and not gripping it. Anatomically the third, fourth and fifth fingers are closely bound together by tendons and strings. This means that if the fifth finger is too tight, the third and fourth are also restricted. This free fifth finger makes it harder to pull the instrument on to the lips, thereby reducing pressing.

Basic Check: To Find the Best Position for the Left Hand

It is important to experiment with the left hand's holding position, until the most comfortable setting is found. The more direct the line through the forearm and hand to the trumpet, the better it is. The less the wrist is at an angle or cocked sideways, the better. This allows the weight of the instrument to be supported in the naturally strongest way, which is important when the player tires after long spells of playing.

The stability of the instrument throughout the act of fingering must be a prime consideration when trying out holding positions. A badly balanced trumpet will bounce around on the embouchure. A trumpet is rarely perfectly still while being played, but good positioning of both hands will minimise interference.

Slide adjusters must be checked for the same reason. Many players accept the positioning and size of these aids without questioning whether they fit or not, as if we all wore the same size shoes! The triggers and rings may be in the wrong place and/or too large. Ask for them to be moved, changed, or otherwise adjusted as part of your deal when buying the instrument. Otherwise get them altered to suit you at your local repairers.

The shifting of these tuning adjusters needs practice. For example, the shifts to and from C sharp to D sharp, and other pitch combinations, must be practised in isolation to ensure smooth working. Surprisingly few students do. Most players make these shifts without consideration and at the very last moment. These adjustments should be made as early as possible in any passage where they occur, perhaps during a rest or a breath. This will serve the player's comfort, and release any short term air lock caused by extending the third valve slide late.

Long Days Holding the Trumpet

Playing for many long days on end will lead to diminishing physical alertness and mental awareness. These are the main causes of undue mouthpiece pressure on the embouchure and less efficient breathing. During my own career as a player I regularly used handweights three or four times a week, for ten minutes or so, in order to keep some extra 'tone' in my arms and shoulders. (CR Physical Conditioning) This ensured that my arms did not tire and that I did not unconsciously lean the instrument on the lips.

The Rotary Valve Trumpet: Fingering Position

On rotary trumpets, the finger position tends to be more curved because of the lever positions relative to the body of the instrument. The lever design gives a totally different response compared to the valve. There are musical and stylistic differences in players for whom the rotary valve is native. There is more of a click to the rotary change, giving a naturally cleaner legato. The bore is also different to that of piston trumpets, being much more akin to the bore of a cornet. (I have always held the view that the German classics would sound better played on the cornet by players used to the piston trumpet. It is hard to imagine a more politically incorrect idea than this!) The piston has a great deal more speed facility, and can be operated to produce, for example, blue-notes, smears, and finger glissandi - effects which are hardly possible on the rotary trumpet.

The Rotary Valve Trumpet: Holding Position

The rotary trumpet enjoys the ideal holding position, open and strong. In comparison the piston instrument allows a much wider variety of positions, many of which are constricted and sometimes contorted. Cornet players are particularly prone to this difficulty due to the left hand being held cocked and close to the body, making the twisted wrist position potentially very awkward.

FINGER DRILLS

These drills can be used for relaxation breaks in normal practice. The instructions are a repeat of some from the chapter on Fingering, which discusses the matter more fully.

- Note the natural position of the fingers when relaxed; usually a gentle curve. Place them on the valves in that shape, with the middle of the end finger pads on the valve caps. Ideally the fingers should stay at rest on the valves.

- Press the valve down, then let the valve push the finger up by releasing the pressure. Do not lift the fingers. The finger action should always be quick, but without a bump.

- Avoid arched or claw fingers, because the fingers then have to be lifted. The muscular tightness which lifting creates in the back of the hands hinders fast fingering. The tension created by this faulty process then spreads up the arm, into the shoulder, and to a lesser degree into the breathing and throat. It is impossible to shut off one part of the body from the others. Tension in one area spreads, ripple-like, to the whole.

- Choose speeds at which the hand and fingers are comfortable.

The first set of staves gives some variations on a simple two valve sequence. The second system gives further valve combinations. The articulations given will have a very beneficial side effect on finger-to-tongue co-ordination.

PHYSICAL CONDITIONING

To a small degree the performing musician is an athlete, using the body to create music. Good physical conditioning ups energy levels so there is more to use.

A General Position

Brass playing is an athletic activity, requiring peak performance from many parts of the brain as well as the appropriate muscle groups. It goes without saying that all of these functions are affected by the body's general health.

Human constitutions vary so much that strict rules do not apply, but it can be said that the adoption of a sensible lifestyle will ensure that any person, without too much discomfort or over-discipline, can function effectively as a musician. The younger the age at which a comfortable routine is set the better. It should take in diet, exercise and leisure.

Many people treat their bodies as if there were no tomorrow. When the body is young it can absorb a great deal of punishment, but changing bad habits only when the body is older and slower is very difficult indeed. Look around you! Any fantasy the human race has about being rational is disproved in the field of health alone!

An Exercise Routine

Choose forms of exercise which can be sustained. Over-elaborate systems of keeping fit are always quickly abandoned. Better to play golf, which is very popular with musicians, or to swim regularly, than to start a routine which is unrealistic. Walking is said by experts to be the best general form of exercise, and can often be incorporated into daily life without loss of time. Stretching is a natural form of animal preparation for action, and can be used without inconvenience. Walking and stretching are my own exercise activities into which I put four or five hours a week. Fitness is not stored in a bank like money. It must be constantly renewed.

Binge exercising is distinctly dangerous to the body. (CR Practice) The body will sharply remind you to respect it, with pulled muscles and other signals of disapproval. Occasional binge practising will also do nothing but cause trouble.

A Reasonable Diet

Eating habits are ingrained in us at the deepest levels. Altering them requires a self-discipline not given to many. For the purposes of common-sense living, a varied diet, which includes both food that is enjoyed and the good-for-you variety, seems to be most practical. Puritanical avoidance regimes caused by vanity, ethical or other considerations put a strain on people's moods and feelings.

Quantity of food relative to exertion is also important. Excess of food is an overload to the digestive system. Beyond the point of need, food is a dangerous drug as much as any other. Entertainment, social and family eating are deeply embedded in our natures. The key point to remember is that our individual body is a once-only resource which cannot be traded in for a more up-to-date version once it has been trashed. The whole-body-brain, or identity transplant, is not yet widely available!

Drug Abuse

Most humans enjoy appropriate changes of mood for social situations and facilitate those changes with drugs both legal and illegal. The bottle of wine between friends is one of civilisation's most pleasant moments, the cigarette the silliest, the needle in the back room the nastiest.

Drugs are quite ruthless in their ability to search out weaknesses of personality and intelligence. They are commercially available everywhere, and when reinforced by the type of music which invades and dominates the nervous system, they take over completely. Young people are today under perpetual attack.

Coda

The specific hardware of our performance may be the trumpet. Ideally we should regard the whole person, mind and body, as our instrument. Treat it well. It is the only one you have.

POSTURE

Quality of posture influences our breathing and therefore our playing. Our posture controls the balance of our body, and influences our health and our moods.

The Basic Person

When a person's posture is balanced and positive, the body's musculature will do its work perfectly well. The body receives its instructions from the brain and enacts them with the maximum efficiency. Habit gives an often misleading sense of comfort, causing us to think that what we are doing is fine, when it may be that we are just used to it. The majority of people hold themselves tight around the neck and shoulders, resulting in permanently tender muscles and restricted breathing.

Confidence is an ingredient in all successful activity. Look up, pretend to be confident, and you are! The world looks better through the middle of the eyes. Watch the way people walk. If they look bright and confident that is almost certainly how they feel and operate. The section on Anxiety Control gives a series of checks for posture.

The Playing Person

Good posture allows good breathing to happen without interference. Playing posture should be as close as possible to the person's best normal posture, without exaggeration or awkwardness. In particular, bad posture limits the movement of the diaphragm and the ribs, thereby restricting lung capacity and usage. (CR Performance, the section on The Performer's Physical Presence)

The Itch to Interfere

In the context of an activity such as playing the trumpet, any detailed instruction to one's body to do this or that in order to achieve a specific result is fraught with danger; it will almost certainly insert a new malfunction into the system. It is my considered view that any conscious attempt to pinpoint one muscle or group of muscles is doomed to failure. The inter-relationships of the whole body's musculature cannot be sensed or controlled. Make one shift of tension or weight in the body, and it will be counterbalanced by a hidden responding tension elsewhere.

Try out these actions.

- Stand up straight, head erect, feet together. Lean the head backwards as far as possible. You will notice an immediate muscular effort in the back and lower parts of the body. It is stopping you falling over!

- Feeling loose, stand on your toes. If your posture is good there will be little or no readjustment of the head in relation to the body compared to the standing position. Most adults have to re-adjust the head position, or fall over.

- Flex a bicep. You will feel the tension centred on that specific muscle spreading well outside the intended area, into the lower arm and into the shoulder. This tension is not creating useful action, and is spreading its negative effect to neighbouring muscles.

Breathing and Embouchure are the two subjects most open to interference and abuse in this way. (CR these Chapters) Every player has had the experience of pulling in here or pushing out there with the breathing, or smiling here or puckering there with the embouchure. The result is always the same, a brief improvement and then a relapse into something slightly worse than before. Any interference in the form of deliberate, targeted tightening creates static, hidden tension.

If there is anything which a physical activity such as playing a musical instrument does not need, it is an excess of negative tension which locks the body up rigidly. So the result is twice negative, both muscularly and in terms of taking the player's attention away from the real target: the musical sound to be made.

A very common response to high range work is for the player to tighten inwards and downwards in the throat and chest area. This squeezing down gives a satisfying sense of effort, but in fact operates against the player. Any sensation should be 'upwards and outwards', allowing the natural combination of the throat, mouth and embouchure to work without hindrance.

How We Start

Assuming that we are born free of defects, as babies we are in a near perfect condition. As a species we hover between being an all-fours creature and an upright one, but as we begin to sit in awkward chairs, sleep in unsuitable beds, suffer a string of accidents, small and large, we gradually lose our best posture and condition, and become crippled in small hidden ways. Watch a baby sitting, its straight back, its relaxed strength.

And How We Continue

In former times, children would be told to sit up straight, that is, maintain their posture. A vigorous regime of physical exercise at school and less comfort at home ensured a strength and stamina, physical and mental, which are often missing from the development of the young of the present-day western world. Today 'stress' is spoken of as a negative force. I see it as the energy created by challenges to which the response can be positive or negative. Response to challenge is one of nature's principal methods of testing us, usually in some form of competition or contest with others.

My own view is that lack of consideration for the whole person is largely to blame for modern inability to cope with negative stress. The young child has as much of a need to experience challenges, in a setting of both caring and discipline, as it has for food and shelter. (CR Anxiety Control) Good breathing, based on good posture, allows the personality to confront challenges without panic.

A good upright posture, the head held high with shoulders relaxed, improves the whole person's mood. This is not simply an old-fashioned thought but the result of modern research which says that the body and the brain work best in this position, as opposed to the slouch. The bio-chemistry of the body is at its most efficient when posture is alert and bright. The primary 'look' of the body is forward and up, with the result that the body lengthens and widens.

In the section on Performance I discuss the use of the eyes. My comments there also apply to normal living. The eyes are the channel for most of our contact with the world and with our routine sensory intake. When the eyes are alert so is the mind.

RANGE (HIGH AND LOW)

Effective and reliable range, both high and low, must be built with steady, patient work. No quick fixes are available.

Two Types of Range Work

1. Sustained work in both ranges has a wear and tear effect on the embouchure, although the stamina and audibility factors together make the problems of high range more obvious.

2. Brief sudden death entries in either range represent some of the sternest of tests for the orchestral trumpet player. Composers have shown a liking for this type of trumpet entry, presumably because of its shock value as a contrast to other quieter music. The Principal Trumpet's first entry in Strauss's Sinfonia Domestica is as good an example of this type as can be imagined.

General Principles

The internal mouth shape controls the airstream which 'makes' the pitch. The external embouchure complements the internal shape as it does in speaking. The syllables 'uuh-eeh' illustrate the movement both internally and externally. The tongue is by far the most important agent in this process, with its ability to alter the mouth shape and volume. This ability to respond in speech and in playing is totally natural and instantaneous, having been developed by evolution. Many great players never give a thought to the matter, except to 'do it'. (CR Embouchure)

There are other factors involved, particularly the pharynx, or lower throat. Pulling down the pitch of notes is achieved by the pharynx, in a quite natural way. For example, play a low C, then pull it down to a B without using the valves, before letting it return to C. For the opposite effect squeeze up a low C by a quarter tone, then let it drop back to its starting point.

Petering out in the top range occurs when the surface of the lower throat has become rigid with effort, thereby producing the effect of the thin, hoarse high note. The rule is therefore to keep the lower throat as open and unstrained as long as possible during ascent into the highest range.

I have no doubt that some players are physically better suited to one range than another. Today players are expected to cover an extended range both high and low. The way has been led by the virtuosi from popular music and jazz. Listen to a great performer such as Derek Watkins delivering superb playing in the highest ranges, only to sweep down and produce the warmest, smoothest, richest low register sound!

Low Range

The need to develop expertise in the low range is frequently ignored by students. Yet it is the range in which most of their early professional work will be done, and the range in use in the orchestral positions which they are most likely to fill at the start of their careers.

As the pitch lowers so the tongue drops, opening up the mouth shape, producing a matching shape in the embouchure. Having said that, the embouchure needs deliberate shaping work to establish a precise position for each note at varying dynamics. Work on pedal notes in particular is helpful in manipulating the mouth and embouchure. John Wallace roomed with me on tours many years ago. His addiction to Claude Gordon's book on pedal notes is still fresh in my memory! He contended that pedal practise was pure gold for every aspect of playing. His sensational technique, impregnable stamina, and vividly wide range are an example to everyone.

High Range

With students I discuss range in terms of layers.

- The middle range is overlaid by the upper middle, which in turn gives way to the high range. These layers vary in pitch according to the player; some students' useful high range may well be a fourth higher than others.

- Above the high range is the petering out zone, when the sound quickly becomes airy, finally disappearing in a squeeze of total effort, as described in the third paragraph of the section above entitled General Principles. Most work must take place in the upper middle register, establishing comfort and ease. As this range is improved so the upper range is lifted. The petering out zone should be entered only very rarely, and not in the regular course of affairs.

Here it is worth repeating some words from the section on stamina.

- Develop the power of the breath stream. The more powerful the breath stream is, the less burden falls on to the embouchure, therefore the freer its response will be. Have the feeling of supporting the lips with the airstream.

- Check general posture, and minimise undue mouthpiece pressure.

- The best starting material for stamina, sound quality and range work is available in the early pages of the Arban Tutor and in hymn books. Gradually transpose them upwards into the higher ranges, concentrating on breath support, comfort and good sound. Avoid squeezing up into the highest areas where the sound becomes airy and peters out.

- Scales and arpeggios can be used in the search for higher range. They must be played without straining, both in the approach to the topmost notes and in turning round at the top. The player must maintain an even flow of effort, without squeezing, and accept, without response, any notes that fail. 'Squeezing' is an action which guarantees that high range problems will be perpetuated.

An Exercise Common to Low and High Range

The On/Off Routine

1. To learn the routine, choose a mid-range note.

2. At a tempo of crotchet (quarter-note) metronome120, play the note for a minim (half-note), then take the instrument from the lips for a further minim. Repeat exactly in tempo. The placement of the mouthpiece back onto the lips must be instantaneous and *not* careful. If it goes back onto the 'wrong' spot, that is part of the value of the routine.

3. What will be found on repetition is that both the external embouchure and the interior of the mouth shape up for the note much more positively than usual.

Example 1

4. Now work with a low-range note. Again make no allowances for setting the embouchure. After a few trials you will find that, as in 3. above, the embouchure and mouth find the necessary shape for the note much more quickly and definitely. In the case of a player with poor low range, work downwards from, say, low C.

5. A high range note (not too extreme) can now be selected and the routine repeated. Again, no allowances for setting are to be made. If the mouthpiece lands off centre, so be it. That is part of the exercise.

6. Now play the exercise at the top of the range.

SLURRING

Harmonic slurring is a daily drill which tunes up the whole playing system.

Fingered slurs are generally easier, but they have hidden problems which can go undetected and uncorrected, to the detriment of the student's progress.

The Key Elements

There are three types of slurring movement.

1. The first is the slur made on the same harmonic series without a change of fingering. A note is moved from one harmonic to another on the same series by a movement of the tongue inside the mouth (the internal embouchure) and a complementary movement of the external (visible) embouchure. These actions alter the tension of the airstream, which alters the pitch of the note.

2. The second involves a change of fingering to a different harmonic series. The same factors apply but less critically, as the fingering action is very helpful to making the change.

3. Thirdly an alternative or false fingering is occasionally used to slur to a note which is shared by two or more series, in order to ease the slurring.

Any change of pitch between two or more adjacent notes needs steady, unchanging support from the airstream. When the slur is over a wider interval, any element of change must be delivered smoothly, or, in the case of a wide slur upwards, be set in place at a convenient moment before the slur starts. (CR Breathing)

Any fingering change must be co-ordinated with the exact instant of departure from the note.

Most players develop slurring skills without experiencing problems along the way. Contact with a good teacher usually resolves any temporary difficulties.

Problems and Solutions

When problems become serious there are certain causes likely to be responsible. As in most situations, anxiety is the probable underlying reason. (CR Anxiety Control). Primarily the player must maintain a sense of musicality, freedom and smoothness when slurring. It is the easiest skill to lose under excess tension, when the player has in effect stopped listening in favour of worrying. Before playing, imagine the quality of smoothness needed, then keep it at the front of the mind.

- *The basic airstream should flow without any interference from the muscles of the lower throat.*

The tongue movement which alters the size and shape of the mouth chamber should be just that and no more. Squeezing the airstream with the lower throat at the note change is a common habit which creates other problems as a result. Players squeeze in order to try to make sure of the note-change. In slow motion, the result is that the tone thins just before the change, squeezes through the gap, and then expands after arrival. This produces the well known 'twaa-twaa' effect. The solution is to project the air through the note-change without any drop in airflow pressure and without any interference by throat movement.

- *The tongue, mouth and embouchure movement should be undertaken as late as possible before the next note.*

Faulty slurring is very often due to the movement starting too early and slowly in order to squeeze the note into its next slot. Late movement is economical movement. It minimises the opportunity for distortion and the 'twaa' effect.

- *When fingering is involved, the movement of the finger should be as late, quick and smooth as possible. (CR Fingering)*

The squeezing of the fingers/valves invariably accompanies the squeezing of the lower throat. Together they often kill the slurred sound between notes. How many otherwise simple fingered slurs are spoiled by the sound disappearing! It hasn't been lost, it has been strangled by the player!

- *When slurring upwards, put the air support for the highest note in place at the last breath point.*

Do not leave the increase of air support until the moment of change, unless you like gambling, or glissandi slurs! Slurs over very wide intervals can be flipped up as if by a yodel movement inside the mouth.

- **_When slurring downwards just let the note drop, as if by gravity. Do not push it down, because it will resist._**

Should the landing on the lower note be bumpy, simply ensure the breath support remains steady through the drop. There is a natural tendency for much more air to rush through as the mouth space opens. Steady air support maintains a level airstream volume, thus avoiding the splash landing.

The Right Solution

The best solution for slurring problems is for the player to improve the musical thought in his or her mind. Concentrated listening and discernment will gradually and naturally reduce the margins of error. This principle applies to all problem solving. (CR Practice Routines) Choosing the precise moment to move is the key element in slurring. The movement should be as late as possible before the moment comes for the next note.

The following routine helps towards good slurring:

- Auralise the following passage (CR Auralisation). Imagine it played perfectly by the finest player.

Example 1

Trumpet in B♭

- Vocalise it in a completely confident, smooth manner, mezzo forte. (CR Vocalisation) Listen intently to the clean quality of the slurs and the fullness of the sound.

- Only when the first two steps have been successful, play boldy and fully, matching exactly the ideal which you have imagined and vocalised. Ignore potential failure totally. Project only the perfect performance.

Any moderately competent performer who has a problem with slurring is practising his or her worrying rather than imagining and listening. This is a matter which no teacher can resolve. It has to be cured by the player adopting musical motivation rather than giving in to fear of failure.

The Fast Mixed Slur

The following brief examples are (Example 2) a test for fast slurring on harmonics and (Example 3) for harmonic and fingered slurs mixed. The prime value of these passages is that their speed makes it impossible for the player to exert note-by-note-control. Let them skid! Gradually a different more general sense of control will take over.

Example 2

Prestissimo

Example 3

Prestissimo

The Lip Trill

When normal slurring has been mastered, and speed work builds up, then the so-called lip-trill can be developed. This is a misnomer because, in effect, it is a tongue trill, the tongue moving back and forward in the mouth in order to cause rapid changes in air tension and therefore pitch. Practise firstly around F's and G's around the top of the stave, using simple varied rhythms. Play comfortably, without concern for tidiness and immediate perfection. Stay loose.

SOUND

The sound or tone-quality which a player makes is his or her most distinctive and important musical fingerprint.

The Quality of Sound

In the judgement of musicians the sound which a player makes is his or her most essential, personal, and valuable attribute. Ideally it combines the opposing elements of warmth and brilliance, each of which can be brought to the fore according to the musical context.

The quality of sound which a player produces is the exact reflection of the musical and physical effort made when blowing. To the expert teacher a student's sound is like an x-ray picture of the playing process, its make up being unique to him or her. The teacher should be able to read a sound and diagnose basic problems in a student's technique as a doctor reads a patient's symptoms.

The Feeling of Sound

Sound is not simply what we hear or play. It is equally a feeling which exists in the body while playing and listening. For musicians, this special harmony of sensation between sound and feeling is one of the basic satisfactions in performing music. The deep response created in a player by his or her own sound, when it is well produced, takes over the whole person.

For most players their choice of instrument was influenced by the attraction and thrill of its unique sound and personality. The most basic reason any musician has for playing an instrument is its sound, feeling, and therefore what it can express. Often it seems as if the instrument chooses the player.

There are occasional examples of players who, having been given an instrument by chance, found it sympathetic, and went on to a fine career. These occurrences are not common.

The Ideal Method for the Placement of Sound

The musician must imagine (auralise) the most beautiful sound before playing starts. This should happen during the brief instant before playing. For master players it becomes simultaneous with the production of the note.

If the student player imagines, in musical terms, both the tone and the type of articulation to be produced ***before playing*** then musical quality quickly and consistently develops. By this means the mind prepares the body quite naturally to undertake the actions necessary to play. This approach requires boldness. Boldness creates technique.

The priority for most players is blemish-free pitching. This very limited approach is mistaken and contrary to the development of sound and personality in playing, and is an important reason why most players fail to develop their potential fully.

Varying Placements of Sound

A well produced sound is usually described as 'centred.' It is as if the note being played were circular and the player had aimed accurately at the middle of it. The practice of long notes is often prescribed as the best way to produce good tone quality. However the mere playing of long notes by themselves does not in itself produce improvement, unless the work is guided by acute and intelligent listening.

When the airstream is squeezed by the throat, the embouchure, and the ribcage in combination, the sound becomes thin, dull, harsh and grating. Players who do this are squeezing 'up' in the circle, above the centre. Most poor tone quality is produced in this way.

If the throat spaces are opened too wide, drawn down together with the embouchure, a dull vacant sound ensues, lacking brightness or shine. This is 'down', below the centre.

These flat and sharp timbres may be perfectly in tune when measured by a machine, but will sound uncomfortably like their character (up or down) when intonation is being considered. Inexpert musicians, who frequently resort to tuning machines, are often confused by this crossover of quality and pitch, mistaking one for the other. (CR Intonation)

Practical Methods for the Placement of Sound

Practical experience has taught me that the best placement for a player's sound lies just above the point where the downpull begins to take effect. The following routines will make this clear.

First Routine:

- Play a long low C.

- When settled, gradually pull it down in pitch using the back of the mouth (the soft palate and tongue) and throat (the pharynx, which is the yawning space). This happens naturally. The embouchure will also flatten and pull down automatically. Firstly the sound will become duller, then it will lose pitch. (CR Practice/Low Range, for another use of this action) For those who habitually squeeze their sound up, this movement downwards may well be a substantial one. It will feel strange.

- Repeat the process until familiar. When ready let the note rise from its depressed position, *listening intently for a change in quality*. This change will come at, or just above, the point where the note floats naturally. The sound should be warm, colourful and glossy.

Second Routine:

- Warm up gently.

- With a practice mute inserted, blow as strongly as possible through a series of low notes. Empty the lungs totally and aggressively. Repeat the process for some thirty seconds or so. Pay no attention to musical quality of the notes as this action is totally physical. This forces the breathing into vigorous action, pushing the airstream past all obstacles like the lower throat and the embouchure.

- Repeat at short (say ten minute) intervals during practice. (CR Practice)

These routines are a quick way to improve sound. CR with the Breathing chapter is essential, in order to develop an understanding of the inter-relationships involved.

The Wider Picture

In the beginning was the sound. Sound is the first factor in music performance and is the primary carrier of the emotion of music. (CR Performance) Whether in Baroque or modern music, in jazz or popular music, for the listener this is where the first response lies. Improvement in sound quality automatically enhances all other aspects of playing; they improve naturally.

The performing musician is always in danger of losing touch with his or her sound for the reason that mistaken short term priorities crowd it out. Pulling off faster 'technical' passages, achieving that extra high note, often become mini obsessions which obscure the picture. While players often concern themselves with technique and safety, audiences love beautiful and interesting sound and the flow of fine tone through the notes.

I chose to study at the Royal Academy of Music with George Eskdale simply because I had heard him (on a battered old radio) play the solos in Vaughan Williams' Fifth Symphony with such a shining, lyrical sound that it was just like falling in love. I didn't at that stage understand, I just knew!

When, a few years later, while still a student, I was working briefly as an extra in a provincial orchestra, a grizzled old pro said to me 'You'll make a lot of money with that sound,' I didn't understand what he meant. I do now.

SPEED PLAYING

High-speed playing began to be seriously explored in bands, popular music and jazz, in the latter part of the nineteenth century and onwards. Practising this aspect of playing, which is still largely ignored in serious brass music, has many benefits.

The Background: the Traditional View of the Trumpet's Role

We expect the violin, the flute and the piano, among others, to be very quick on their musical feet, but the trumpet, especially in its orchestral role, is mainly expected to be the provider of statuesque sound, with the occasional flourish of facility.

The New Trumpet

The Germanic orchestral repertoire dominated the development of the trumpet for a long time. From the close of the Baroque until the turn of the twentieth century, composers writing for the trumpet used it essentially as a tutti instrument, to add rhythmic clarity. Occasionally the instrument's military background was recalled with fanfares and similar musical gestures.

Towards the end of the nineteenth century, the game changed. Technical development of brass instruments had advanced so much that even serious composers in the Germanic school of composition realised that here was an old voice with a new presence. The increasing demands made on players by Wagner were increased by Bruckner, but especially by Strauss and Mahler. However, new ideas from different musical sources in Russia, France, America and Britain were calling up new musical accents, and languages and therefore fresh opportunities for the trumpet.

The most dynamic injection of new life into trumpet performance came from an entirely different source. Jazz and popular music put a completely new musical face on the instrument, releasing it from the restrictions of the old concert hall. The range of performance required across these fields of popular music is enormous. The heroic playing deeds and razor-sharp ensemble of big band musicians, the rebirth of improvisation under the quicksilver fingers of hundreds of jazz stars, the exuberance of a host of soloists in popular music, and the sheer joy of showing-off, all lit up undreamt-of possibilities for the instrument.

All of this came from outside the confines of the orchestra, and the limited thinking of serious art composers. For the trumpet, it shows the way forward to those who see musical life beyond the museum culture of the traditional orchestra and the concert hall.

The cornet, the trumpet's sister instrument, was also a channel to freer expression and technique. In the USA, the virtuosi of the popular touring wind bands became household names, while in Britain the wider freedoms of brass band repertoire, with its adaptations of orchestral, instrumental and vocal music through arrangements, encouraged a different style of performance, together with a limited form of virtuosity.

The brass band route today can be followed through New Zealand, Australia, Europe, Scandinavia, and increasingly Canada and the USA. To this day the heavy brass sections of British orchestras largely consist of players who developed initially in brass bands. The same is true of the majority of players in British jazz and popular music. (CR The Brass Band)

In the section on Technique I underline the need for playing to be imagination-led. Nowhere are the benefits of this approach clearer than in jazz and popular music, where 'technique' is nowhere learned. It is created naturally by the wish of the player to do whatever the imagination demands. These players' academies are the night-club and bar-room, not the concert hall.

The Practical Benefits of Speed Playing

The benefits of speed work are as follows:

1. The development of quick thinking and positive playing.

2. The boost to confidence resulting from 1.

3. Improvement to finger technique: speed, evenness, and quality of the fingering process. (CR Fingering)

4. Developing familiarity and speed of musical thought around the complete instrument, not just on the main roads of C, G, F etc.

An Example Discussed

Regular work on simpler forms of slurred playing at high speed can bring great benefit, especially to poor and medium quality players. Speed work allows the player to improve a number of areas which are often ignored in normal practice. It also re-emphasises the need for common-sense organisation of work, as it applies both to practice and performance.

The main steps are as follows:

1. Play a few single octave scales very fast. The evenness of the fingering will be the first element to be exposed. To improve this, alternate fast work with slow work which uses varying rhythmic and tonguing patterns. When playing fast, vary the speed, making sure that an extreme speed is attempted frequently. Risk going into the unknown. Only by daring what cannot (so far) be done will it become possible! (Refer to the sections on Scales and Arpeggios, and Practice, for a full description of rhythmic and tonguing patterns.)

2. The sostenuto quality of the sound while slurring is an equal priority. Careful listening focused on the evenness of the sound will reveal any blemishes. The temptation for the anxious player is to accept a passage as satisfactory if there are no pitch errors, or if the musical quality of the playing does not actively offend the player. The anxious player, whose attention is almost always somewhere else and not on the here-and-now, is only alerted by note errors and not by quality ones. Listen again and again to improve quality listening.

3. Check the quality of sound *through* the finger changes. The section on Fingering points out the need for effective valve depression. A surprising number of young players are at fault with this, squeezing the valves down rather than depressing them quickly and cleanly. Again the main point is the quality of imagination and listening taking place; if the player has a clear pure legato in mind, and is listening for it, the fingers will deliver it. If the attention is elsewhere, on safety, or on internal physical feelings such as the embouchure, the player will not notice.

4. The factors which most usually spoil the legato are the very ends and starts of notes which are joined by the legato. (CR Legato) The player with moderate or poor legato will tend, as described above, to squeeze the fingers up and down, creating an unintentional glissando, and thereby dirtying the sound. This will interfere both with the end of one note and the start of the next. (CR Fingering)

5. At high speed, the habit of throat squeezing is somewhat neutralised because the notes are happening too fast for interference. At speed, check the fingering. The valve depressions must be complete or the sound will be blurred. The scratchy, uneven effect which characterises many players in moderate speed legato work is the direct result of these two interlinked malpractices. The type of player who uses throat and finger squeezing at each note change will almost certainly be tightening in the soft palate and lower throat areas, with a consequent negative effect on high range. (CR Range)

6. Remember that slow legato playing needs clean fingering as much as fast legato does.

7. Speed and sharpness of thought characterise all good performers, slowness and dullness poor performers. Like all human faculties, the right usage and exercise of the mind will help players of all standards to become better. The brain should be thought of as a muscle; if it is worked hard, it will become stronger. Yes, it also hurts to be exercised, just like a real muscle!

8. The result for a player who significantly increases speed capability is greatly enhanced confidence. This is not an illusion of the transitory mood-swing type, but a genuine gain in skill. Regular physical exercise gives a sense of well-being. Equally, mental challenge-and-response tones up the mind and improves its mood-weather.

9. Speed work takes the player beyond the point of safe control, which is an upsetting feeling for some players. For others it is the excitement of trying something dangerous and attractive. If a player never ventures outside what is secure, how can new and better techniques be created? How else can a player change for the better?

TECHNIQUE

Q: What is technique?
A: The capability to fulfil musical thoughts.
Q: What is the most effective way of acquiring it?
A: Boldness creates technique.

A Case of Mistaken Identity

The majority of performers think of technique as something separate to their musicality, to be earned by hard work and to be kept in good order by steady painstaking effort. They have the idea that technique must be gained first and only when it has been gained can attention be given to playing expressively.

A few lucky players are regarded as having a good technique as if it were a gift from the appropriate good fairy. They seem to have come by their technique not by practising but by 'just playing.'

As usual the truth lies in between the two extremes. The idea that the development of technique must come before musicality is the product of anxiety. The wish to be tidy, respectable, and not to lose face through making blunders has become the prime concern. Quite a few players make it into professional music by using this approach. Most, however, never arrive at a convincing all-round style and end up with a stiff, unresponsive, rather wooden quality of performance whose main virtue is reliability. (CR Velocity)

The Correct Emphasis for Technique

The primary impulse for all playing should be musical. A strong expressive idea as to how a phrase should be played will, if followed with persistence and intelligence, gradually create the capability (technique) to bring it about. The realisation of the musical impulse needs time, but the main motivation must always be a musical one.

Exercises and studies are however necessary and desirable; they create order out of everyone's natural tendency to be chaotic. While it is obvious that most exercises and studies are not pieces of music as such, but are abstracts of musical situations, they must be played as music. That effort - to find 'music' where it is obviously missing - is part of the essential discipline of technical work as it develops the player from the state of being amateur to becoming professional.

The Learning Process for Technique

Progress will be slow if the process of improvement is through the bored repetition of exercises. *Scales and arpeggios, long notes, flexibilities and tonguing work should all be played as if they were pieces of music.* However unlikely it might be, imagine that the exercise being played is part of a concert work, and that there is an audience listening to it as music.

Even where a student is undergoing remedial work in regard to major difficulties, the mechanical, technical-as-opposed-to-musical approach is mistaken. Conceiving exercises in musical terms, for example a scale played with a tongued legato espressivo, engages the whole musical personality.

Musical impulse stimulates, but technical anxiety stiffens.

'Technique is the consequence of the dominating concept. Change the concept and the technique will change.' Who said that? Not a trumpeter, not a musician, but an American painter, Willem de Kooning. This exactly agrees with the idea of musicality leading and technique following. There is in fact remarkable agreement across many disciplines that the idea and the feeling, powered by boldness, create the necessary technique.

Why are good players good? Because they are bold enough to conceive good playing, and are audacious enough and patient enough to work towards their ideal. Why are great players great? They think great (musical) thoughts! How does your favourite trumpet artist achieve those special effects? He or she had the courage, the musical nerve and imagination to think them up, and then the nerve to try to make them happen.

There is no other method of becoming extraordinary. Otherwise we do that which is ordinary, like most others. We all make our choice. We all achieve the performance we deserve, because that is what we ask ourselves to do. We play what we think. We become what we think! Attempt the impossible!

Poor players will not try to play to an ideal: they want to wait until it is safe, until they have the technique! When a baby wants to walk, it gets up, falls over, gets up again, falls over, bangs its head, cries, tries again, and in the end, after hundreds of failures, bumps and cries - it walks! The baby doesn't wait until it has the technique to walk before it tries. It would still be waiting!

Babies don't mind taking risks or hurting themselves if they can get what they want. Poor quality players won't take the risk. They fear failure. They don't want to look stupid to themselves or others, and don't want to hurt their brains with the hassle of re-thinking their attitudes, their strategies, and ditching their habitual bag and baggage. Above all they don't want the mental pain of being brave. So they choose to improve as slowly as possible or not at all. Putting it harshly they prefer being no good, rather than risking looking foolish.

Recapitulation: The Main Method

The trumpet is not an instrument for those who wish to hide. Everyone in the hall hears a trumpet mistake or split. Curiously enough, quite a number of people who temperamentally shrink from exposure and danger are drawn to the trumpet. (CR Careers and Talent)

Conceive the idea, then do it as soon as possible. This remains our basic human method of progressing. Poor players are poor because they repeat a cycle of poor thoughts. They can be heard everywhere, repeating the same errors over and over again. If something doesn't work change it, re-think it. The baby explores, tries, fails, rethinks, regroups, tries again - and so does the successful musician. (CR Practice)

Repeat! Repeat! Repeat!

SECTION THREE

PERFORMANCE

INTRODUCTION

This group of chapters is very closely connected to those in Section One. In one or two cases the assignment of chapters to this Section may seem arbitrary, but they are intended to deal with the outward face of mind skills.

Performing is a separate study to practising, a fact which is often ignored by teachers and students alike. The assumption is made that if the work in the practice room is good then the performance that follows will also be good. Nothing is further from the truth. In practising, players work analytically to improve themselves, while in performing they must deliver as much as they can in a once-only setting.

Performing itself needs to be practised.

ACCOMPANIMENT

Dealing with accompaniment and accompanists is a special skill. It is equally difficult to provide effective accompaniment.

A Knowledge of the Accompaniment is Essential

It is rare for a soloist to pay close attention to the accompaniment, except in difficult moments. It must always be remembered that the soloist is just one part of the overall piece of music. Certain performers are the finest because they are aware of everything that is happening in the piece, and can therefore give a complete account of it.

When we look at concerti for the trumpet such as the Haydn or the Hummel, the accompaniment contains slurs and dynamics missing in the solo part. The full orchestral scores contain much of this missing detail and can tell the soloist much about the appropriate way to play. I am here referring to original editions which contain no editing, as opposed to those which add a large amount of editorial detail. (CR Music Editions)

This example, from the soloist's first entry in the Hummel Concerto for Trumpet, shows detail in the accompaniment from which we can infer how to play the solo part. (All examples from this Concerto are given in Eb, the key in which it is usually played.)

Example 1

Allegro con spirito

Note the third bar: the final three quavers of the accompaniment are marked staccato (in one original edition given as semi-staccato), while the solo part is not. This continues until the fifth bar, when the staccati ceases at the fourth crotchet while the next bar is marked slurred. From this I would infer that the solo part should be played as follows.

Example 2

NB. The concept of the staccato as a half value note is very misleading. In music of the Classical period at least, it should be read as only slightly marked. This tends to give a slight separation. The vertical dash mark is intended to produce the half length staccato.

Depth of Knowledge

For the student who wishes to give the best possible performance of a solo work, the accompaniment should be learnt thoroughly. During preparation, significant cues should be added to the soloist's copy, and should be imagined through during personal practice and rehearsal, even including bars' rest. This method will help memorisation of the solo line by creating a continuous context.

Fully professional preparation requires not only memorisation of the solo part (CR Memory), but a complete memorisation of the whole work. This essential knowledge allows the soloist to realise the work as fully and securely as possible. The superficial run-through, however cleverly managed, is not honest music making or good professional practice.

Problem Moments in the Accompaniment

Knowledge of the accompaniment must also include an understanding of the degree to which an ensemble or orchestra can respond to rubato in certain musical contexts. If a soloist wishes to adopt a particularly wayward interpretation of a passage, then it is important that the context can stand it. An extreme rubato with an intricate accompaniment will cause poor ensemble. Against static chords, any amount of rubato is practical.

Working with Piano Accompaniment

Performing with piano gives rise to three problems, of which intonation is the first. It must be remembered that the harmonic series which rise from each fundamental note on the trumpet contains notes which are sharper or flatter than the norm, as well as those which are more or less in tune. (CR Intonation) Pianos, however, are tuned as evenly as possible.

The second problem is the variability of the player. Unlike the give and take which can be exercised among 'natural' instruments, where the trumpet is among friends, the piano is totally unable to vary its tuning. If the soloist is becoming overheated during a performance in a hot room, or because of a high level of exertion, the trumpet's pitch may well rise. The piano's pitch however stays the same, causing conflict.

Thirdly, the piano never knows whether it is playing a C sharp or a D flat, by which I mean it has no sense of key or tonal centre in the way a brass instrument has. Context means nothing to the piano, whereas in 'real' tuning it is vital. This matter is discussed much more fully in the chapter on intonation.

The second movement of the Trumpet Concerto by Haydn throws up most of the aforementioned problems for the unwary soloist. For example, written low C's, often sharp on the instrument, are set against Eb on the piano: the effect is almost always jarring. In bars 21 to 24 inclusive, the top line of the trumpet is doubled by the piano accompaniment, which can be similarly awkward. Much better to ask the pianist to leave out conflicting notes in both these examples, or better still, edit them out of the piano copy.

The positive aspect of piano accompaniment shows up strongly when the pianist is a fine musician and able to show rapport and sensitivity to the soloist. A positive partnership then ensues which almost totally minimises the disadvantages.

Working with Conductors

Very few solo performances are thoroughly rehearsed with the accompaniment, because orchestral rehearsal time is always short. On those rare occasions when working with an orchestral accompaniment is possible, the soloist has to deal with a conductor. Few conductors enjoy accompanying, because not only is it a secondary role for them, it is also their most difficult technical challenge. Listening to the soloist while controlling the orchestra means that the conductor must be technically competent. (CR Conductors)

Only experience can equip you to deal with the conductor as accompanist. For the soloist from the orchestra's ranks, direct experience is rare. Use the time playing in the brass section to weigh up the methods with which conductors handle concerto situations. Read their personalities, how other soloists respond, and imagine the varying circumstances into which you might be thrown. Above all be certain of your interpretation, so that positive delivery will give you the advantage. Be prepared to assert yourself quickly, firmly, preferably quietly, but publicly if necessary.

Taking the Lead

The vast majority of solo situations occur with accompaniment provided by pianists not of your choosing. This can be a tough test of your musical character if the pianist is struggling, but it can be a most enjoyable experience if he or she is thoroughly expert.

Always indicate your tempo with total clarity, and then assert it at all times, leaving the pianist adrift if necessary. The ability to be strong minded will be to your advantage, because experienced musicians will understand what is happening and will appreciate your determination to have your tempo, come what may. They will have suffered it themselves. (CR Auditions)

Above all beware of the moderate pianist or conductor who gently drags tempi back into their own comfort zone, taking that vital edge off the soloist's performance.

Being a Good Accompanist

On those occasions when you are in a one-to-one situation accompanying a soloist, or playing a solo line in the orchestra, the priorities are as follows:

• Listen as carefully as possible to the soloist at all times.

• Watch the soloist as well as the conductor, so that you can detect visual signs which will help the detail of the performance. This means that you, the accompanist, must have virtually memorised the key passages in order to have attention to spare. (CR Memory)

ACOUSTICS

The acoustic environment is the musician's canvas. The performer must be ready to deal flexibly with any new acoustic according to its character. In certain circumstances it can affect the performer's playing and the achievement of good orchestral ensemble.

The Helpful Acoustic

Some acoustics add resonance and sheen to a sound. The concert hall which helps to smooth out the legato, and to plump up the tone, is always enjoyable to the performer. However, there are comparatively few of these halls.

The disadvantages are that firstly, this acoustic can cause the performer to play too loudly for the orchestra; secondly, the sound can become confused in a reverberant acoustic, making accurate listening difficult. Ensemble will suffer as a result.

The Dry Acoustic

The dry acoustic subtracts some or all of the flattering elements from the sound. In a particularly dead acoustic there will be no shine on the sound at all, while the dynamic range will be severely restricted. This acoustic response may cause the inexperienced player to force, making too much effort to replace the qualities which are missing. Often this can lead to over-blowing and distortion of sound quality when competing against a full symphony orchestra.

For practice purposes, however, a dry room is much the best, as it stimulates the habit of strong full breathing when playing.

The Traditional Concert Hall

The older eighteenth and nineteenth century halls are ornamented with abundant plasterwork. The effect of this decoration is to break up and diffuse the sound evenly, adding a very smooth decay to the sound. In this kind of hall any excess reverberation tends to be reduced to a comfortable amount by the audience. Without any doubt these halls are the most receptive to performance.

The Modern Concert Hall

The basic acoustic sound of the modern hall is likely to be synthetic, unnatural and uneven. All modern concert halls now have electronic systems to mimic the sound of a natural 'acoustic' concert hall. Hundreds of microphones and speakers pick up and relay reverberation, trying to put back what the architects should not have taken out in the first place.

The shape of the hall will also give a clue as to potential problems for ensemble. The traditional rectangular box shape is probably the best. The wider the hall, the more difficult hearing, playing and balancing become. Playing is therefore rarely straightforward in these halls.

The Use of Baffles

For players and audience, direct acoustic response is helped by baffles placed behind the musicians, because sound tends to diffuse equally around a player and is only partially directional, even for the brass. Empty space behind a brass section means that 'it' will probably sound late. (See below, Orchestral Playing (Ensemble and Articulation). Baffles are common in recording and broadcast studios as separators i.e. for recording purposes.

If the 'ensemble' is a problem because of the acoustics of the hall, and baffles are available, ask for them to be used. When placed as a surround for an ensemble, they can pull the sound and ensemble together in a very positive way, both for the players and listeners, for reasons described above. It never ceases to surprise me that expert musicians can be so uncaring about the poor acoustic environments in which they play.

Orchestral Dynamics and Balance

The acoustic of the hall must be taken into account by the performers. For example, a small or noisy hall will just not have the capacity to take the biggest modern fortissimi. Unfortunately some brass players ignore this fact and play equally loudly in all halls. It is very easy to adjust the range of dynamics and it is un-musical not to do so when the acoustic requires it.

Improvements in manufacture have resulted (among other things) in brass instruments becoming much more powerful. It is always tempting to play up to the upper dynamic limit, even though destruction of the musical balance results from that.

In an orchestra with only moderate or thin string tone the brass will always sound too powerful even at moderate dynamic levels, but a full-blooded string sound allows the whole range of brass dynamic to be used.

Musical Noise

All musicians should develop sensitivity to musical noise, both for musical benefit, and for the wider good of our world which is increasingly being drowned in noise. Our senses are ruthlessly played on by those wishing to bring themselves to our attention and by others who wish to make money by creating appetites for more and more extreme sensations. (CR Time and Rhythm)

Orchestral Playing (Note Lengths)

Each kind of acoustic needs different note lengths. For example, a dry acoustic needs longer and fuller lengths to make up for missing resonance, whereas a booming hall which has plenty of resonance needs shorter notes to give definition. This kind of adjustment needs first class team work and awareness.

Orchestral Playing (Ensemble and Articulation)

Perhaps the most important acoustic fact of life for the brass player in an orchestra is the distance at which he or she sits from the conductor, the rest of the orchestra, the audience or microphones. Even in the best halls, the geography of standard orchestral seating means that the brass will need to play 'right at the front' of the tempo, that is, to be as early as possible without actually being ahead. The conductor's beat is not the critical factor that most people think. The players' awareness is.

The seating of the brass at the back of the orchestra dictates the basic articulation to be used in routine orchestral playing. For most orchestral brass situations the standard attack must be clear and definite. This sends the sound across the orchestra with maximum clarity. Remember that volume is not clarity.

The inexperienced player is sometimes puzzled by the strong, clear articulations used by experienced symphonic players. The clarity of impact relative to sound often needs to be much more than the beginner expects. The professional is thinking differently; not how it sounds close by, but how does it sound in the hall, or how is it going to sound on the recording?

In my early playing days, I learnt a great deal by constantly listening to recording playbacks. Even though the recording studio is an artificial environment, it is another important situation in which the player can learn a great deal. The master performer must continually calculate the projection of his or her sound. Does it balance? Does it lead? Can it be heard? Is it too loud?

Orchestras' Individual Ensemble Characteristics

All orchestras have their own personalities which persist through the years and through total changes of personnel. The London Symphony Orchestra plays in much the same way now as it did when I first joined it in 1960. These orchestral habits of sound, attack and ensemble are as individual as fingerprints. New members of any orchestra are chosen only if they feel tempo and attack in the same way as the section. Judging the acoustic is an important part of this. Guest freelance players are in the most difficult position. They have to vary their response as they move from orchestra to orchestra, instantly adjusting their playing to the new blend.

CADENZAS

A well-played, musically effective cadenza can add tremendous value to a Baroque or Classical concerto performance.

The Cadenza's Purpose

The traditional cadenza allows the performer an opportunity to display a wide range of abilities on an empty musical canvas.

The Cadenza's History

The cadenza's emergence in musical history runs parallel with the development of the individual performer as star, when outstanding musicians were seeking any and every opportunity for showing off their talents.

The cadenza evolved in the Baroque period as an improvisation, placed at the final main cadence of a movement or aria. (The word 'cadenza' is Italian for cadence.) Throughout the late eighteenth century, the instrumental cadenza developed rapidly in scale, after which the cadenza opportunity also began to appear at other additional points, in all movements. However, as composers began to exert more and more control over all aspects of their music at the expense of the performers' input, cadenzas were also taken over. Within a few decades of Mozart and Beethoven writing down their own improvised cadenzas, the performers' improvisations had disappeared.

The Cadenza Today

Today the performance of music contrasts very strongly with the past. In the eighteenth and early nineteenth centuries, musicians had the education and intelligence to venture on improvised cadenzas: it was an expected part of their performance. (CR Improvisation) In addition, the concert manners of the audience were less inhibited than now. A poor performance, especially of the cadenza, would be shouted down in no uncertain terms. Our current habit of presenting music as an unvarying, quasi-sacred and, ultimately, sanitised ritual, would be thought very strange by our ancestors.

Today the performer is never trusted to improvise, except in very limited circumstances and with multiple instructions. (CR Contemporary Music Performance)

The Cadenza Itself

The good Baroque or Classical cadenza must have a convincing shape and present an effective link to the tutti. The audience must be carried along not only by the performer's playing skills but by the musical progression of the cadenza. Whether short or long, the cadenza must be musically literate or it will not be convincing. Only on this basis can a player fully control the audience's attention, by provoking, surprising, toying with and finally satisfying their expectations.

Performing the Cadenza

How often does the cadenza in the Haydn Trumpet Concerto or a Baroque concerto sound like a chore, only played because custom demands it? How many players create some magic for an audience? Uninterrupted by the accompaniment, the soloist can display his talents to the full. How many do?

In the cadenza the player is alone. More than ever, just playing well is not enough. In most cadenzas, the music is almost static, with the performer frequently stopping and starting the action. In this situation he or she must play with the audience, teasing it, amazing it, making it wait. As an expert actor times the lines, the musician must time the pauses, spaces, rallentandi and accelerandi. Here, above all, the musician is an actor with sound. By these means the master musician transforms the simplest cadenza material into gold.

The Standard Printed Cadenza

Late Baroque and Classical concertos are usually printed with a mediocre cadenza, courtesy of the editor. The player of taste must create his or her own cadenza and be prepared to take great trouble with it. Cadenzas which do nothing but repeat two or three motifs from the work are too predictable. Motifs should be used, but are only interesting if woven into a stimulating context.

The Baroque Concerto

The movements of the Baroque concerto do not have the clear character differences found in the Classical concerto form, but when writing a cadenza the approach should be the same: pick up the mood of the movement and exploit it. The cadenza concoctions which are found in most published editions of Baroque concertos are inadequate, uninteresting and should be avoided.

The Haydn Concerto

The first movement cadenza should match the mood of its setting, and should explore a wide range of expression. Whether the start is quiet, building steadily towards the trill, or whether it begins boldly, giving way to quieter moments, *the underlying harmonic progression must make sense*. When the cadenza modulates or goes through harmonic sequences, the progressions of harmony and the resolutions of notes must be coherent within the rules of traditional harmony. This harmonic progression traditionally (and sensibly) arrives at the tonic 6/4 chord (the second inversion) when, and only when, the cadenza is ready to finish with the grand trill on the dominant chord. This sense of direction and irresistible arrival is only possible if the preceding harmony is coherent and logical.

My view is that the last movement also cries out for a cadenza, short and brilliant, a witty one-liner which does not interrupt the movement's impetus.

The 'Modern' Cadenza in the Haydn Concerto

Some enterprising players compose cadenzas for this Concerto in one of the musical languages of the twentieth century. This is an approach which, whilst arguably valid, is very difficult to bring off successfully. Any Concerto must be enhanced by the cadenza, with which the player must be able to interest the audience without it feeling shocked. If it feels jolted or offended then the point of the cadenza is lost and the audience's continuity of attention will be destroyed by the shock.

CONTEMPORARY MUSIC

Composers constantly make more complex, novel demands on performers. The musician must be willing to meet these challenges without any prejudice against the unfamiliar.

Attitudes to Contemporary Music

Performers (and listeners) have open minds about any piece of music which comes before them - until they hear the composer and title! After which they are likely to respond according to their existing tastes and expectations. If it is a piece of unknown contemporary music, the response will be guarded and potentially negative before a sound is heard. Only the professional musician with a specialised interest in contemporary music is likely to maintain a genuinely open mind. Though there are exceptions, today it is normal for public taste to run at least seventy-five years behind the calendar.

The Unwelcome Challenges of some Contemporary Music

There are composers good, bad, and indifferent, who like to write 'difficult' music. Professional musicians may well see this kind of material as an unwelcome challenge, as first impressions will usually be confused and therefore unpleasant.

It is important not only to stay flexible in response to new playing challenges, but to keep an open mind as to the quality of the music. So many examples exist of the greatest works of art initially being dismissed as nonsense that it is reasonable to guard against similar mistakes and not to close off the possibility that one may be wrong.

To Like or Not to Like

The musician's judgement against a work may be right, but the negative attitude which many performers instantly adopt to a certain type of music is mistaken. Liking music is not a primary part of professionalism, whereas performing to one's highest competence is. To enjoy the music being performed is a bonus, not a right. Use the difficulties of any new music to expand instrumental skills and horizons.

Developing New Skills and Upgrading Old Ones

When new music offers new challenges the result will be the constant upgrading of players' techniques, and the expansion of the expressive range of the trumpet. The progression towards complexity can be clearly seen over the whole of music history, and should surprise no-one.

The main challenge of today's music is that, like its predecessors in their day, it presents the performer with ever more complexity to resolve. Each independent strand, whether of pitch, rhythm or dynamic, is more and more detailed, therefore the effort to combine them into a whole has to be constantly upgraded. When a difficult piece has been overcome and is replayed after a period of months or years, there is no longer a problem. The mind has absorbed the challenge, resolved it and made it its own. It becomes 'normal'.

Aleatoric Music

This type of controlled improvisation is now commonly met in contemporary music. Presented as single notes or groups of notes, in boxes or in some other situation with instructions, the performer is invited to 'improvise'. In every situation of this kind that I have encountered, a good deal of organisation is necessary to produce an acceptable result. Unprepared spontaneity tends to produce noise!

Theatricality in Contemporary Music

Much contemporary solo repertoire has a theatrical character. Sometimes it is obvious, as in Stan Friedman's Solus, where the series of shouts is a very dramatic interruption of the playing - a wonderfully successful inspiration.

In a different and less obvious way, a great deal of contemporary music is constructed from small motifs, rhythms and other features. These are essentially theatrical and gestural, in which case a matching response however restrained, can be very helpful to the performance. Peter Maxwell Davies' Sonatina is a good example.

DYNAMICS

The development and command of a wide range of dynamics is an important part of playing, worthy of careful attention.

The Starting Point

Good sound is the starting point for all meaningful work on dynamics. Straining to play wide dynamic variations when the student's sound is as yet undeveloped makes matters worse. (CR Sound, Practice) When this has been achieved, work on expanding the dynamic range can begin. The modern scale of dynamics is very large indeed in a powerful symphony orchestra; the student should prepare steadily to be able to fulfil it when the chance comes.

The modern practice mute is invaluable in building up breath power, which benefits all dynamics. It should be used only for very short periods, as - beyond a certain point - it does introduce an element of distortion into the embouchure.

Medium Dynamics

Full sound at *mezzoforte* is the basis from which development of dynamic range can begin. Listening for quality and evenness of sound over the whole pitch range is the priority at this point.

Soft Dynamics

Few brass players are naturally good at playing softly, yet it can be the most embarrassing gap in technique when exposed. The following simple routine usually works.

- Play a middle register passage at *mezzoforte*, concentrating on a sense of comfort.

- Repeat at the slightest degree softer, taking care that the physical effort to play remains the same as at *mezzoforte.*

- Repeat, again slightly softer, maintaining the same physical action.

- Continue till *double pianissimo* is reached.

- Spread out into other ranges.

The key to this procedure is maintaining the same kind of physical effort in a soft dynamic as in a medium dynamic. Squeezing to produce a soft dynamic is the commonest fault, and is self-defeating. It comes from anxiety.

Another important routine is outlined in the section on articulation. CR the paragraphs titled as follows: 3: The Air attack without Tongue. Practising on the Airstream. Focusing the Airstream. 4: The Air attack articulated in the Throat.

When comfortable soft playing has been mastered, then move on to practising diminuendi from pianissimo downwards into the subtone where the sound is more felt than heard. The skill of manipulating volume at this low level gives the performer a virtuoso command of the softest dynamics.

Loud Dynamics

Use of the practice mute is important here, for frequent but brief periods. Regular work will gradually raise the upper levels. Cultivate a smooth, unforced delivery, being sure to produce the best quality of sound at all times and in all dynamics.

Crescendi and Diminuendi

Proceed as above to do a little work often, setting out a planned progression of work. When doing the breathing warm-up, speed up and slow down the airstream, paying attention to comfort and smoothness of exhalation. As always, have the musical image in control as playing takes place.

A common fault with crescendi and diminuendi, as well as with rallentandi and accelerandi, is to make both far too soon. In all these cases in actual performance, they are best made late, where they have the most effect.

INTERPRETATION

Interpretation is the act of turning a written score into a coherent performance.

The Skills Necessary for Interpretation

Throughout the history of music, comparisons have been made between performers and performances in order to compare the effectiveness of different approaches. No two interpreters are the same. Furthermore, no two performances by the same individual are ever identical. The skills necessary to achieve adequate interpretations are assembled by observation, experience and study.

The lack of a broad concerto repertoire for the trumpet has had two main effects. Firstly, the vast majority of players do not play solos consistently throughout their career. This has meant that the ability to interpret has not been developed very far in trumpet playing, in comparison with more favoured instruments, such as the piano or violin.

Secondly, the growth of interest in the trumpet has been based mainly on the display skills of the player. In practical terms, the purpose of the bulk of trumpet repertoire is simply to show off the facility of star performers. Virtuosity and quality can co-exist quite happily, but unfortunately in much brass music this is not the case.

Interpretation in the Orchestra

In orchestral performance, the Principal Trumpet's main musical function is to lead the section and deliver the important solos well, combining a memorable sound, a first class technique and a strong musical personality. An ability to be decisive, professional and calm in the many situations which arise throughout the years, almost always goes with quality musicianship.

In the Principal Trumpet repertoire many opportunities exist for the exercise of fine musicianship, for which a knowledge of the varying styles of repertoire is essential. It should be no surprise that those Principals who are the most musical, and whose interpretative skills are best developed, are those with the widest national and international reputations. (CR Careers)

Interpretation for the Student Soloist

Study gives the musician the knowledge with which to improve his or her ideas about playing. For a start, listening to a number of performances of the same piece by different performers will widen one's appreciation of the options available. For example, when a student of mine is working on a piece, I suggest they listen to a number of recordings. Firstly I ask them to note the overall relative success of the performances, and how each performer shapes the piece. I also ask them to note key points such as tempi, sound, note lengths, accentuations, slurrings etc. Finally we discuss ornamentation and cadenzas.

Not only does this study improve the student's ability to discriminate between performances, it also strengthens his or her own ideas. The student's ultimate priority must be to develop his or her own interpretative abilities. Imitation is only a study method used to widen the player's horizon.

Look for the following points.

Themes and Musical Motifs

These will be of varying importance and will recur throughout. If the performer is simply aware of these family likenesses, then they will come out quite naturally in the playing. Awareness of motifs is particularly important in contemporary music performance. (CR)

Climaxes and Resolutions

These obviously signal the high points of pieces or movements and are normally the loudest moments. Having said that, there is the occasional piece where the key points are soft in dynamic, for example the Hindemith Sonata for Trumpet and Piano.

Bridge Passages and Codas

These passages have specific functions leading towards, preparing for, or coming from main sections.

Tempi

The single most important choice to be made in any piece is its basic tempo or pulse. A tempo can be slackened or tightened, but the pulse must remain recognisably the same. Any variation beyond the recognisable boundaries of a tempo is a serious error of judgement, unless written by the composer.

Form

Knowledge of the overall form of pieces, movements and complete concerti is invaluable. It gives the performer the understanding to vary the themes and motifs according to their internal position in a piece.

(CR with the following chapters: Learning Music, Reading Music, Melody, Time and Rhythm.)

INTONATION

To achieve good tuning requires a constant listening effort from the player:
(1) to his or her own playing and
(2) to the ensemble as a whole.

This listening has to be on two fronts:
(1) to the horizontal progression of notes and
(2) to the vertical harmony.

Natural Tuning vs. Modern Tuning

Natural tuning, or how the ear likes to hear intervals, prevailed until the late seventeenth century, when the need for equalised tuning of the twelve semitones became imperative. Composers had become aware of the whole possible palette of keys and of course wanted to use it. Modern tuning can be conveniently dated from Bach.

Most authentic instrument orchestras play to modern tuning (if not modern pitch) because the public and critics hear natural tuning as simply out-of-tune! For those interested enough it is worth while listening to examples of keyboard music where the instrument has been tuned 'naturally'. It will be a shock for the uninitiated! The reason is that, prior to the development of equal semitone tuning, key centres existed quite separately from each other, and were never mixed by modulation, which did not exist as we know it now. The musical shift must have been equivalent to the change from the flat-earth to the round-earth theory.

Remnants of natural tuning still persist, in the way we like to hear certain aspects of tuning. Watch a fine trombonist make minute adjustments to slide positions for the 'same' note in different chords. These are called enharmonic changes. The trumpeter who uses a false fingering (see below) will be adjusting the position of the note in the chord, either because (1) the normal fingering produces an unacceptable pitch from its position in the harmonic series, or (2) the current chord needs a sharper or flatter pitch, even if the normal fingering produces a good pitch.

Lipping notes up or down is a short term solution for the occasional out-of-tune note, but sound quality is often dulled by the note being pushed or pulled off its sweet spot. Trumpets have various push and pull devices for detailed tuning of slides during performance. They should be used as precisely as a trombonist uses a slide. (See paragraph below, The Same Note in Different Keys)

Notes which 'Tend'

A melodic line, together with its harmony, is always 'going to' or 'coming from', aiming at, or resolving from, a target or climax. This is linked, very subtly, to intonation, creating a sense of direction, a sense of notes tending upwards or downwards. A string player or vocalist or trombonist will follow these tendencies naturally because each pitch has to be made by the player.

Example 1

Quite a few of the trumpet's pitches, which are more or less exactly made by the instrument, need some fine-tuning. I do not list all of them here, because they vary widely according to the manufacture of the instrument, but the commonest ones are as follows:

Example 2

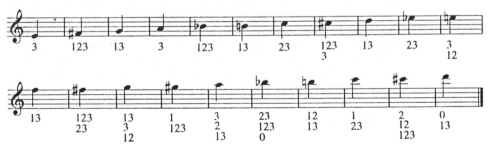

Interval Characteristics that the Ear Likes

Taken in isolation, each interval has a tuning width which the ear likes. This remnant of natural tuning shows itself most clearly in the ear's liking for a bright fifth. The choice of the orchestral tuning A, which can seem puzzling to a brass player, allows the violins to take a level conveniently central to their string configuration, and then tune down to the D and G, then up to the E. Were they to tune up in bright fifths from the low G, the resulting fourth string E would be horribly sharp.

To my ear, intervals go in matching pairs within the octave, usually, but not always, one sharper and one flatter.

- The unison and octave are critical intervals for the trumpet, appearing countless times in Classical repertoire. They ring unmistakably when perfect. When played by two fine players, they are unmatched for beauty and sonority. The octave interval requires the lower part to be slightly louder than the upper, to add warmth and to allow the upper part to float and shine.

- The perfect fifth is also unmistakable when right. Ringing true, it is sharper than equal temperament (piano tuning) allows. This is proven when a progression of perfectly tuned fifths is played upwards. On completion, the final note (the same name as the starting note) will be more than a quarter tone sharp. Its opposite, the perfect fourth, is ideally a narrow interval. As a fourth in the scale it tends downwards towards the third, whether major or minor. (See paragraph above: Notes which 'Tend')

- The major third, and its match the minor sixth, are the most negotiable of the pairings. In natural tuning the third is happiest when very slightly dull. If a series of three natural major thirds were tuned, say, C to E, E to G#, Ab to C, the resultant octave C to C would be flat. Compare this with the cycle of perfect fifths which when complete is very sharp. However, the major third is influenced strongly by the character of the triad which it inhabits, every key having its own feel and personality.

- The minor third likes to be well down, while the major sixth is naturally bright and strong.

- The major second is a full strong up-tending interval, while the minor seventh is a down-tending interval, like the perfect fourth.

- The minor second is a narrow down-tending interval, partnering the bright up-tending major seventh.

The Same Note in Different Keys

Any one note will have a different slant according to the key in which it exists. A G# in the key of A major (the seventh) will need to sound sharper than an Ab (the fourth) in the key of Eb major. This is because our scales have unequal configurations which are not based on twelve equal pitches. These unequal relationships within a key must be understood by the ear before playing of the highest quality can be achieved.

Key relationships are opposed by the configuration of the trumpet's own intonation. The characteristics of the harmonic series are clearly defined, and well known to all competent players: some notes are flatter and some sharper. However, the tuning patterns of these series cross randomly with the tuning configurations required by the key of the music. The result is that often the natural tuning of the note on the instrument is quite wrong for the pitch of the note in the musical context. For any one piece of music, these clashes between the instrument's harmonic series and the music will be different for each pitch of instrument. For example, the fourth-line D of a Bb trumpet is a little dull both in pitch and timbre. The same note on a C trumpet is bright in both regards.

Tone versus Tuning

Variation of tone, note-to-note, is a characteristic of most instruments, although progress is now taking place in instrument design to equalise tone and response. Brightness of tone on a particular note often goes with sharpness, and vice-versa. It is possible to confuse the two, especially with a player whose sound is naturally bright. This type of player can easily be thought to be sharp to the general pitch, whereas it is only an impression. The answer for this player is to add warmth to the sound to complete its character. (CR Sound)

Tuning Characteristics of Differently Pitched Trumpets

It is therefore obvious that competent players must be fluent in the different tuning characteristics of their variously pitched instruments. These characteristics are as infinitely variable, instrument-to-instrument, as is the blow of an instrument. Players must familiarise themselves with every nook and cranny of each instrument, in order to be ready for all tuning problems.

False Fingerings

As a general rule, the smaller the trumpet the greater the distortion to intonation. The Eb, in particular, is now in general use as an alternative to the Bb or C, and therefore has to perform with as accurate intonation as the larger instruments. A comprehensive control of all false fingerings is essential. Watch an expert player with an Eb trumpet and you may find it hard to identify any normal fingerings!

Example 3

Example 4

23

Example 5

13   1312   23   13

The variable bell sizes which used to be offered by Schilke for its Eb detachable-bell trumpet presented a fascinating progression of change in tuning. The largest bell of all, which made a magnificently broad, strong sound, stood all the usual false fingerings on their head. In the right context it was worth all the trouble!

Sometimes a more useful quality of sound - whether richer or duller - can be achieved with a false fingering. D's (fourth line), Ebs and Es (fourth space) are the commonest alternatives, but all options are open provided that the tuning is fully taken into account.

Horizontal Tuning

When the trumpet plays alone it is more difficult to judge the intonation, as there is no harmonic background available for comparisons to be made. However, a progression of single notes builds up a pitch level. The ear remembers the trail of notes left by the instrument, synthesises them into a context, and matches each new one to that context. The moderate or inexperienced player is less likely to remember the intonation of the row of pitches preceding the one being played, being more taken up with surviving. This is the problem about buying a trumpet in the showroom: it is difficult for the inexperienced player to judge intonation in the context of an ensemble.

The player must therefore consciously examine these horizontal relationships, and not just wait until alerted by an obviously bad fault. The following examples illustrate the kind of horizontal examination of intonation required. This quickly produces awareness, after which improvement occurs naturally.

Example 6

Example 7

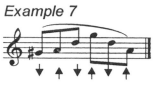

Example 8

Vertical Tuning

The paragraph entitled 'Interval Characteristics' details the relationships of two notes. The vast majority of chords contain a minimum of three notes, often many more. The middle and lower parts of complex chords are where the complications lurk. The controlling note, in terms of setting a pitch level, is the lowest. In order to make some tunings fit it can be necessary to lower the pitch of the bass note much more than can initially be believed. This phenomenon occurs especially in compound chords.

Tuning with the Piano

The piano is the most unnatural and difficult instrument to partner. In the case of preparing a recital with a piano, always tuned just below the pitch at which orchestral instruments normally play, it is often necessary to get used to bringing the trumpet's pitch down for practice several weeks before the date of the event. If a radical tuning down is needed on the day, it will then be too late. The player's ear will keep the pitch up, even though the main slide has been pulled out, and split notes will result. Additionally, the soloist should look to match up the pitch of important exposed notes, particularly at the extremes of range, but especially in the lower. False fingering and slide use should be well prepared as a piano is totally unforgiving in its tuning. (CR Accompaniment)

The Interaction of Rhythm, Note Lengths and Intonation

The quality of intonation is most noticed on longer notes, and on the main beats of the bar, to which the listener's attention is naturally attracted. For example, in a 4/4 bar, the notes occurring on the first and third beats have the clearest audibility. In groups of semiquavers, the first of each group is the most critical. False fingerings which are out-of-tune can be used when the position of the note is sufficiently low-profile. For example, the first fingered flat G# above the stave is a very valuable option at speed, out of the rhythmic limelight.

Example 9

The Importance of Good Intonation

A thorough knowledge of intonation, false fingering, and an understanding of the behaviour of our listening faculties is very important to the complete professional. Quality of intonation can make the difference between success and failure for two players competing for the same professional position. The finer the tuning, the cleaner the impression.

Tuning Groups of Instruments

My system of tuning a group of players of the same instrument is as follows.

- One by one, play a named note, being sure to have a space between each player. The space allows a clear comparison. Playing together does not.

- Repeat the process, with a succession of four or five other notes.

- By this point, it will be clear which players are in tune, flatter, or sharper. Prompt the players to identify the problems for themselves, thus developing their own sense of intonation and responsibility.

- Continue, but not too long, as it is easy to become confused by tuning matters. Best to achieve a small improvement, and then return to the subject at frequent intervals.

My system of tuning a group of players on diverse instruments is to adopt the same process, but first tuning the leading (principal) players on a mixture of unisons and octaves. Then the instrumental groups can be dealt with separately.

Intonation with Mutes

Mutes, often regarded as as annoying and negligible extra to playing, can change the basic pitch of brass instruments by small but significant amounts. Metal straight mutes tend to raise the pitch, while fibre mutes lower it. Cup mutes significantly flatten the pitch, while harmon mutes can vary it in totally unpredictable ways.

One factor which alters the tuning characteristics of mutes is the wearing down of the corks. Not only will there be a gradual alteration of sound quality as they are depressed, but intonation will alter at random. Another factor is the matching of mute and bell sizes; it is important, particularly with the higher pitch trumpets, that the proportions fit, each to the other. What those proportions are, becomes clear with experience and careful trials of various combinations.

Electronic Tuning Machines

These devices are not for serious musicians. For the reasons given above, they are inaccurate for all but the crudest purposes. They remove from the musician the responsibility for listening, judging and refining the sense of pitch. These machines are a good example of technology's drive to de-skill the human race.

MUSICIANSHIP

Musicianship is the ability to shape music in an appealing and convincing way.

Musicianship Described

Musicianship, a word often used by musicians, is a term of high approval, suggesting that the performer enjoys freedom of expression in spite of any technical difficulties.

Ask any number of professional players which quality they would like to be thought to possess and the majority will reply: 'Musicianship!' This is a very unsatisfactory answer. Like goodness, badness, or any other vague quality, musicianship comes in all shapes and sizes.

All trumpet performers have repertoire specialities, whether Symphonic, Big Band, Jazz or Baroque, due either to their inclinations or to a career opportunity appearing in a certain area. Every musician has special tastes and sympathies for certain composers or periods of music.

These affinities become clear to the listener through a musician's performance. The quality through which we judge this rapport is musicianship. When we say that Mr X is wonderful in a Mahler symphony but unconvincing in the Haydn concerto, we are saying that his kind of musicianship is more attuned to the one than the other.

The non-professional listener is able to appreciate the presence or absence of musicianship in a player. The priority is the same the world over: the communication of feeling through sound. This is what the listener wants, and this is what the professional musician is paid to provide.

The danger for the professional is that he or she listens, not for the musical feeling, but for the 'technique' involved, an arid and pointless exercise. Very little of use is learned this way.

How to Develop Musicianship

The key element in developing musicianship lies in the question: 'In what music do you feel most at home? To what music do you respond most happily?' The player's answer reveals the repertoire in which he or she will display most natural musicianship.

Having established the areas in which he or she is most at home, the player who wishes to become as professional as possible should then look outward to extend his or her knowledge and taste into neighbouring areas of musical interest. In this way the scope of a player's professional musicianship and competence is extended.

Musicianship for the Trumpet Player

For the soloist, there are always new discoveries to be made and new ideas to be found. Adventurous musicians constantly redraw the boundaries of their interests. For example, the Swedish trombonist Christian Lindberg has created new areas of technique, expression and musicianship on his instrument, with new repertoire and ideas full of revealing surprises. When fresh, these ideas are startling and innovative, but in time they become accepted and appreciated by many performers and listeners.

For the orchestral section principal, while the basic requirements of the position are style and authority, the right player can expand the musical possibilities of the role to an enormous degree. Setting standards implies the creation of new levels of technique and musicality, which then inspire those who follow. The section orchestral player has to achieve an acceptable ensemble style and apply it with flexibility.

While an orchestral principal can fill the role perfectly adequately without a distinctive personal musicianship, for the jazz artist, a unique creative musicianship is the essential identity card. The role call of great jazz trumpet names instantly brings personality musicianship to mind. Louis Armstrong, Dizzy Gillespie, Miles Davis are amongst the best known names. There are hundreds of others.

So important to jazz artists is this individuality, with its own special fingerprint, that many of them have gone down the drug road in search of heightened inspiration. Needless to say, any bright ideas induced by drugs are a self-delusion, usually with a tragic end to the story-line. The Faust legend lives on in the twentieth century - with a vengeance!

Professional Musicality

It is obvious that   professional musicianship varies according to repertoire, so players must develop the appropriate type of musicianship for each situation they are likely to meet. A particular aptitude for certain repertoire can be beneficial to a musician when starting a career, but it is important not to become typecast. When a musician becomes too identified with a certain type of music, it can hold back his or her career prospects outside that particular area, thereby reducing other opportunities for new artistic stimulations. (CR Professionalism)

The Potential for Musicality

Musicality can be heard in players of all standards, although it requires a wise teacher to identify it and nurture it, particularly in beginners. One of the most enjoyable experiences for musicians is to hear natural musicianship in the very young.

The potential for musicality in a performer can be hidden by a poor technique on the instrument. Good guidance and teaching is vital at an early stage in order to set up the balance of the young player's work from the start. A poor start is very hard indeed to overcome.

It is possible for a player's musicianship to reveal itself gradually. There are many players whose rise to the top of the musical ladder is steady rather than sudden.

The Disappearance of Musicianship

Talent which appears to wither after an excellent start is a well known phenomenon. There are many young players spoken of as future stars who somehow never realise their full potential; when a musician becomes absorbed in technique for its own sake and loses the sound of the music, then trouble develops. The main purpose of performance - the communication of feeling through sound - is lost when attention is wholly focused on technique.

'Play the music, not the notes!' If a player is described as having musicality it tells us that he or she can make music interesting beyond the notes. True musicianship exists when expressive feeling and technical skill are both present and indivisible. (CR Talent)

ORNAMENTATION

The decoration of the musical line is achieved by specific limited ornaments, inserted by the composer or the performer, or by unlimited variation of the line itself by the performer.

Ornaments

Early in musical life everyone is shown rudiments books with precisely notated examples of ornaments. Trills for example are usually written out in demisemiquavers (32nds). The truth is that the real-life performance of ornaments varies according to instrument and context. The spirit of the ornamentation is what is important. Ornaments played mechanically contradict their character as decoration.

An ornament is a decorative gesture, added to an otherwise straightforward musical melody or line for expressive reasons, but sometimes for the purpose of technical display. An ornament must always be performed lightly, gracefully, and where appropriate, with virtuosity.

Ornaments are often treated as annoyances by performers, for two main reasons. Firstly, an ornament is usually an awkward group of notes to be inserted at speed, and secondly, retaining the pulse behind a tricky or lengthy ornament is sometimes difficult.

Ornamentation of the Musical Line

From the Renaissance to the Baroque, improvised or additionally composed ornamentation of the musical line by the performer was the common practice. Passages played 'da capo', where the music has turned back to the beginning for a second performance of its first part, are the ones to be specially treated with ornamentation. This is distinct from self-contained ornaments placed on the score by the composer.

As a full revival of interest in pre-Baroque music has taken place only in the last fifty or so years, our knowledge of this repertoire and its performance is still growing. Examples of quasi-improvised decoration by the performer can be heard in all modern recordings. Students should beware an editor's ornamentation masquerading as the original. When a student has sufficient expertise, it is better to invent his or her own ornamentation, rather than copy another musician's version. (CR Music Editions)

In obligati for the trumpet, such as Handel's 'Let the Bright Seraphim' (from Samson), players are usually expected to decorate the melodic line on its second reading. As in Renaissance repertoire, ornamentation should be in the form of quicker notes invented or improvised in close relation to the original.

Example 1

Trumpet in D

On the other hand there are obligati, such as some by Bach, which, in my view, do not welcome additions from performers. (See 'Hail, Mighty Lord!' from the Christmas Oratorio.) The ability to judge when and how to ornament develops through listening, study and experience.

Baroque Ornaments

Baroque ornamentation is a subject on which many books have been written. For the brass or wind player who only occasionally performs this repertoire a knowledge of the trill, its start, continuation and finish, the simpler mordents and the appoggiatura will suffice. For string and keyboard players there are many others to be learnt, remembering that different groups of composers, and different countries, had their own distinct and parallel traditions of ornamentation. These traditions blended together in the nineteenth century as composition, performance and publication became spread more evenly over the whole of Europe.

Correct practice places a short appoggiatura at the start of all trills and mordents. (The shortness depends on the musical context and the judgement of the performer.) It is, however, historically wrong to do so when the first note of the trill or mordent has already been approached from the note immediately above.

Example 2

The trill and mordent are often played too fast, giving a frantic rather than graceful quality. It is surprising at how slow a speed a trill can be played successfully!

A turn at the end of a trill is rarely appropriate except at the end of a major passage or movement. There is currently a growing habit of stopping the trill on the last beat before its resolution, the only reason for which can be convenience of fingering, or the re-assertion of an insecure pulse. Musically it should be avoided, as the effect is awkward.

Early Classical, and Romantic Ornamentation

Types of ornamentation are not imprisoned within academically convenient periods of music. The ornament, as noted by a graphic sign, gradually faded from use as composers began to write out their music in complete detail. Yet in the Early Classical period, a mixture of new and old performance practice still existed. For example, only at the very end of the eighteenth century can it be said that Baroque ornamentation finally faded away.

In the trumpet repertoire perhaps the clearest indication of ornamentation at the cross-roads is in the second movement of the Hummel Concerto, where a curious mish-mash of ornament signs exists. In the available recordings, a wide variety of options are taken throughout the movement because of uncertainty of the meaning of the signs.

By the time the nineteenth century was fully into its stride, for the first time in musical history performers were effectively barred from joining in the creative process. In modern times, the ornament and the improvised line provided by the performer have more or less ceased to exist in serious music. The composer is now utterly in charge.

Common Problems with Ornaments, and their Solutions

• The usual cause of difficulty is quite simple: the player loses the music's pulse due to the anxiety which he or she feels in having to fit the ornament into the context. This anxiety usually causes the tempo to drag or, less often, to hurry. In the event of any problem, play the melodic line without the ornament. Having done so, replay while auralising (imagining) the ornament into the line. The ends of trills or extended mordents are the weak points for loss of tempo. Calculating the end-turn causes difficulty to a surprising number of otherwise able students.

- Trills are the ornaments most encountered by the trumpet player. Here the commonest fault is to play the trill too fast. In a standard *allegro* it is surprising how little above the semiquaver speed it is necessary to play for the trill to sound well. Sound quality also tends to deteriorate with over-fast trills unless the finger action is excellent. For the trill, most players adopt a rigid arm movement in which the valve does not travel fully down or up, resulting in a smudged sound quality. It also looks ridiculous! (CR Fingering exercises)

Example 3

Examples of practice

- False fingering should always be kept in mind for awkward trills and other ornaments.

- In playing matching trills with another instrument, the speed of trilling and the placement of the final turn should be synchronised.

- In playing groups of acciacaturas, two faults commonly occur.

    1. The gracenote often sounds like a standard notevalue of the tempo, e.g. a semiquaver, instead of being suitably crushed.

    2. When these crushed notes occur in groups, they frequently cause a rushing of the tempo.

The Spirit of Ornamentation: a Sideways Personal View

Ornamentation, improvisation, and the improvised cadenza (CR Cadenzas), have been squeezed out of music as it has become increasingly composed and serious. The spontaneous ornament and the spirit of improvisation are, however, alive, well, and jumping for joy in the world of popular music and jazz, where, significantly, the performer is still king.

The serious composer's mistrust of the performer as participant in the creation of the musical experience, and the resulting reduction of the performer's role to that of the neutered, obedient servant, has been a very mixed blessing for the development of music and the musician.

Specialisation for musicians, whether composers or performers, has meant the sharpening of playing technique but the reduction of musical input from the performer. The second half of the twentieth century has seen a quite ludicrous cult of the serious music super-star, developed for egotistical and commercial reasons. This has at least kept the orchestral bandwagon rolling, but now that the public is tiring of this game, the bleak commercial future for serious composed music is becoming more and more obvious as the public shows less and less interest.

This cross references to the subject of careers. How many of the best players move out of performance halfway through their careers, to look for more stimulation elsewhere? Given the dominance of popular music and jazz as the musical expression which match the public's mood, where will the trumpet students of today find their work in twenty, thirty and more years' time? Keeping a close eye on possible long term developments in music is one of the most important activities for young musicians and their teachers. Popular music and jazz offer wide and exciting targets to aim at when considering a life and career in music.

In practical terms, the victory of popular over serious music would today be totally complete if it were not for artificial subsidies, donated for wholly non-musical reasons. It is quite clear that these subsidies for serious music will largely wither away in the years to come. On the other hand, the public's appetite for, and consumption of, music played by the personality performer grows by the day, where the exciting spirits of ornamentation and improvisation continue to reign.

PERFORMANCE

'To perform' is much more than just 'to play'. Musicianship and technical capability by themselves are not enough.

Performing is for the audience. It must be rehearsed in as many aspects as possible, because it requires a different form of attention and concentration to practising. Performance skill adds the essential professional dimension to a player's work.

The Musician as Performer

In the same way as an actor uses words, the musician uses musical sound. The ability to perform is quite separate from playing the instrument, or from musicianship. Many fine musicians will never be expert performers because they assume that musicianship and technique are enough. The performer must project a performance so that it captures the audience, whether of three or three thousand people. The most expert performers play with an audience like a cat plays with a mouse.

As in teaching, performance skill develops on a platform of rapport with the audience. Rapport gives the audience the sense that the performer is playing for it and not simply allowing it to listen as a group of outsiders. The performer must deliberately practise awareness of this contact, in order to perfect ways of performing and manipulating an audience..

The player who accounts for every detail when studying can then feel free to improvise when performing.

The Audience's Eye View of a Performance

The audience is present to hear and to see the performer's interaction with the music. The public is fascinated to hear and see how performers respond to a wide range of repertoire. Performers must remember that each one of the audience has made a substantial effort in order to go to a concert. A concert ticket, a programme, travel, food and drink are, taken together, very expensive. Having made the effort, the audience wishes to enjoy itself.

Therefore it is the duty of the performer to provide enjoyment in the best sense of the word. To come into contact with a personality expressing itself through musical performance is always a riveting experience for the audience. The relationship between player and listener cannot be taken to pieces and described. The performer creates it simply by wanting to communicate, in the same way that we are individually welcoming (or not) to another person.

The Creation of Performance Skill for the Soloist

1: Before Playing, after Playing and Platform Manners

A performance begins the moment the performer is first seen by the audience. Thereafter, until he or she disappears from view for the last time, all behaviour adds to or subtracts from the overall effect of the performance.

For a recital or concerto performance, the whole routine must be examined, re-examined, mentally run and re-run, time and time again, until it flows smoothly. (CR Visualisation) Walking on, bowing, tuning up, the adoption of a settled manner of standing while not playing (e.g. control of fidgeting), the acknowledgement of applause, of the accompaniment, the walking off, with or without the accompanist, the return and re-acknowledgement of applause - these must all be appraised. When the routine can be envisioned seamlessly, the performer's total confidence rises and the last barriers between the performer and audience come down. Repetition is the key.

The natural performer communicates freely with an audience and needs only a little guidance. This skill can and should be learnt by all players. Each musician must create his or her own skill, because it is the individual personality that is being displayed to the public. I will describe how I try to develop it in students.

Firstly, the use of the eyes is critical in establishing that the hall is the performer's domain. The moments of entrance to the stage begin the audience's appraisal of the performer. If the performer's eyes drag along the floor or are equivocal in any respect, the performer is at once weakened in relationship to the audience, which should be regarded by the performer not as many individuals but as one creature. The use of the eyes takes control; non-use of the eyes cedes control. The performer must 'own' the hall as his or her territory. Welcome the audience with your eyes.

As the performer walks on, his or her body language must also be convincing. A smooth but alert walk, timed, if possible, to match the size of the hall and the length of the audience's welcoming applause.

The use of the hands and arms can be an especial sign of unease. For example, if when talking to the audience the performer holds the hands in what I have heard called the crotch clutching position, the impression given is instantly defensive. Freedom of arm and hand movement is essential.

Any speech must be delivered a little more slowly, and with the voice slightly lower in pitch than normal. Care should be taken to keep enunciation clear and the vowels sustained. Breathy speech does not travel to the back of the hall. Phrase the sentences positively towards the key words, especially titles, composers and foreign words. Musicians especially should be professionally concerned with good pronunciation of foreign languages. The delivery of faulty pronunciation and the ensuing embarrassment demean the speaker.

A mistake, error or disaster must *never* be acknowledged or revealed to the audience. Always behave calmly even if you are internally engaged in a fight to the death. To do otherwise is un-professional.

The bow needs rehearsal until fluent. It is a matching response to the audience's appreciation and should fit the scale of the room or hall and the type of performance being given. The large Romantic concerto suggests one thing, a small dry piece of modern music another. A smile is always appreciated in any circumstance!

2: During Playing

I always direct the student's attention towards an imaginary audience. 'Play to the back of a large hall'. 'Project your music above the back row of the hall'. The limitation of the usual small practice room can easily stunt the musical personality, therefore the player should constantly have the audience present in his or her imagination. The command to 'Always play to someone other than yourself' directs the player's attention beyond the self and towards the outside world. Not only does this simple concept produce an attitude change, it also improves the musical and physical quality of the playing. It is one of the first things I say (when necessary) to a new student.

Thereafter a few supporting ideas help to develop the player's audience awareness. For example:

- If the music is being used, the stand must be placed in such a way that it is not a barrier between the player and the audience.

- If the music is being used, the player must give the impression that it is only being referred to and not read. Music being read too carefully imprisons the performer and prevents the essential contact with the audience.

- If the music is being used, at the start of a solo performance and until the first entry is well under way, the performer must keep his or her eyes on the audience. As in conversation, eye contact enhances intimacy and understanding. Eyes which are elsewhere suggest the person as a whole is not with you. Throughout the piece, each new significant entry after a tutti should start in the same way.

Once this awareness is fully developed, our inherent ability to create relationships takes over. Each performer must use his or her native wit to develop the necessary contact skills. The initial impact of how the performer looks is crucial to making the best possible first impression with his or her playing.

The Performer's Physical Presence while Playing

The performer must appear comfortable. The audience, which watches as well as listens, will instantly assess the presence and mood of the performer. If the player appears ill at ease or otherwise uncomfortable, the audience will immediately sense it. Enjoyment is the whole purpose of the performance, therefore sensing discomfort in the performer spoils the experience.

Ease of presence whether real or apparent can be achieved by simple means. It also produces associated benefits for the player, in the same way as I outlined above in the example of playing to the back of a hall.

I ask a student to do the following:

- Stand with the feet approximately eighteen inches apart.

- One foot should be a little in front of the other.

- The hip, knee and ankle joint should feel free and ready to flex and move.

- I then ask the student to move the weight sideways foot to foot, and also forward and backward. This allows quiet movement and positional change without moving the feet. This subtle mobility, or 'flow', suggests ease and comfort to the audience, which will relax, respond and be ready to react **with** the performer. For women, any shoes that can be described as high-heeled, look awful! They distort the posture and therefore the breathing.

Preparation for a Solo Performance

All players give solo performances at some time or other. Everyone knows how tricky first experiences can be. Passages which seemed safe in the practice room go wrong, while some that were dangerous come off surprisingly well. Making the transition from this kind of pressured and unreliable playing to calm and secure performance needs very careful and solid preparation. The level of performance which master players produce almost without fail has to be earned over many concerts.

At some point all players who wish to become truly professional master players must undergo substantial periods of gruelling preparation for high pressure events. The value of the lessons learned during these periods will be directly in proportion to the intensity of the preparations.

It is a characteristic of the best players that they do not allow themselves to be fazed or thrown off balance by small blemishes, whether their own or other people's.

An Example Preparation: The Degree Recital

The degree recital which comes at the end of college study is a mini Everest for all students. In spite of the many recitals or concerto performances they may have given along the way, the demands of this type of event are extreme. In many branches of education in Britain, such pistol-point examinations of ability have been abandoned as too cruel. Apart from the fact that, as in top sport, failure at music performance is a harsh and unforgiving experience, the value of the experience lies in its 'cruelty.' The performer's fear of failure is a spur which should be used to fire up his or her effort to improve.

- The programme should be finalised several months before the recital. (CR Recital Planning)

- The programme must be played through every day, on a five day-a-week basis. This play-through is quite separate from any other practice or work in hand.

- Ideally it should be preceded by a brief warm-up, and then a five minute gap before the play-through.

The play-through must be without stopping of any kind. The tutti rests are counted, and spaces are left between pieces as in the event itself. If the programme items are to be introduced by the soloist then this element should be included. Normal daily practice is quite separate to this play-through. (CR Practice)

What is being done here? Performing is being practised! How rarely this happens! To survive the rigour and potential boredom of this preparation is to make the journey from being amateur to being professional. Boredom is unintelligent and amateurish. The intensity and duration of the preparation matures the player musically and personally.

This process is to be carried out together with the visualisation as outlined in the paragraph on Platform Manners. Some weeks prior to the examination the student must take a couple of weeks completely free from the recital pieces, allowing the mind to freshen up.

After taking up the repertoire in the final days before the recital, the student and the teacher should accept the level of performance that has been reached. They have done the best they can. There should be no struggle to achieve last minute improvement.

The whole aim of this procedure is to mimic the event exactly as it happens on the day. The student will then be totally accustomed to the procedure, and will feel as comfortable as it is possible to be. It means, most importantly, that every conceivable sequence and combination of errors will have occurred and will have been survived.

Even if the student is not on top form come the recital day, the resilience given by this deep preparation will carry him or her through. The player's form will not drop below a certain level.

Performing in the Orchestra

When as a young player I first sat in an orchestra with some of the great players of the time, I immediately became aware that musically they commanded centre stage at the right moment. Their ability to frame a solo, to draw attention to it musically, added an electric charge and an aura to a performance which was indescribable, but totally unmistakable. For example, the first Solo Horn entry in Bruckner's Fourth Symphony can be one of the most magical moments in music, as it was when played by such artists as Alan Civil and Barry Tuckwell.

All that is necessary for a performer to achieve this 'framing' is an awareness that it is possible and indeed necessary. When the performer has this awareness, it gives stature and magic to the playing.

Contrasts and Similarities with Popular Music

In popular music, where the only income derives from satisfied listeners, the performer has to fulfil the audience's needs or be discarded. In serious music, where most classically trained performers eventually hope to work, there is a distinct corruption of the relationship between performer and audience. Somehow because high art is thought of as an unexplained 'good thing', many musicians give no attention at all to the audience as the reason for the performance. In the minds of many musicians the audience is negligible, a necessary evil.

This attitude results in poor concert manners on the part of many performers. Watch the behaviour of the average orchestra before a concert and during the applause! At the time of writing (1997), attendance for most concerts is falling fast, and many former concert-goers are taking their free time elsewhere. The vigour and brio with which popular music addresses its audience is in marked contrast to the almost religious tone of much serious music presentation. In popular music, when the public loses interest, the performer meets instant obscurity.

The musician who thinks of the public, and becomes as good a performer as possible, is unlikely ever to lack an audience.

VIBRATO

Vibrato warms the musical expression. Its absence keeps the expression cool. Vibrated sound also has the quality of transparency while straight sound mostly seems opaque.

The Use of Vibrato

The use of vibrato varies from player to player, country to country, and between kinds of music. Unlike dynamics, with which it is partially connected, vibrato is rarely specified by composers. Some players use it frequently, others rarely.

Vibrato is one of the player's most valuable expressive tools when well used. Though the word vibrato covers an infinite number of sound variations, there are some basic types which can be outlined. Any competent orchestral player must develop a useful range of vibrati in order to be able to fulfil the musical and stylistic demands of different composers. Those players who avoid vibrato, or use it all the time, are failing to provide a full range of expression.

Types of Vibrato

Vibrato is the application of minute pitch variations, above, and/or below, the note. Some vibrati also thin the sound as the vibrations occur, making it more transparent. More rarely nowadays, it can be minute horizontal dynamic variations, without any changes in pitch.

1. Vibrato created only by vertical movement of the chin is mainly associated in Britain with brass band style from the thirties to the seventies. The musical effect is rather mechanical, but when allied to a light feathery sound it can have a faded period charm associated with sentimental ballads and salon pieces. It is rare today, except within a very limited and diminishing school of cornet players.

2. The standard vibrato in use today is created partially by chin movement but mainly by the vibration of the airstream as it reaches the embouchure. This latter constituent allows true colour variation of the sound, including, in soft dynamics, the effect mentioned above - the changing of the sound from opaque to transparent.

3. The type of vibrato mostly in use in the American school of playing consists of a side-to-side hand movement on the valves through the fingers. The sound quality remains the same through the vibrato. Hand vibrato does not colour the sound, but overlays it.

4. An older type of vibrato, not now favoured by modern brass players, is created at the diaphragm. It is capable of great beauty, but when overdone is referred to as 'nanny-goat'.

Examples of this method can be heard on recordings of the cornettist Jack Mackintosh, and on recordings of French trumpeters, such as Foveau and Sabarich, from the early part of the twentieth century. Cornet sound, as heard in these recordings, was much brighter and more brilliant than its modern equivalent. This was partly because of the higher basic pitch then in use, but was largely because performers' conception of sound was more robust and masculine than the effeminate style which followed it.

The French trumpet sound of this period should be heard by all trumpet students. It is one of the most beautiful ever heard. Like other French brass and woodwind sounds, except on recordings it is lost.

The Two Main Applications of Vibrato

1. The traditional kind of vibrato is evenly applied to all notes. This can only be applied when the basic sound is also produced evenly. It is the brass equivalent of the singer's *bel canto*. Any variation of width or speed of vibrato is related to the shape of the overall phrase, rather than being on on a note-by-note basis. It requires sustained breath support and when produced successfully it is of the utmost beauty.

2. The modern style of vibrato, originally developed by jazz, cabaret and popular singers, alternates cool and warm notes in an improvised off-the-cuff manner. The style is basically speech based, casual in feeling, and inappropriate for traditional melodies or melodic lines. This type of slang vibrato is unfortunately common everywhere now, not just in the repertoire where it is at home. (CR Style)

The Absence of Vibrato

The musician has the choice of manipulating sound in a variety of ways. While warm and cool sound are equated with vibrato and non-vibrato respectively, there are types of sounds which cross the divide between them. Straight trumpet sound can be both cold, hard and unresonant, or generous, resonant and warm, depending on the able player's intention. The good player can manipulate straight sound to be hard and direct, or warm and indirect as he or she wishes.

These characteristics can be underlined by changes of mouthpiece or leadpipe for different situations. The metal of bell sections also has a significant effect on straight sound. The beryllium bells produced by Renold Schilke for his trumpets are outstanding, while the gold beryllium four-valve Eb which he made at my request in the early seventies, and now in the Schilke catalogue as a standard model, is superlative in all respects. Straight sound on this metal is infinitely colourful.

My own preferred way of thinking of vibrato is through its expressive effect. The image of temperature is very appropriate to music, from 'cold' across the spectrum to 'hot'. Harry James and hot jazz, cool jazz and Miles Davis are names and descriptions which are immediately identifiable with different styles of vibrato. Warmth is created by generosity of vibrato, its width and speed, whereas a slow moderate vibrato creates coolness.

Vibrati are infinite in their variety and value. I stress time and time again in this book that all players should try to develop their own musical ideas. The best ideas for all players are their own, born of their own musical feeling. The Russian school of trumpet playing as typified by Timofey Dokschuster is a perfect example. In his recordings he shows a unique range not only of musical expression, but also of sound colouration with which vibrato is linked.

SECTION FOUR

PRACTICE

INTRODUCTION

In this Section the playing skills of Section Two are put to work. The practice room is the player's workshop, to which patience and musical intelligence are the keys.

Practising is the hardest test for the musician's mind, from which many turn away because of its difficulty, preferring to learn by 'just playing'. This is a perfectly acceptable strategy if it produces results. It may work for the few; for the majority, however, it guarantees the slowest possible form of progress.

SECTION FOUR

PRACTICE

INTRODUCTION

AURALISATION

Most people can imagine music in their minds. Using this process is essential to the full and continuing development of musicians. The rehearsal and performance of music in the imagination is the creative side of listening.

Use of the Inner Ear

Auralisation is to the inner ear what visualisation is to the inner eye. When used consistently to develop interpretations and phrasings, its value to the musician is immense.

The Value of Auralisation

1. The best process for producing fine sound is to hear and feel it the instant before playing. The body then naturally tries to match the one with the other.

2. The player can quickly become familiar with a work being studied, quite separately from playing it on the instrument. This has the benefit of freeing the player from dividing his attention between reading the score and playing the instrument. The more certain the player's knowledge and reading, the more positive the playing actions will be. Unsureness of 'what comes next' in the score inhibits the actual playing. Once fluent in this type of practise, the learning time for new pieces is cut radically. (CR Vocalisation)

3. Knowing positively which note comes next frees the player from confusion and uncertainty. Bad seeing and reading habits are therefore avoided. For example, when reading partially or wholly unknown works many players have the habit of peering forward at the part. This induces poor quality breathing and the development of postural faults. (CR Posture, Reading Music)

4. The ability to develop interpretations of works of music is one of the essential skills of the master performer. Most musicians form a judgement of the way to play a particular piece while learning it and playing their instrument at the same time. This makes it likely that the overall sense of the piece is rarely considered - only the details as they pass.

5. In order to produce musically adequate results with worthwhile music, it is essential to spend time alone with the score. In order to consider and decide on the direction of a performance, the sometimes confusing demands of the instrument must be absent. All musicians 'allow' for technical difficulties on occasion, but unless that 'allowance' is kept in severe check it soon comes to dominate. The musician should run music through his or her mind time and time again, weighing it up and trying it out until the sense of it is convincingly established. Concern for technicalities should be a separate process.

6. The method of thinking about the piece of music only while it is being learnt is typical of the normal human failing of not being able to separate short and long-term considerations.

7. Freedom to imagine the daring option and to indulge in flights of musical and technical fancy rarely come with the instrument in hand, when safety is the usual priority. The player who does extraordinary things with the instrument, does so only because he or she thinks and conceives them at a time other than playing. Freedom to let the imagination wander comes first, then the new idea must be backed up with the bravery to try it out. Developing an inner musical life can be endlessly interesting, whether it is to do with current work, general matters or past memories.

8. The interactions of the senses bring visualisation and auralisation very close at times. A fingering problem-passage is best solved not by constant replays, but by thinking through the notes and their fingerings. This should be done without shadow fingering on the instrument, which for some reason slows down the learning process. (CR to Learning Music for more detail)

9. It is perfectly possible to achieve very high standards of playing by just playing, and no more; players who can do this are the exceptions. This level of quick-wittedness is unusual, but the fact that there are many individuals who never play and think separately does not mean that they might not have achieved more.

The Normal Player

As outlined above, learning solely by playing is a very slow method of improvement and leaves the player with no alternative methods when that one stalls. For players without superfast responses, the lack of a strong imaginative process will be a bar to full realisation of their talent. Not only will the nuts and bolts of technique be inaccurate and incapable of consistency, but those players will lack the musical interest to keep improving.

Together with auralisation and visualisation, the most important ingredients for success are patience, persistence and the ability to listen and discern. Patience is the ability not to rush into action with the first thought that enters the head, persistence is the control to play a longer game, which is difficult for musicians (especially when practising). The skill of listening accurately and with discrimination is the rarest of all, and belongs to the few who give full attention all the time, without preconceived ideas.

The Exceptional Player

Sports scientists can find no physical differences between athletes of Olympic standard and moderate athletes. The only difference that can be identified in any way, shape or form is that the great athletes think about their event all the time, mentally rehearsing every element, time and time again.

Likewise the musical performer who consistently thinks about style, technique and different ways to play will continue to improve, will develop as fast as possible, and will come as close as humanly possible to realising fully his or her talent.

PRACTICE

1: GENERAL

Practice is the most demanding organisational activity for the musician. In practice all the parallel strands of the physical and mental skills of playing are woven into one, ready for performance.

Introduction

Across the whole range of student performers there should be something for everyone in this section, when linked up with the appropriate cross references. The player who is a complete artist will have travelled this way already and have settled on his or her pattern of work. Above all, this section is intended for the middle rank of student players who need direction, method and a sense of progress to their work. If a player's form stagnates for too long it means that their practice routines are not working. It may not mean that the player's talent has run out.

The Pre-Warm-Up

The warm-up is the most personal part of practice. Experienced professional players reduce it to an essential minimum, through many thousands of trials. For the student player, developing the warm-up is part of the learning process.

- Breathe half a dozen deep breaths, open throated, some vigorous. Use the wall breathing exercise from the chapter on Anxiety Control.

- Introduce counting for further breaths as follows

IN	HOLD (with open throat)	OUT (through shaped embouchure)
4	4	4
6	6	6
8	8	8
2	4	2
2	8	16
2	8	32
1	-	4 or 6, 8, 16 etc.
1/2	-	as above

- Vary the speed in order to stretch your lungs.

- Once into these exercises, think of the variety and quality of sounds you are going to produce, whether the warmest, softest, loudest, smoothest, most brilliant, and so on. These are the sounds to make when you begin playing.

- Take the mouthpiece, and buzz a few long notes to shape up the embouchure.

- Take the instrument; adopt playing posture, with the mouthpiece a couple of centimetres from the lips. **Sense the freedom that <u>not playing</u> gives**. Maintain it, then play a full, free-sounding note.

The extra value of this process is that it focuses the player's attention on quality of sound and the work to be done; and it wakes up the player's engine, the breathing. Those bad days which afflict all players are largely done away with if this simple routine is followed consistently.

The Warm-Up

- The warm-up should be just that, and nothing more: a preparation to play. Do not confuse it with real practice, which should be a planned process.

- A warm-up should be as short or long as necessary. An experienced player knows the short cuts, the less experienced must be sure to cover everything.

- Firstly some long tones in middle and low register, concentrating on fullness and quality of sound. Then a little undemanding flexibility work.

- Warming up the tongue is as essential as the embouchure. Legato tonguing into low long notes, with special emphasis on looseness and freedom. (CR Stamina and Recovery)

Take a Break

Stop when ready to practise. There is a very good case for taking a short break, say 5 minutes, to check out the day's work. This may seem unnecessary and time wasting, but it is important to avoid drifting from one thing to another in the practice sessions.

Practising: Outline Comments

- Each musician must develop his or her own practice routines. The suggestions below are just a guide for creating a dependable routine. I ask students who are starting to study with me to follow them for a month, so that the benefits of planning can be appreciated and some stability established. After that they are free to continue or develop their own.

- The student who is going to succeed professionally must get away to a fast start at college. I have known only one or two exceptions to this rule. If, at this point, time is wasted, it has gone for ever. This is the period of life when society encourages students to have full time education, when the foundation of good habits must be laid to serve for the rest of the playing career.

- In most subjects it is possible to undertake study in later life to improve our mental skills. In music performance, however - as in sport - the physical nature of the skills to be learnt limits this period biologically to a very small number of years.

- Clear, steady thinking, good practising and fine performing go together. So do muddled thinking, ineffective practising and unreliable, patchy playing.

Practising: Setting up a Routine

- List, in writing, all the elements to be worked on daily, such as

    Pieces of music for performance
    Studies
    Articulation in its various forms
    Flexibilities
    Long tones
    High and low range
    Dynamics
    Scales and arpeggios
    Orchestral repertoire
    Sight reading

- The starter student should practise in periods of 30 minutes, *and no more.* Take a break of at least fifteen minutes, and do something quite different to refresh the mind. The rule is, stop before you want to. The opposite - to go on beyond your best attention span - is damaging, and sends you backwards.

- In practising you are trying to learn new things, and trying to improve old habits; therefore your concentration has to be at its highest level. The concentration needed for practice is of a different kind to that for performance. Keep freshening up by taking breaks.

- Two hours per day is the minimum time a serious student should spend on practice. Make out a schedule of four periods of half an hour to take in all the elements. This is a suggested schedule, with the time in minutes:

  Session One
  - 0 - 5 Long tones mixed with flexibilities
  - 5 - 10 Varied articulations
  - 10 - 20 Scales and arpeggios
  - 20 - 30 Piece or study

  Session Two
  - 0 - 5 High range work
  - 5 - 10 Sight reading
  - 10 - 15 Long tones with extremes of dynamics, crescendi etc
  - 15 - 25 Piece or study
  - 25 - 30 Flexibilities

  Session Three
  - 0 - 5 Low range work
  - 5 - 20 Orchestral repertoire
  - 20 - 30 Scales and Arpeggios

  Session Four
  - 0 - 5 Articulations
  - 5 - 10 High range work
  - 10 - 25 Piece or study
  - 25 - 30 Flexibilities

- Sessions can be repeated or new ones written if need be.

- It is vital that the timings are observed exactly, because there is then a sense of work to be done before time is up, rather than: 'What shall I do next? Can I stop now?' The need to work well and fast becomes the prime motivation. Stop exactly on time. In this way full attention is maintained. Attitude is changed from passive to active.

- Continue this highly organised practice for a definite period, such as four weeks (a minimum) or three months. Only then look back to assess its value, especially the improvement in consistency.

Practice: General Comments

Most of these comments are no more than common-sense. It is a strange phenomenon that pressing a mouthpiece against the lips seems to stop the brain working!

- At all costs avoid the 'patchwork' practice habit for pieces and studies. In this process the player starts off, only to stop at the first serious blemish. After tinkering with that, he/she proceeds to the next blemish, again stopping, tinkering, carrying on, and so on until the end. The piece is never performed complete and uninterrupted as it is in performance, and so a performing context is never established. This is the worst possible practice strategy.

- When a piece has been learned in outline, revise the difficult passages, either by practice or preferably auralisation, then play through as a performance. If necessary revisit the difficult passages, then put it away. Do not nag anxiously at problem passages. Treat them lightly. Re-think or ignore, rather than repeating failed practice.

- Once a piece has been thoroughly learned, the best strategy for progress is to play it in long, complete passages, ignoring blemishes of any kind. This strengthens attention and determination, and gradually trains the focus outwards rather than negatively inwards.

- Studies especially should not always be started from the beginning. The music will divide into paragraphs. Start in a different place each day and play in a circle. They are usually written as technical and stamina challenges, as if asking a runner to run sprints and a marathon.

- With studies, auralise the difficult bars, without shadow fingering, then play-through.

- Do not over-practise problems. When the student has a specific priority, say the improvement of speed tonguing, each time a new section is started take the first 30 seconds on that subject. Little and often is the golden rule for improving areas of technique; then put it out of the mind.

- Often a student will choose a priority and then decide to spend several weeks concentrating on it. The result after a few days is that the player's work deteriorates. The student often concludes in desperation and frustration that practice is bad for you! The conclusion should be: *'Bad practice is bad for you!'*

- What has happened is the normal balance of the playing has been severely disturbed. The overall capability of even moderate players is more complex than can be imagined. Obsessive concentration on one aspect of playing wrecks this balance. All players know more or less where they stand in relation to their own capability. When that balance is disturbed, panic results. Frustration is created by the lack of fulfilment of unrealistic targets and ambitions.

- Sensible aims which can be fulfilled quickly are those such as (1) learning faster, (2) reading more efficiently, (3) improving knowledge of style and repertoire. These will improve the background competence of the player's work and gradually filter through to performance.

- On my own single days off, when I didn't want to practise but had a tough piece the next day, I would leave three or four trumpets around the house. When I passed each of them I would play just one note, always a different one. I found that this kept the embouchure nicely in trim.

- Remember that all skills are based in the mind.

- Remember also that the next generation of players will be better than yours, and that unless you continue to improve you will be overtaken.

The Importance of Time

In terms of technical achievement, the accuracy of a player's control of time is paramount. For a definition and discussion of time together with related terms, turn to the chapter entitled Time and Rhythm.

Put briefly, *the exact choice of the right moment to play* is the prime co-ordinator for the basic elements of technique. The only common factor which the elements of playing - the breathing, the tongue, the fingers and the embouchure - must obey, is the instant at which each note starts. These elements are in use all the time when playing, but their individual difficulties may vary enormously according to particular demands of the notes being played. For example, while the tongue has an easy double tonguing passage to play, the fingers may be struggling with awkward combinations for that passage, resulting in missed or blurred notes. When the player has mental control of time, the fog lifts from these problems and solutions are quickly found. The Time Pattern Exercises expose the state of any player's grasp of timing the start of notes.

Ensemble playing demands an agreed accuracy of timing and style of rhythm, particularly in the commonest groups of notes.

- Players in an ensemble must be able to read these groupings accurately, and in the same style. Orchestras have styles based upon fine detail being felt unanimously. Sound, rhythm and intonation are the three prime musical priorities looked for in applicants for orchestral positions. (CR Careers)

- Different time patterns demand varying exactitudes. A modern romantic tutti melody will benefit from a small amount of asynchrony, that is, not sounding exactly together. Within narrow limits it can add a richness of effect, as in the Janacek Sinfonietta.

- On the other hand, a different type of work - for example, the Stravinsky Octet for Wind - requires the utmost clinical precision. Precise timing in two new forms comes in music of the second half of the twentieth century. As an example, five notes in the time of four demands accuracy, but eleven in the time of twelve can only be an impressionistic gesture, beyond the point of discrimination by our musical ear at its present level of evolution.

- When ensemble players have contrasted values against each other, such as two against three, or three or five against four, the performance is only valid if the timings are accurate. It is also necessary to be able to play these notes, which may be rhythmically against the context, in the appropriate musical manner. When players have to consciously count against the pulse, the style of their playing can become stiff and mechanical. There is no substitute for 'knowing' in advance how to play any normal grouping, at any tempo. That knowledge can be gained only by repetition and/or mental rehearsal.

- Perfect mechanical synchronisation only exists in machines. It is impossible for humans to achieve, and - with a few exceptions - it is totally anti-expressive in effect. Good time and rhythm must be achieved within certain small tolerances and variables, whether it is the placing of individual notes, or small groupings of notes. (CR Time and Rhythm, and Interpretation)

PRACTICE

2: IMPROVEMENT ROUTINES

The first two routines cover a good-sounding melodic line, and playing in time. The third routine produces good articulation.

These routines (algorithms) can be used separately or together. They improve the quality of the player's whole performance by improving the concentration of his or her listening. Once achieved, good listening is a skill which never deteriorates. (CR Time and Rhythm)

ROUTINE No. 1

Using the the opening phrase from Haydn Trumpet Concerto as illustration, the first routine produces a melodic line which is coherent and even sounding.

Example 1

- **Step 1**

  - Play slurred, filling in the rest.

  - Repeat as many times as necessary, until absolute evenness is achieved.

  - Listen again and again, even when the performance has seemed good. Keep matching it against your ideal sound. When the ear hears well the body automatically adjusts to perform better. It does not need descriptions or analyses, it knows what to do - or will find out.

  - Unevenness in the legato is to due to unevenness in the airstream. If the airstream is smooth at all times there will be no lumps or bumps in the musical line.

- *Step 2*

  - Introduce the tongue into the slurring. It should work as lightly as possible and be hardly audible as an articulation. The even sound must be maintained totally; in effect it is a tongued slur. If the airstream becomes broken, spaces will appear between the notes. These gaps will be accompanied by a slightly thin sound at the start of the next note, and then a mini crescendo as it swells to full value again (the 'twaa' effect). The tongue should come forward to the contact point as late as possible and leave as quickly as possible, thereby avoiding a break in the airstream. Players finding it difficult to avoid gaps should look to Routine No. 3 for correction of this fault.

    Example 2

    Example 3

- *Step 3.*

  - When competence in this has been achieved, gradually introduce more normal tonguing into the phrase, inserting the rest into the second bar. A sense of continuity and evenness must remain in the playing, even when the music is not legato.

    Example 4

Summary

This routine can be used for much more complex passages, even very staccato ones. The principle of good sound connected by a line, whether hidden or not, is one of the absolute basics of good performance.

ROUTINE No. 2

This routine involves the creation of a short loop, in which a problem moment is repeated in strict time, over and over. This can be used for a variety of purposes, for example to shape a short progression of notes, or to clear up a time or rhythmic inaccuracy.

- In the Haydn Concerto many student players have problems completing the last three notes in the following phrase, both with the length of the last note (too long) and with failing to shape the phrase away from the first beat of the bar. This time-loop forces the player to focus attention on the problem moment. The process of re-balancing the rhythm and phrasing of the notes occurs naturally, as a totally musical comparison, without verbal explanation.

Example 5

- These various examples of loops focus the attention on detail that might otherwise fly past only approximately right, without ever being totally correct and reliable. The time patterns in the Exercise section give many samples of more complex groupings of note values.

Example 6

Summary

This routine blinkers the player's attention so that it is aware of nothing else but the basics (the timing) of the problem. Attention becomes concentration. Once concentrated, the player automatically corrects the detail.

ROUTINE No. 3

This routine firstly forces the tongue to move in as late as possible to its contact point, and come out as soon as possible. Secondly, the speed of the tongue's movement guides it to its best possible contact point. Thirdly it corrects any tendency the player has to move the jaw while tonguing. The player simply has to remember the tongue action which has been created and apply it during normal playing.

Play on a variety of notes, not just the given ones.

Example 7

Summary

All skills have a natural speed at which they work most effectively. For example, many players can tongue clearly in a fast tempo, but unreliably in a slow one. This routine highlights the best tonguing action in such a way that the player can feel it clearly, and then apply it to other speeds.

Coda

These routines may seem too much trouble to the player gifted with natural facility. My experience shows that players of all standards benefit from servicing their listening in these ways. In the end it is always the ear and mind that we are training; the body can only follow the mind's instructions.

Even for the master player who has total musical and technical competence, there is a value in refreshing the absolute basics of his or her playing. The stylistic habits which give a player a recognisable personality also represent a cul-de-sac which goes nowhere. It may be a very nice cul-de-sac, and the player may just want to stay there and not disturb anything, but all the same it goes nowhere. These very simple routines allow the player to back out again and continue exploring and progressing.

PRACTICE

3: COMPLEX PROBLEM SOLVING

Master players know how to solve complex problems before anyone else notices that there are any. They are mentally flexible, quick-witted, and choose the right options even though many of them may not know consciously how they do it.

Outline

These various suggestions are designed to focus the player's attention on problem moments in such a way that the solution emerges with the minimum of fuss.

The First Priority

Younger student players often feel themselves overwhelmed by the huge amount of material that has to be learned. In this they are mistaken, because it is not so much the volume of material to be learned, as the development of the ability to read and absorb fast which is important.

The basis of all reliable playing is accurate timing, which exposes the problems of difficult passages. The following example, shown in stages, illustrates a quick route to resolving problems.

Example 1

Allegro

Extract the rhythm of the passage, minus ties, and examine for total accuracy.

Example 2

Add in the ties. Make sure that the rhythm immediately after the ties is accurate.

Example 3

If any particular moment in the phrase is proving awkward use the loop routine (No. 2) from the previous chapter, Practice 2.

Example 4

ROUTINE No 4

Variable Tempo Practice and Its Benefits

I recommend this most valuable practice technique very strongly indeed.

- Variable tempo practice allows the playing of difficult moments in context. Everyone is familiar with practising difficult moments, getting them right, but finding that, on putting them back into the context, they go wrong again. This technique avoids that situation.

- Variable tempo practice develops the player's ability to control his or her tempo within the basic pulse. It develops the player's ability to balance himself or herself both as a problem approaches, and then while playing the problem. In performance a tempo can be varied by as much as 10% slower or faster - 20% overall - without the average listener noticing.

- The ability to be level-headed through difficult moments is often the difference between the successful and the unsuccessful performer. This element of 'balance' refers to the expert player's sense of danger around the corner. When one falls and hits the ground, the moment is painful and annoying, in the same way that an obvious error is to the performer. The cause of the fall, however, is the trip and loss of balance which precedes it. On many occasions the same process applies to playing; a steady lead-in to a problem, followed by a controlled passage through it, will produce surprisingly effective results.

- All players respond differently to tension and crisis. (CR Anxiety Control) **Many players** rush when approaching a problem, thereby making disaster all the more likely. This unawareness is overcome by variable tempo practice. The player with this control can make time and space within any tempo.

Many players find this technique very difficult indeed, because it demands that the mind has awareness beyond the notes actually being played. Some have said that it hurts their brains! It is a type of thinking which is also useful in normal life!

It works as follows:

Example 5

ROUTINE No 5

Timing Control and Its Use

Be inventive in getting round problems; they rarely dissolve with a frontal attack. The following examples may be thought too easy by better student players. If so they will be mistaken, as all work undertaken which focuses listening sharply improves that player.

Here is a relatively straightforward passage from the first movement of the Haydn Trumpet Concerto.

Example 6

Proceed as follows:

Examine the timing of the passage, playing it on one note. The timing is the absolute priority for the whole of this sequence.

Example 7

Introduce some of the melodic 'shape' of the passage, *still concentrating on exact timing.*

Example 8

Increase the shaping towards the original.

Example 9

Now play the original. If the process has faltered at any point, go back in the sequence, *always concentrating on the timing.*

The cornet solo from Petrushka by Stravinsky can be played quite well by most students. However, the quality required for professional performance is far in advance of a casual run-through. Security and style can be developed relatively quickly if the solo is built up sensibly and not just played. The need for exact timing in this solo is underlined by the accompanying side drum.

In those passages with even slurred semiquavers (bars 3 and 4 of the cornet part), break the slur into twos, threes, fours and also into dotted rhythms. In addition, transpose the phrases into nearby keys in order to give them a different 'feel'.

This kind of practice will equalise the fingerings, take out the 'lumps,' and smooth the slightly awkward intervals. Overall this practise will inject security and consistency into what is a notable little solo. *It will also bring reliable results as quickly as possible.*

Timing Control Practice, when used with imagination, patience and persistence, can organise and make secure most problem passages. This routine can be applied to any passage.

Sundry Points of Interest

1: Fingering

- Awkwardly fingered fast passages can often be eased by the use of false fingering. Where the speed of note is fast, these alternatives are valuable even though they may be out of tune. Careful listening shows that even a good ear finds it hard to judge accurately the tuning of each note above a certain speed. If possible avoid an out of tune false fingering on the main beat of a bar, as these strong beats have a high audibility factor.

Example 10

2: Target Notes

- Certain notes in any phrase are technically more important than others. If these notes are secure the notes around them tend to fall into place. These are target notes and are often on strong beats or are at the high pitch points of a phrase. Evenness of air support, and restricting the movement of the embouchure downwards, are useful points to remember.

- In the case of a phrase in which the pitch jumps around a great deal, it is often useful to steer a course through the middle of the phrase shape, rather than jump the playing system up and down for each individual note.

Breathing

- Saving breath can often be a better way of lasting through a passage than grabbing at emergency breaths. Smooth playing (i.e. an even airstream) saves breath. Equally, soft playing is economical of breath.

- Many players take in breath only in major amounts and at major gaps, whereas smaller sips taken at minor points can very usefully top up the volume of breath as well as the oxygen content of the lungs.

- Circular breathing is certainly worth learning. The storage of breath in the cheeks ready to be expelled at the same time as a quick normal intake of breath is a difficult trick for some players. Patience over a number of weeks or months will secure the technique for most players.

- When a high note is being approached via lower notes and not directly after a breath, experiment to find the best moment to set the air support. It is rarely wise to leave it until the moment of the high note's arrival.

SCALES AND ARPEGGIOS

The daily practice of scales and arpeggios offers the fastest route to competence on the trumpet.

N.B.

I refer to Scales and arpeggios throughout by the initials 'S&A.'

The Rule

I have found very few exceptions to the following rule: that the best players are very good at scales and arpeggios. Whether S&A help to make a good player or whether a player can play S&A because he or she is good, whichever way round is irrelevant; they almost always go together.

For the moderate (or worse) player, S&A offer the best practical hope of steady and encouraging improvement. Not only do S&A lead the player around the instrument completely, the very nature of the work instils regularity, discipline and method. The lack of these qualities in the first place is the probable reason for a player's mediocrity. For this level of player I can only describe the value of S&A as enormous.

The Exceptions

The playing of a few players can develop perfectly well without S&A. This does not make a general rule, however. In their early playing life *they will have had enough work of the right kind, and at the right time in their development, to build up their playing intelligence and good habits*. In these instances good luck allied to talent produces effective grounding. (CR Talent) Thorough work on S&A ensures that everyone receives good grounding.

The Value of S&A: Fluency and Confidence

- S&A create fluent and reliable playing knowledge of those patterns of notes which regularly appear in music. The same sequences of notes are constantly written and rewritten by composers in varying ways. Scales deal with adjacent notes, while arpeggios (generally) deal with the non-adjacent ones. Arpeggios are invaluable in strengthening the player's harmonic sense.

- Once this knowledge has been gained, it gives confidence to the player, who then knows that almost all possible note-to-note relationships and angles will have been mastered. If this work has been thorough, consistent and demanding, the player can feel sure that his or her skills will stand up to the highest pressure of public performance.

- A scale or arpeggio should be regarded as a mini-study - a piece of music with an expressive character. Seen in that way, it is not an irrelevant mechanical exercise, divorced from musical reality, but part of the normal act of making music.

Specific Areas Improved by S&A

S&A guide the player equally through all parts of the instrument, not just the easy areas. The Bb instrument in particular seems to encourage players to stick to the sunny spots of C, G and F majors. The sharper keys especially tend to be avoided, yet these are just the ones in which most orchestral music is written. These shady parts of the range, usually involving third finger notes and distant keys, are often missed out in random, unplanned practice.

Familiarity with the note-families which make up all the various keys gives added fluency to reading, sight-reading, and transposition. In transposition work, when guessing is the last option left, the dice are heavily loaded in favour of the player with a knowledge of S&A patterns. (CR Reading and Transposition)

Throughout the book I refer to the brain as a resource to be deliberately exercised and improved. The brain, being no different to any other part of the body, needs stimulation, challenge and work, without which it will not function well. Mental improvement is essential for increasing our musical value to those who use our services.

The mental effort demanded by the study of S & A gives the brain serious exercise. Academic work in music has gradually been abandoned in British schools, with the result that the ability to think in music is not being created. The effort involved in the study of S & A will go some way towards remedying this lack, supplying experience of the basic interlocking maps of musical relationships.

Used imaginatively, with variations of musical style, rhythms, pitch patterns and dynamics, S&A become mini studies. Being limited in duration, and not presenting the endurance problems of most studies, the player can give full attention to the musical task in hand, without being negatively concerned with stamina and just surviving to the end.

Two simple examples:

1. A Db major two octave scale, continuous staccato quavers (eighths) at crotchet (quarter) 104, played piano, will give the player an excellent picture of the reliability and evenness of his or her articulation.

2. A Bb harmonic minor scale, slurred, mezzo forte, semiquavers (sixteenths) at crotchet 104, will give an excellent readout on the player's legato. The qualities of sound and fingering will be clearly exposed. (CR Fingering, Sound)

Quickness of mind in problem solving is an essential for all professional musicians. (CR Professionalism) Familiarity with the whole territory of the instrument is mentioned above, but many otherwise good players remain uneasy outside the common main-line keys. The short but sharp challenges of S&A give the player excellent training in problem solving and thinking under pressure.

Memory-recall under pressure is one of the most valuable life skills which we can acquire. Exercising the mind while coping with outside distractions is not easy. In the beginning it may worry or hurt, but it is good for you, both as a musician and as a person!

A Selection Method for the Practice of S&A

1. On individual slips of paper, write out all the scales and arpeggios to be practised.

2. Take two jars or containers, putting the slips into one.

3. Draw out the slips one by one, and play the scale or arpeggio listed.

4. If played well, put into the second jar.

5. If not, mark with a cross and put aside.

6. In conclusion, practise the scales and arpeggios marked with crosses.

7. Put them also in the second jar.

8. Continue round and round, adding new slips on each circuit.

Memo

Repetition is the path to the mastery of any subject.

The Values of this Selection Method

- It achieves random but consistent work on all scales and arpeggios.

- It ensures that you have a record of those S&A of which you are uncertain. As you repeat this system, the weakest ones identify themselves by a growing number of crosses.

Practice Routines

Adopt a set routine when asked for a Scale or an Arpeggio.

1. *STOP!*

2. *THINK!*, review all details and only then

3. *PLAY! without stopping under any circumstances*. This ensures that you develop firstly, good recall of what is to be played and secondly, a determination to see it through.

What usually happens is quite the opposite. *PLAY, STOP* at first fumble and then *THINK*, but too late. A brainless anxiety results, with further false starts, and fingers hacking away in the hope of reaching dry land. Stop, think (that is, mentally recall and review until sure), then play, is a routine which creates calm, steady playing, which will be unflustered and will survive any superficial blemishes. The *THINK!* moment may be embarrassingly long to start with, but it will quickly decrease. This method also sets a pattern for all successful thinking under pressure.

When you are not sure of a SorA, mentally revue the whole SorA before playing and without shadow fingering. Avoid this habit when thinking through a scale. For reasons I do not understand, just thinking the notes through, results in faster learning. I assume that it is another example of the brain working best when doing one thing at a time, before attempting coordinations.

Achieve fluency without touching the instrument. The notes of all S&A are best learned and revised without the instrument in hand. A great deal of valuable practice time and effort can be saved this way, and the ability to learn away from the instrument is strengthened. (CR Learning)

The return part of each S&A is always more accident prone than the opening section. Remember to use deliberate variable speed playing, slowing into an awkward passage, and then quickening back to tempo once past. (CR Problem Solving) This also strengthens the player's sense of control and balance when approaching dangerous passages.

A Selection of S&A

I include examples of S&A for use in daily practice in **Scales and Arpeggios: Examples**, which is placed at the end of this section. While there are infinite variations possible, I show some which will test the player thoroughly. These examples offer advanced patterns and difficulty levels not found in the usual trumpet S&A books.

Style

At all times be aware of musical style. Treat each S&A as a very short piece of music. There is no such thing as boring practice, only bored and boring players.

Practice Points

- When fluency has been achieved, start on a different degree of the SorA every day, e.g. on the second or third of the S or A. Start at the top or thereabouts, as the majority of difficult entries begin higher up in the range.

- Introduce different rhythms. See the examples.

- Go up on one S or A, and down on another.

- Change on to another S or A at each octave.

- Add extraneous notes, in ones, twos, etc. See the examples.

- Practice in groups of players. Not only will this sharpen quickness of response, it will help you learn not to be thrown by others', and your own, mistakes, an essential skill for the professional performer. Errors can spread like wildfire in an ensemble if players are easily rattled. See example 4.

For a much fuller listing of S&A, see the examples following.

Memo once more: Repetition is the path to technical mastery.

SCALES and ARPEGGIOS: EXAMPLES

All scales and arpeggios should firstly be mastered within an octave, extended to an octave and a fifth, and only then to two octaves. The achievement of fluency at each step is important. Once the student can play them freely within the normal two-octave range, extensions to the low notes can take place. Finally, the student can extend all scales and arpeggios into the upper ranges. For the Bb trumpet, therefore, the target range for all scales and arpeggios should be from low F sharp to high D. The ambitious player with a good range can then go further.

This set of examples is in C major, but are intended to be used in all keys, both major and minor.

This set of examples introduces broken scales and arpeggios. These are only a few of the endless possible variations.

Below are the five series of arpeggios in fourths. It is curious that this interval has been ignored in S & A books and examinations. The fourth, both perfect and augmented, is as commonly used in the twentieth century as is either the major or minor third.

The following diagrammatic examples are suggested for use with the series of fourths given above.

In these examples, perfect and augmented fourths are incorporated into the standard two octave arpeggio format. The starting note of G was chosen for its convenience. Once these are familiar, they can be transposed to all starting pitches.

Further Scales and Arpeggios

The addition of extra notes to standard scales and arpeggios creates new challenges. I give a few C major versions. Application to all other keys and types of scale and arpeggio should follow. Visualise first!

Once the idea of developing quick thinking has taken hold, add two, then three or more extraneous notes for further tests. Think first!

STAMINA and RECOVERY

Stamina is the by-product of mature good habits. In itself it is not created by muscle building exercise. The ability to recover quickly from heavy playing develops with experience and the application of common sense.

The Nature of Stamina

Stamina in playing is commonly thought of as strength of embouchure. In truth the key to embouchure resilience lies in the support given by the airstream to the lips, *at the lips.*

Stamina improves by economy of effort, which, in itself, allows the quickest growth of muscular strength. Embouchure comfort under pressure is the yardstick by which the player should judge his or her playing. If comfort exists, consistent progress will be made. In most players' minds, the stamina question is inseparable from the high range question, for the good reason that energy is lost more quickly the higher the range. (CR Range)

Unlike runners, who specialise at specific distances, professional brass players must be able both to sprint, i.e. to deliver bursts of high energy playing, and to stay, i.e. to survive well over the course of a long and sapping piece of music.

Some student players abuse their embouchures with constant exhaustion practice, as if the lips benefit from pumping mouthpiece iron. Playing a brass instrument, while being very physical, is not a violent contact sport.

A Strategy for Stamina

Many players become obsessed by the development of stamina. If a player decides to focus on stamina as a priority, then a long time scale must be adopted. Six months is the minimum period for a meaningful check on progress. The virtues of patient planning and persistence yield the best results, as always.

- Develop the power of the breath stream in a variety of playing ways, but not by interference, for example, pulling up, pushing down, in, out etc. While artificial breathing processes are occasionally adopted very successfully by some big band trumpeters, these may be inappropriate for orchestral, chamber and solo performance as they are likely to produce sound of a type very different to that needed. (CR Breathing)

- Ensure that the weight of the mouthpiece is evenly distributed between the top and bottom lips and teeth. (CR Embouchure)

- Check general posture, and excess mouthpiece pressure.

- Cross Reference with Range.

The Material to Use

The best material for stamina (and sound quality) work is available at the start of the Arban, in other standard tutors and in hymn books. Gradually transpose them upwards into the higher ranges, concentrating on comfort and good sound. Avoid squeezing up into the highest areas where the sound becomes airy and peters out. The occasional test to destruction and beyond should stay out of this squeezing zone.

Leave aside difficult technical studies and compositions as they confuse the issue and take the attention away from the priority that matters: good basic playing habits.

Recovery After the Day Before!

Stiffness is caused by the exertions of the groups of contrary muscles which pull against each other in the mouth and throat area. The tongue in particular works as hard as any and needs to be revived also.

- At the end of a hard day's playing, take the trouble to 'warm/cool down'. After some middle and low range flexibilites, finish off with a couple of minutes of pedal notes. Allowing the muscles to wind down like this disperses the lactic acid which builds up during severe exertion. The benefit will be felt the next day.

- The mornings before and after especially strenuous playing, make extra time for warming up. Check out basics such as breathing and general physical condition, doing some stretching if necessary.

- Spend a little extra time buzzing the mouthpiece to wake up the facial muscles.

- The tongue is as likely to be as stiff and tired as the embouchure. A little tongue stretching (in private!) should be followed by an extended legato tongue warm up in the low and middle range. My own view is that the tongue is much more important than the embouchure: it is the largest of the muscles anchored in the throat. Five minutes with legato tonguing always solved the problem for me.

The Small Matter of Physical Conditioning

The ability to absorb hard work without too much of a stiffness hangover and to recover fast, is improved mightily with good physical fitness and with a good night's sleep.

When it proves really hard to rouse yourself, take a leaf from the rugby players of the Pacific regions. The haka, originally a dance to prepare for war and frighten the enemy, is used for sporting arousal by the All-Blacks. The pummelling of the body, as they do, is a very good way of waking up. The back, the arms and especially the thighs, welcome an increased blood flow after a few minutes brisk beating. The message soon gets to the face and head! (CR Physical Conditioning)

TEACHING

All worthwhile teaching is based on the existence of good rapport between the teacher and the student. Rapport allows the teacher to develop the student's feeling for music, the instrument, and to awaken the student's interest and intelligence.

Rapport is also the channel for the regular injection of energy which helps to carry the student forward through the uncertainties of the early and middle learning years.

The Teacher: Accepting a Student

At the advanced level of teaching and playing, the teacher must consider the following.

1. Can I deliver the right kind of guidance for a particular student?

2. Even though I enjoy teaching this person, up to what point am I the right teacher for this student? I regularly say goodbye to students, not because I have nothing more to teach them, but because they need the stimulation of a change of environment.

Teaching must be regarded in the same light as medicine or any other profession which takes a practitioner into an important inner part of another's life. The element of trust is vital, especially where the potential career of a young player is at stake.

My Own Teaching Practice

My own practice as a teacher is summarised below. The detailed thinking behind my view of playing and teaching is laid out in the Recapitulation which appears at the end of the book.

I often say to my own students that I don't regard myself as a teacher, in the traditional sense. Rather, I simply try to keep the student pointing in the right direction, to help them to teach themselves by constantly restating the musical and physical fundamentals, developing their independence, resilience and individuality at the same time.

This period of life is the last when the student will have the benefit of regular teaching contact, so he or she must be weaned off undue dependence on the teacher. Above all, I encourage the student's own musicality and feeling for the trumpet, rather than producing an imitation of mine or anyone else's.

The teacher's easiest option is simply to tell the student what to do. At some points early on in the relationship this may be right, but carried too far it is an abdication of the teacher's true role. Every personality is unique. The more completely the student's individuality is realised, the more secure and fulfilled he or she will be.

Inside this velvet glove however the teacher must exercise a firm hand. The teacher must have a comprehensive knowledge of the following essentials:

1. The physical basics of playing

2. The primary styles of performing

3. Repertoire

4. All forms of teaching and learning

5. The arts of persuasion, i.e. the use of the carrot and the stick

The teacher's knowledge of these areas allows the student to develop within them. Just being a good or great player is not an adequate basis for teaching, as teaching needs communicable knowledge. In many master players the knowledge is there but in the sub-conscious, from whence it cannot be brought. The key ability is that of being able to pass on, through the channel of rapport, that which produces the maximum improvement, whatever it is.

The Creation of Rapport

The creation of rapport is the responsibility of the teacher, although the teacher must retain an internal separation from the student. Rapport exists when a positive relationship comes into being between people, allowing the teacher to energise and inspire the student. The well-motivated student will match the teacher's effort.

Occasionally rapport cannot be created, in which case the student should move to another teacher. It should be obvious quite early whether a relationship is going to be productive or not. The wise teacher will recognise this before the student does.

In those cases where there is a lack of rapport, it is not a matter of placing blame, but of simply recognising that rapport is not present. There are the occasional students who perpetually look for something or somebody else, rather than examining their own shortcomings. (CR Being Taught)

The Teacher as Performer

I have always regarded teaching as a kind of performance. As in public performance, the teacher must switch on his or her attention and interest like a light. The teacher's energy opens up the student to accept and absorb what is said to them. I also avoid as far as possible making verbal points in the negative, always using the positive.

Teaching well is a very tiring activity, requiring constant concentration.

Verbal Communication in Music

The appeal of music bypasses words and links directly into feelings and their arousal. Therefore all musicians agree that too much talk about music is a bad thing in the conduct of musical activity. This is a sensible if crude guideline to follow. What should be said is that the wrong kind of talk is a bad thing.

To lay out the principles of playing in such a way that all expert brass players agreed on the wording would result in the following. 'Place the mouthpiece on the middle of your lips and blow.' Further explanation would cause immediate disagreements about wording.

There are of course general areas of agreement, but even so we are into words and our individual use of them. Those master brass players who just 'put it on the face and blow' are not empty-headed because the words are simplistic. Their heads will be full of musical and practical ideas, but they may not be able to, or want to, put them into words. For such players words have no real relevance to playing and music, and in fact get in the way.

The Teacher as Communicator

So how does the good teacher talk to the good student, if too much talk is a bad thing, and example is not necessarily all it is cracked up to be? If a teacher regularly talks a great deal, then he or she is not a good teacher. It means either a lack of discipline, or an inability to be precise with knowledge.

From time to time the good teacher will talk more than usual, probably to convey inspiration and energy. This is in contrast to the process of passing information, which should be concise and to the point. If the passing of information is not short, sharp and immediately understood, it will confuse the student. The onus is on the teacher to choose what is necessary at whatever moment.

The good teacher must therefore be economical with words, and above all know when to stop talking. Words may seem to be our main means of communication, but research has shown that we make our judgements of people and situations largely on the basis of non-verbal cues: body language. This brings the matter back to rapport. The teacher must offer the appropriate sense of rapport by all these various channels of communication.

The Teacher's Use of Imagery

In my experience, the most successful verbal technique for producing an inspired response from a student is that of the image, the simple figure of speech which matches the musical response necessary with an image which is direct and vivid for the student. This is a very old technique which has fallen out of use, but which is one of the most valuable if used with imagination.

Consider the following situation. A student is playing a legato melodic passage, but the result is patchy, because the legato is not 'smooth' in the shaping of the phrase, in the individual notes, or in the detailed movement note to note. The teacher then has three options in order to effect an improvement.

1. Firstly the passage can be discussed as a series of failures 'This note was far too pear-shaped, this one was softer/louder than the others, this one was out of tune, at this point the legato was lost between notes.....' and so on.

2. Secondly the teacher can discuss the basics of legato production, perhaps explaining that unevenness in legato is caused principally by an uneven airstream, or by throat interference.

Alternatively the teacher can offer the student an image of smoothness such as the pouring of oil (Mozart's own choice), the feel of silk, or an image of level-ness, such as the horizon at sea, or a still calm lake. It can then be suggested that the student matches the image in sound. Having offered the student an example or two, the teacher should then ask for the student's own image of smoothness. This will naturally be more powerful for the student than the teacher's own image.

Time without number students have described this process to me as a thoroughly pleasurable way of achieving better playing. Sometimes the image can be unusual: a former student chose the eating of a bar of milk chocolate as her image of smoothness. Her performance of a lyrical passage improved enormously with no technical explanation given!

As a follow up, the analytical description of what was previously wrong can be used to underpin the success of the image-based performance. This uses technical knowledge in a support role, which is where it should always be. If analytical description is at the front of the mind, it causes confusion. Paralysis by analysis.

The greatest value of this method is that it focuses the student's attention solely on the expression and the feeling of the music. The student is only aware of the one strand of interest, and is not trying to translate several strands of verbal analysis into action. The mind is uncluttered and free.

My Teaching Strategy

The unvarying strategy of my teaching is to simplify the student's idea of playing until there is just one thought: the music. The simpler the idea, the better the skill. This underlies all the seeds that I plant, the strings that I pull, the tactics I use.

When one hears or sees a master performer at work, in whatever sphere of action, it looks simple. It looks simple because it is simple. All the parallel strands of knowledge have been woven into a single strand. Obviously this is an illusion, because the complex knowledge is there, but is has been absorbed and blended into this one strand of attention. The practitioner of any skill progresses towards mastery by doing less and less. The great sportsperson does just what is needed, the poor one ten times as much. 'To the eye the actions of a skilled athlete seem simple and effortless'. (CR Recapitualtion)

Handling the Dangers

As very young children our activities and skills are unhampered by too much knowledge. Failure is relatively unimportant. At the student stage, there is a sudden bombardment of information, possibilities and comparisons. The difficulty facing the student is that of effectively handling this mass of complicated information, impressions and ideas, which is why the student must have skilled teaching to maintain a balanced attitude. It is the most dangerous period for any developing player.

Many aspiring student players see progress as a process of picking up as many tips and hints as possible, thinking that once they have amassed enough of these they will then play well. What really matters is the consistency of approach of the student and the teacher in developing strong musicianship, basic skills, and an understanding that simplicity is the goal, not complexity.

The Over-Intense Student

If the student player is too intense about improving quickly, progress can be blocked. (CR Anxiety, Progress) Over-intensity can be one of the most severe handicaps with which to deal. The teacher must evaluate this factor in deciding how to treat the student, even down to the point of using a consistently calm tone, and slow speed, of voice.

It doesn't need conscious thought to decide on a tone of voice. Tone is created naturally from a sense of rapport with the student, allied to experience of how long it can take to lead a musician out of anxiety. If the student is guided correctly - and it only needs a few words at the right moment - the student will come to the teacher and say 'I've decided just to play and not to worry anymore' or words to that effect. It can be earlier or later, no-one knows or can predict. The teacher must wait patiently.

My Tactics: The First Priority....

Having assessed the student's playing as a whole, I then choose one priority area for attention. I continually keep an eye on all parts of the student's playing, but at the start I shine a full light on only one area at a time. My experience is that any change in one part of a player's performance, however small, will cause a reaction throughout the rest of it. To burden the player with more than one change at a time inevitably results in confusion. Even a poor player has an idea of his or her own capability. It is important not to damage that identity by attempting too much at one time.

If as a last resort the teacher believes that drastic rebuilding must take place, say in the form of remodelling the embouchure, then a full understanding of what is involved must be worked out beforehand, as the whole basis of the student knowing 'where he or she is', is going to be removed and replaced. The human mind hates to change a habit and is easily confused. (CR Embouchure)

If the change resulting from focusing on one area is good, it will bring unexpected benefits to other parts of the player's capability. I refer to this method as the 'logjam method' of teaching. Releasing the specific log causing the jam allows the logs to flow down-river. The next jam is then released - and so on, until the destination is reached.

.... *Sound*

In most situations, my initial attention is given to sound quality. (CR Sound) The sound a player makes is the exact musical reflection of their blowing method, a mirror image of what is being done in the act of playing. It tells the master teacher what is going on at each point in the physical act of playing.

The airstream is the prime factor in sound production in the way that the act of breathing is the basic act of being alive. While this principle has always been understood by brass players, I have grave doubts about the usual teaching methods of adapting our normal breathing habits to the special act of playing. (CR Breathing) More often than not, more negative tensions are created than positive ones by undue talk of doing this or that to the diaphragm. I use the general word 'support' in a context of good posture. (CR Posture)

The Creation of Good Sound

The creation of a good full sound boosts and encourages the player the way nothing else can. The effect can be seen in the player's face. It lights up, the posture becomes alert, and the whole person is brighter and less tentative. The sensory pleasure of good sound is as primary to a musician as vibrant colour is to a painter, or the ring of words to a writer. The background reason is that the player will be making a better sound only because he or she is breathing correctly, which is in itself a cause of well-being.

The teacher now has something with which to work. A good sound gives the teacher a basis from which to move out into wider areas of playing. The very act of breathing correctly and making a good sound will have changed and improved those areas of playing which had been earmarked as needing improvement. Above all, the player will be much more positive, co-ordinations will improve and the student's playing effort will be naturally more confident.

Both the student and the teacher will have cause to feel that the journey which they have begun together has made a good start, and that a fair distance has been covered very quickly. Usually the euphoria of good sound production relaxes the student, which then gives the teacher the opportunity to create a realistic, unhurried expectation of progress. For the student, if anxiety can be calmed at this stage, a realistic tempo of work and expectation can be created.

Working with one priority means that improvement is much easier. Learning one lesson at a time rather than two or more, the obvious question is which is the next priority?

The teacher must judge what the next thing is from experience. In fact the easiest area of playing to fix makes itself obvious both to the student and teacher, taking into account that the student's confidence and well-being are of the utmost importance. We all find it difficult to take two steps at once in any process of thought, trying to go too far too fast. Missing out a step in any progression of learning leads to confusion. Behind all of this is the constant effort to improve the student's listening ability.

In Addition

With all students, I begin discussions about their career aspirations at an early stage. This is not with a view to fixing a path as soon as possible, but just to lay out the possibilities so that I can gauge the natural response of the student. (CR Careers) The teacher must decide how much or little to say, based on the realism or unrealism of the student's spoken aims and ambitions.

Thereafter the teacher must steer by the star of the student's own musical and instrumental personality. For example, in the matter of interpretation, rather than handing down 'the interpretation' of a piece, or randomly suggesting 'try this or that' over some detail, I try to encourage the student, however naive, to develop his or her own version in relation to the principles of interpretation. They often find something I have not heard or imagined before!

One of the first works I study with a student is the Haydn Concerto, not for an extended period, but to establish the basics of appropriate style. During a four year period I will return to it perhaps a dozen times. It allows both of us to plot the course of the student's development. The quality of the music reveals the player's own quality unerringly.

Finale

Giving inspiration is a different process from giving information, and is much the more important of the two. I avoid pointing out those flaws which students know themselves. In fact I guide students towards paying no attention to surface blemishes.

With regard to surface blemishes, I insist that when a passage has been started, it must be finished, no matter what! There is more impetus to achieve when that rule applies. Real life performance is like that. If players know that they can stop, it is a get-out clause, an easy option to semi-fail, start again, in the hope of better luck. Many will start a second time without re-setting the embouchure, thereby avoiding another fact of life: in real performance the player always has to start on a freshly set embouchure.

TEACHING 2: BEING TAUGHT

The student's input into the teaching relationship has to be honest and straightforward, otherwise very little progress can be made.

The Student: the Choice of a Teacher

The student must answer the following questions.

1. Can the teacher take me where I need to go?

2. Is the teacher's approach the right one for me?

He or she should talk to the students of a variety of teachers. It will become obvious from their responses which ones are dedicated; the student must feel that the teacher is positively on his or her side.

If the teacher has the ability and attitude, the next important question concerns the attitude of the student. Am I capable and willing to work to the degree which is going to match the teacher's own interest? The answer to this question must be a resounding 'yes' otherwise the student should question his or her own career aims and ideas, before spending any more time and money.

The Student: a Working Attitude to the Teacher

The student must understand that the teacher is a guide only, and cannot program anyone and everyone to play well regardless of talent and application. Expecting the teacher to pour information into the student's mind like water into a jug is completely misguided. The student bears the responsibility to work along the path laid down by the teacher, even though the direction of that path may not at first be obvious.

All students must accept that an expert teacher will have a personal vision of playing and performance, developed over many years into a consistent whole. This vision will work best for the student only when accepted completely. The student should not treat the teacher's various advices as an a la carte menu, to be dipped into merely when it suits. The good teacher takes the long view created by experience. Experience is exactly what is not available to a young person.

Practice is the area requiring the most thought and consideration. (CR Practice) The well organised student makes the least excuses, the fewest complaints and the best progress. Each student is responsible to themself and to the teacher for the adoption of patient long term aims. (CR Aims and Goals)

For example, young players often develop an obsessive interest in, and anxiety about, high range and stamina. Any experienced teacher will offer guidance on these subjects which will inevitably counsel a steady course of specific practice. The unintelligent student 'wants it now,' at once, and goes about picking up a rag bag of tips and hints from anyone who will talk to them. They then proceed to fritter their time away with self-destructive hither-and-thither practice in the hope of quick solutions. Serious students must learn how to teach themselves, as part of preparation for professional life. It is a vital skill for all students to acquire. (CR Practice)

Once a teacher is chosen, in the short term any change of teacher must be undertaken with the greatest care. At College level one change of teacher is understandable. Two changes begin to suggest that the student is a problem.

The Student at College: the Choice of a Teacher

A key mistake which can made by the student entering music college, or undertaking advanced study while still at school, is to equate a well-known player's performing abilities with his or her teaching skills. They do not always go together. Across the range of master players we find those who are totally 'natural', i.e. those whose thought processes are entirely hidden even from themselves, and who say they just do it. At the other extreme we find players who have an ability to describe what they do and have developed the craft of communicating. This requires very highly developed verbal skills on the part of a teacher. Teaching is a skill quite separate from performing.

A fine player will of course inspire by example. As a student this is how I chose my teacher. If they are also the 'natural' kind of player, analytical help may not be forthcoming when needed.

Some teachers assume that what works for them, however individualistic, will also work for the student. This faulty logic assumes that the fundamentals of playing are perfectly displayed in their own work. The rigid pronouncements of some player-teachers, particularly on that most emotional of subjects the embouchure, can cause more problems than they solve. (CR Embouchure)

Brass teaching has very few practitioners who operate in the same way as the leading string teachers. When I once asked a violinist about the noted violin teacher Ivan Galamian, 'Did he play?,' I received the instant revealing response 'Oh no! he didn't play, he was a teacher!' Dorothy DeLaye (violin) at the Juillard School and Aldo Pariso (cello) at Harvard University, both 'only' teach. Bo Nilsson in Sweden, Hardenberger's first teacher, focuses now almost entirely on teaching. At this virtuoso level the skills of teaching are very highly developed indeed.

TRANSPOSITION

Regular practice, for very short periods of time, soon dissolves this minor reading problem.

The Problem

Transposition can seem a daunting challenge to the beginner. As soon as it is faced intelligently, the problem begins to disappear.

The Solution (for Beginners)

Assuming that the Bb trumpet is being played, and that major keys are employed, use the following system to learn the commonest transpositions, listed below.

- Choose the simplest exercises in the Arban tutor. Play them in the C transposition, up one tone. Therefore play in the key of D major when they are printed in C major. The key for transposition will always be two keys sharper than the original. Any accidentals extra to the key are read as exceptions to the key.

- Do this daily, one exercise every ten or fifteen minutes, for only thirty seconds or so. The simplicity of the exercises ensures that wrong notes identify themselves. The golden rule is to practise often and briefly, because each time a transposition is practised the player has to recall and review the techniques needed for each one. The more repetitions the quicker the recall each time.

- Achieve absolute fluency with the C transposition before moving on to the next. The process will then be clear and confidence will be high.

- Move to the F transposition, up a perfect fifth, and repeat the process. The reason for the choice of this transposition is that it is visually the easiest. The eye runs on the wide parallel quite easily. Space reads as space, line as line.

- Following this take the D transposition which is read up a major third, four keys sharper, in E major.

- Then take the A transposition which is down a semitone, read either at pitch with seven flats (Cb major), or as the key which is one semitone down (B major). As the A transposition mostly applies to cornet parts which often have their own key-signatures, only when the original is in C does the addition of five sharps (B major) apply unadjusted.

- On to the Eb transposition, which is up a perfect fourth, and always visually awkward because a line reads as a space and vice-versa. This can be read in the key of F major.

- The E transposition, up an augmented fourth, is one of the most awkward, as it is keyed in F#, with six sharps. Many of the most difficult parts in late Romantic repertoire are written in E.

- Most awkward of all are the trumpet parts of Richard Strauss. What look superficially like predictable or chromatic passages always have the 'wrong' note inserted. What look like predictable phrases almost always contain the unexpected twist. The safest course is to memorise them completely, so that reading has only the slightest role in the performance.

Further Transpositions

There are in fact transpositions on all semitones of the scale, from low to high F. Transpositions in F#, G, Ab, B, to Db(C#) occur very infrequently, only one or two examples being seen regularly in the orchestra. Some of these can be found in published excerpt books.

Techniques

Each player builds up his or her own transposition system from a variety of techniques. The possibilities are as follows:

- Each transposition has a key relative to the Bb trumpet, which can be used as a basis for thinking out the notes ahead. Reading in a key allows the player to assume a good deal about the notes (pitches) coming up, leaving attention free for the variables like accidentals, expression and tempo changes. Looking further ahead becomes easier. This process is improved when the player is skilled in scales and arpeggios: the track of the notes can be guessed even more easily. Obviously this system is best when only a few accidentals are present.

- When the pitches become too chromatic, or the music is atonal (i.e. not in a key), the key system is more a hindrance than help. Most experienced players read so much and often that their skills of reading become automatic, and therefore note-by-note, rather than in-the-key. Most 'serious' composers today have standardised their scores at concert pitch (Trumpet in C), with parts intended for other instruments such as D, Eb, and Piccolo Bb being transposed to be read as printed, untransposed. These instruments should be played regularly in order that pitching them 'against' the fingering does not cause disorientation.

- A few composers, such as Britten, write in C and also use key signatures. This creates treacherous reading problems, because the key signature has to be thought into the transposition.

- Always make a priority of reading the rhythm correctly. It is surprising how many right pitches come out! If the pitches take priority in the player's mind a mess almost always ensues.

The Effect of Different Trumpets on Transposition

Trumpet playing today requires total familiarity with at least four or five trumpets: the Bb, C, D/Eb, piccolo G as the fifth, and piccolo Bb/A. It is plain that the ability to transpose has to be infinitely flexible. Every player, especially in the Principal Trumpet position, makes different decisions regarding difficult passages.

VOCALISATION

When a performer's playing is musically 'stuck' and less than convincing, he or she should vocalise the phrase or rhythm. This chapter may be one of the shortest in the book but it is one of the most important.

Vocalisation?

Singing, lah-ing, dah-de-dah-ing - these are all vocalisations. The voice is our most natural instrument and, for this particular purpose, the less trained the better. Useful vocalisation can even be just a shape - vocal gesturing without exact pitches. However good or bad the result is as vocal sound, a positive vocalisation frees and releases the natural expression of the music. The word 'positive' is of utmost importance; unless a fullblooded vocalisation is created the musical realisation will remain stilted and incomplete.

The Value of Vocalisation

Players who are 'stuck', as far as the musicality of their trumpet playing is concerned, almost always sing better than they play, which is obviously an unsatisfactory situation! When a performer is playing unconvincingly, whether it is a phrase, rhythm, or longer passage, vocalising will revive the positive musical response. Vocalising puts the player back in touch with their basic musicality and allows them to be freely expressive of the music's feeling and sense. Artistry and musicality are often buried under anxiety. Many a player worries about the instrument as if it were an enemy. The pain of past failures, and potential future failures, blot out everything else.

The Use of Vocalisation

When a player is musically inhibited, unsure, or unable to achieve a convincing phrasing of a piece of music, he or she should vocalise each passage aloud in a totally uninhibited manner before playing. Having vocalised with real conviction, only then should the player perform the passage, matching the performance to the vocalisation. This releases the player's own personality more clearly than any other musical act; it can come only from his or her deepest instinct for music.

Music as Gesture or Mime

In exploring ways of releasing musical feeling that has been submerged, I have found that matching gesture to music gives a very similar result to vocalisation. It is very valuable, particularly with reference to phrasing and the balancing of phrasing. (CR Musicianship) Try, for example, putting two-handed mime gestures to Arban Studies numbers 1, 2 and 13.

Music, after all, is the shape and gesture of pitch as it travels through time. Whether the gestures are vocal or physical the actions tap directly into our wells of personal feelings.

If a student feels embarrassed by vocalising or gesturing, this is all the more reason to persevere. Severe shyness is a disqualification for a career as a performing musician. A musician who is seriously bothered by someone else's attention should review their future as a performer.

SECTION FIVE

CAREERS and SITUATIONS

INTRODUCTION

Background knowledge is the theme of this Section. While some of the chapters relate solely to the trumpet, the majority can be read as applying to most instruments.

ARRANGING FOR BRASS

Arranging for brass is a skill which all brass players should acquire to a reasonable working level.

The Main Reasons For Arranging

To be an effective arranger is to be useful to others. To be a very good arranger is to be very useful indeed. Arranging is one of the great enabling skills of music: it makes available to performers and listeners music which would otherwise remain locked away. In brass music this is especially important as brass instrument technology has peaked far too late for those composers who have created the core repertoire of serious music.

In career terms it is not possible to know what the course of a lifetime's work is going to be for any individual musician. Even for those who have a totally clear career goal, additional related skills like arranging can be very productive in opening up a variety of further career options. Players who also conduct or direct ensembles, from the youngest to the most professional, always need new material.

1. The Freelance Career

The freelance player-arranger will always be sought after by those who are creating new ensembles. If pursued consistently over a period of time, arranging can supply useful income through combinations of commission fees, performance, recording and sales royalties.

2. New Avenues of Musical Activity

The practical musician realises that a career in music rarely runs in a straight line from start to finish. Arranging opens up new avenues of musical activity unconsidered previously. For example, arrangers are often asked to conduct their work. There will be circumstances lying in wait for everyone which offer new opportunities. The more skills the player has to offer, the more employable he or she is.

3. Development towards Composition

Arranging music from one medium into another develops knowledge of repertoire, insights into how instruments relate and function, and awareness of how music is constructed and how composers work.

It is also a big first step towards composition, as the arranger can progress from simple transcription, to creative arrangement, to complex re-composition. Former trumpet players who have become composers, such as Malcolm Arnold and Elgar Howarth, pursued their interest in composition while still playing. Some continue with both careers: for example Stan Friedman, Anthony Plog and Thomas Stevens. Today, with an increased acceptance of the need for lifelong flexibility towards work, many talents can be unearthed from inside our minds.

Further Discussion

The demand for new brass material is rising as the number of new ensembles multiplies with the increase in players. It puts the arranger in a strong position to start his or her own ensemble and facilitates the establishment of a clear musical identity for the group. It allows repertoire planning by the arranger without dilution by others.

If the arrangements are successful, and are scored for a mainstream combination of instruments, other musicians and groups will want to buy them. (Or rather they will probably want them for no more than the cost of the photo-copying! CR Self-Publishing) Early application for memberships of the Performing Right Society and the Mechanical Copyright Protection Society must be a priority for any arranger with more than a dozen or so copyright works to his or her name.

Unless committed to a straight-line career in one post - and who can guarantee that? - it is unlikely that any player will travel down a predictable road throughout the whole of his or her working life. The number of positions where this is possible or desirable is very small indeed. Personally I cannot imagine anything less attractive, and indeed in 1976 I resigned from the position of Principal Trumpet at the London Symphony Orchestra in order to take up new challenges.

It is becoming less and less likely that any person will be able to state confidently where they will be in five years' time. I have no idea what I will be doing one year from now, and actually don't want to know. Arranging, and latterly some composing, have been two of the new activities which I have taken up more or less out of the blue. They have opened up many new channels of interest. (CR Careers)

For example, when I began to teach regularly I knew that I would enjoy it, but had no idea however that teaching would become such a fascinating and enjoyable subject for me that I would spend countless hours writing a book about it!

It is not necessary to be active as an arranger to become a master performer. Performance skills can be developed without the player following a wide range of musical interest. There is research to show that a significant number of expert performers have only a minimal interest in music outside their own narrow field. However, the performer who arranges and/or composes is brought into close contact with a much wider repertoire than just that of brass. In short, the performer will be developing his or her musicianship, adding to his or her stock of knowledge of music while increasing career possibilities.

Very Simple Guidelines for Arranging

- Choose extremely short, easy material with which to begin. Arranging is like any other activity; skill will develop steadily if it approached sensibly.

- Avoid pieces that are too pianistic (e.g. left hand arpeggios) or characteristic of their instrument. Allow for the effect of pedalling in piano pieces: when pedalling lengthens chords significantly, pencil in the notes' true duration, until your ear and eye have got used to allowing for them.

- Look at your score like a picture. Does it look commonsense? Would you mind playing each part yourself, for range, for stamina, for interest?

- Complete five or six simple arrangements for small combinations before attempting anything too ambitious. Almost everyone is within reach of a computer system which will allow playback to check out errors. Avoid cheating with the computer by using it to tell you about faults in your thinking and errors in the harmony. Only use it to find copying mistakes.

- Make up parts and try them out as soon as possible.

You will now begin to feel confident and able to tackle larger projects.

AUDITIONS and AUDITIONING

The musician who wishes to have an orchestral playing career must be able to audition well.

The Audition Format

The orchestral audition has a standard format world-wide. It begins with a solo work, before moving on to orchestral material and sight reading. The solo work may or may not be chosen by the panel. The bulk of the orchestral excerpts will be taken from the romantic and modern repertoire, notified in advance and will be almost exclusively from First Trumpet parts, even for section positions. This is not as curious as it may seem; the panel will want to test the candidate on basic playing skills. The more position-specific skills will be revealed during a trial.

The Audition Own Choice Work

When the candidate is able to choose a solo work, it is important to select intelligently. On the one hand, choosing a piece to show off one's best points, and suppressing the least good, is to be recommended. It will engender a sense of confidence and comfort in the player and will bring out his or her best playing. On the other hand, any choice which is too slanted in this way will not deceive the experienced musicians who will be listening. Expert musicians can place an auditionee on their scale of values within a few seconds of the audition starting.

The choice of music itself is always revealing. Most importantly, the panel will know what is missing, and will explore those points during the latter parts of the audition.

Specific Audition Repertoire

The best advice is to choose music which shows your playing skills *as suitable for orchestral playing.* The Arutunian Trumpet Concerto played in an extrovert hearts-'n-flowers style may bring out some smiles of enjoyment, but is unlikely to impress as much as that of a first class performance of the Haydn or Hummel Concerti or impressive accounts of the Jolivet and Tomasi Concerti. The Hindemith Sonata for Trumpet and Piano demands many of the characteristics looked for in good orchestral playing, but it is musically too plain and sombre for most players' tastes.

Modern Music

At all costs, the auditionee should avoid the very advanced modern work which uses the latest extraordinary techniques. It will be quite irrelevant to the matter in hand, which is to proceed to the trial stage of the vacancy. This is not a value judgement on the type of music, but a recognition that orchestral playing is rarely concerned with this repertoire. The danger for the auditionee is that the panel will switch off, until the real audition can start with the excerpts. The candidate should remember that, at the first audition, there is a very limited time in which to impress.

The Audition Panel

This is a variable factor depending on where the audition takes place. Most auditions in Britain for section positions will be conducted by the brass section. On the continent of Europe and in America, it is usual for all principals including strings and woodwinds, and possibly the conductor, to be present. Their taste in repertoire and very different performance priorities may change the situation as far as style of playing is concerned.

In these circumstances ask the advice of someone close to, or in, the orchestra. In European auditions it is not uncommon for brass auditionees to be favoured by the brass players on an orchestral panel, but to be excluded by non brass members.

The Audition Curtain

One further variation in method, which is mandatory in many countries, is that candidates are required to play unseen behind a curtain. The purpose is to avoid discrimination against individuals on grounds of sex or race, or the predisposition of anyone for or against a candidate. There are examples of appointments being made solely on the basis of auditions, without trials, but this is a rare and risky procedure because of the need for co-operation within sections. I have conducted orchestras and groups where silent (and not-so-silent) warfare existed between players, in one case for well over two decades. Of course it is a nonsense that orchestra managements don't knock heads together to sort out this kind of situation, but sometimes they don't! The requirement for a section to work well together is not just a social matter, but a musical one. There is no doubt that a co-operative atmosphere leads to the best possible playing.

Depending on its thickness, a curtain will dampen the upper frequencies, thereby favouring the louder players.

The Volume of Applications

Be aware that in Britain there will probably be a hundred or so auditionees for each orchestral position. No more than five or six will be selected for a trial, and amongst the good players, a one per cent advantage can determine who secures the position. I mention this fact to emphasise the need for every element of self-presentation to be considered. Remember that the audition situation is blatantly competitive.

All Round Impression

The panel will not necessarily be concerned with faultless performance, but will look for the right person to fit the working atmosphere. At all times the panel, and particularly the auditionee's potential section colleagues, will be assessing the candidate as a person with whom they may have to work; therefore self presentation is very important. Guard against an excess of physical movement which might seem natural in a standing solo performance. It could seem intrusive if transposed to a seated position. In other words, the players on the panel might think 'I couldn't bear that person sitting next to me'.

Audition Accompanists

It is unlikely that an accompanist will be provided for a routine audition, but where one is in attendance take good note of the difficulties of playing not only *with* an unknown partner, but *with/against* a piano, that most treacherous of musical companions. (CR Accompaniment) Be sure above all to establish and keep *your* tempo.

Prepared Orchestral Excerpts

The way in which orchestral excerpts are dealt with at audition is very variable. The minimum requirement for the candidate will be to play the passages from the repertoire which have been specified, with fluency, security and stylistic accuracy. Playing the excerpts from memory will add another proof of thoroughness, but this should be done without ostentation. Occasionally refer to the music, don't read it.

It may be that the player is asked to play an excerpt twice. Regard this request as positive. If the auditionee is a non-starter the panel's main aim, with perhaps fifty more candidates to go, will be to get rid of him or her as soon as possible.

It is likely that the Chairman of the panel will ask the candidate to alter the tempo, dynamic or style of a particular passage, in order to test the player's flexibility of expression. Variety of tempo preparation, together with a fluent understanding of different styles, is an important ability to develop. The player must be especially aware of those faster passages which may be taken across the tonguing change from single to double or triple. (CR Articulation) For the panel to ask for this kind of flexibility is very sensible, as most conductors vary tempi between rehearsals and performance.(CR Orchestral Repertoire).

Unprepared Orchestral Excerpts

Usually this is the last part of the audition. It will test the depth of the auditionee's knowledge of orchestral repertoire. After all, if the candidate's career goal is orchestral playing, he or she should be able to display a virtually complete knowledge not only of the highways but the byways.

In addition to a knowledge of the specially published excerpt books, a sensible precaution is for the candidate to prepare the material which the particular orchestra is playing, or about to play, at that time. Leading professional players are busy people, and will often use what is at hand rather than seek out the perfect testpiece.

Equally, the auditionee must show the ability to handle unknown material, with or without transposition, which will be yet another challenge to his or her ability to cope under pressure.

The Successful Audition

The successful audition will lead on to a trial. Even if the player gets no further than the trial (CR Trial) it will be possible to quote this fact on a future CV, as a proof of achievement, and good quality experience gained.

The Unsuccessful Audition

Failure to proceed from audition to trial occurs to 95% of those who enter, and should not be read as a disaster. Most players will need to play a number of auditions before proceeding successfully. The read-out from these auditions will let players know fairly accurately where they are in the pecking order. If the possibility exists through direct or indirect contacts, an auditionee should try to get a detailed view on their performance from at least one of the panel members.

One former student of mine, who is now Principal Trumpet in a London orchestra, played his first two auditions in the same week, performing to approximately the same standard on both occasions. The first audition was for fourth trumpet in an opera orchestra. He was discarded in the first round. The second was for the position of Principal Trumpet in a BBC provincial orchestra. He was offered the position immediately after the conclusion of the first round of auditions. As this anecdote reveals, there is a significant element of 'fitting' into a particular position and into a particular orchestra. A small number of failures can be disregarded, but if the number rises steeply, a re-examination of long term career goals is the only sensible option.

In the Orchestral Repertoire Section, I list a selection of works which make up the bulk of orchestral concert programmes, with one or two operatic additions. The serious student should begin to build up a comprehensive collection of excerpt books and scores as soon as possible.

BRASS BANDS

Most of the leading trumpet performers in Britain developed their playing in brass bands. Making use of the opportunity to play the cornet in a good quality band brings many benefits to the aspiring trumpet player.

The Brass Band: Prejudice, Pride and Respect, Differences and Similarities

Brass banding occupies a strange twilight world. It is a popular music activity, created naturally, self-regenerating, and - in this world of state hand-outs and subsidies for official culture - financially independent. While most of its repertoire is popular and light music, in contests and a few concerts it moves over into serious music.

The Value of Cornet Playing for Young Trumpet Players

The value of brass band experience on the cornet, especially for the young player, whether beginner or advanced, lies in the opportunity to develop a wide range of skills in a competitive and challenging environment. The fact that the majority of trumpet and trombone players in British orchestras started playing in brass bands speaks for itself. My immediate predecessors as Principal Trumpet at the London Symphony Orchestra - Alan Stringer and Willy Lang - were products of brass banding, as I was myself. My successor, Maurice Murphy, a truly great player, both in terms of power and subtelty, has now been joined on Principal by, Rod Franks, an equally fine player with his own style. They both developed in brass banding, before moving into orchestral playing.

The make-up of the brass band cornet section means that the individual players learn co-operation. They learn to follow, to lead, and to develop positive group attitudes. In playing terms there are different types of work to be done, from the less forward roles of the 2nd and 3rd parts, up to the leading position of the solo Bb cornet and the Eb soprano.

The Nature of Brass Bands

The brass band is an ensemble in itself, and not a part of a larger grouping. Brass instruments in brass bands have a totally different function to brass in orchestras. Its musical material encompasses all kinds of situations, the cornet section carrying the bulk of the musical interest in the way that the first violins do in the orchestra. Therefore there are melodies and melodic lines to play, and extended passages over the widest diversity of tempi, dynamics, and range.

The expressive scope of the repertoire is very extensive. The huge volume of music arranged from nineteenth and early twentieth century orchestral repertoire gives the brass band player the chance to play music denied to the orchestral brass. In addition, the rapidly-expanding catalogue of original works for brass band has added repertoire of the highest difficulty. (CR Arranging)

The Historical Perspective

The soloistic use of the trumpet, so much to the fore in the Baroque period, was mainly in abeyance during the nineteenth century. In Britain it can be seen to have gone underground into the brass bands, which by the middle of the nineteenth century were in the full flood of development. Trevor Herbert, in his examination of the Cyfarthfa Band (which was run by a South Wales industrialist in the middle of the nineteenth century) leaves no doubt as to its comprehensive performing skills. John Wallace has brought some of the Cyfarthfa Band's repertoire alive by recording it on contemporary instruments. The very high quality of performance of those early professional band musicians becomes very obvious. As now, they existed side by side with the totally amateur recreational forms of banding.

The Orchestra Compared to the Brass Band

The orchestra's brass section is one of its four main families of instruments. The brass section's main purpose, in most of the mainstream repertoire, is to bolster the tuttis with climactic dynamics, to supply varying colours to accompaniment, and to call up musical patterns with traditional brass connotations such as fanfares and chorales. These musical materials have dominated the development of the style of trumpet playing usually called orchestral. (CR Styles) The danger of this role is that, unless the player remains musically alert, it can encourage a monochrome and dreary style of performance.

In this mainstream repertoire the brass (horns apart) very rarely carry the leading themes and melodic lines. Strings and woodwind, being at the time of the music's composition much more flexible and expressive than the available brass instruments, are allotted the overwhelming bulk of significant musical material. This marginal role allotted to the brass section in the most popular repertoire only begins to change in the very late nineteenth century. With the twentieth century, the demands of orchestral brass writing, scoring and performance accelerates rapidly.

Orchestral Reservations about Brass Band Style

The chief reservations of a limited number of orchestral brass players centre firstly around the use of vibrato. 'Straight' versus 'vibrato' has been an issue in the past, of the Roundheads-and-Cavaliers sort, and just as silly. The orchestral player who has no command of vibrato, is out of touch and fortunately almost extinct. The trumpet player without at least two effective vibrato styles is hardly employable in a symphony orchestra today. There is now a much increased interplay between all forms of brass playing, including big-band and jazz.

Secondly, for expressive reasons brass band players do not always play in as direct a manner through their instruments as do orchestral players. This is a matter of choosing the right approach and not of inability.

When I am developing a student cornetist into a trumpeter, I do not *change* the player's method, but broaden it to include trumpet styles. In this way the player begins to understand the musical purpose of different styles. Enjoyment stays at the core of his or her playing, and progress is therefore very fast. I always underline the point that if a player does not enjoy their own playing, no one else will. (CR Teaching)

The Specific Benefits of Playing in a Brass Band

- All of the parts, except the high Eb Soprano Cornet and the Bb Repiano Cornet, are doubled. This allows the young player to play without undue strain. In particular the pitfalls of excess mouthpiece pressure and extremes of tiredness can be avoided. The cornet is of a smaller capacity than a trumpet and requires a little less physical effort.

- The varied styles of the music offer wide experience, much more so than the limited diet of purely conservatoire music on which trumpet players tend to develop. This ability to be stylistically flexible remains with the player throughout life.

- The basic style of traditional brass band music is flowing and melodic, which encourages musical phrasing. Technically it develops continuity and smoothness.

- Facility grows naturally as a result of the musical demands made upon the cornets to provide the equivalent of the violin line to the ensemble.

- The group nature of the cornet parts develops musical and personal co-operation. Different parts and roles require varying treatment, within the overall ensemble. Regularity of rehearsals helps the learning process and the need for consistency of attitude. The disciplines imposed by membership are valuable to young people and are well-matched by the brio with which they let their hair down after concerts and particularly contests.

- The player who undertakes the role of principal solo cornet has many opportunities to test his or her skills and nerve as a soloist. In brass banding the rivalry is intense and judgement merciless, but apart from those few players who earn goodly sums from their bands, or as semi-professional freelance soloists, loss of form is not personally, i.e. financially, damaging in the professional sense. Therefore when a solo player is inadequate he or she is quickly replaced. Bands adopt a much more ruthless approach than orchestras, where there is understandably a much more protectionist policy. Ruthlessness is acceptable when livelihoods are not at stake, and enjoyment is the priority.

- For the player with a good high range, the Eb soprano cornet seat offers an exciting challenge. It is a position for the personality who is afraid of nothing and proud of it. The demands of the position often exceed anything found in the symphonic repertoire in the same tessitura. The degree of difficulty of these soprano parts often rivals, and sometimes exceeds, the most difficult trumpet parts of Bach.

- The frequency with which most brass bands give concerts and take part in contests is invaluable as experience in public performance. For the young player it is hard to think of any other branch of music making which gives such a quantity and quality of experience.

- Since the 1970's there has been an increasing flood of original works for brass band by composers who are outside the popular banding tradition. The language of conservative mainstream twentieth century serious music has now come into bands, displacing much of the traditional repertoire, particularly at contests. This repertoire has pushed the style and technique of contemporary cornet playing closer to that of the trumpet.

- Contesting is an activity frequently reviled by musicians outside brass banding, including brass players. Leaving aside these superficial and snobbish opinions, the value of contesting to the young player is immense. Painstaking preparation, and exhaustive and detailed rehearsal of the kind which has long disappeared from the symphonic stage are quite routine. The process of concentration and determination leads to the once-only ultimate performance.

- The reliable delivery of one's best work at a particular moment is a skill of the highest value to the professional. Once developed this strength of attitude and mind is rarely lost.

- The attitude engendered by brass banding is one of positive enjoyment. In bands the players are continually involved, as opposed to constantly counting bars rest in the orchestra. The range of playing is always wide and varied, while in the orchestra, hours can be spent waiting for others to rehearse low interest matters, such as the bowing of the string parts. When playing gets under way it may well be of routine background accompaniment. In the brass band the brass player is king.

CAREERS

1: A General View for Younger Students

Two or three years before going to music college or university, it is essential for the young player with professional ambitions to be independently assessed, and to take comprehensive career advice.

Higher Education: Exploring Choices

The talented student player in mid-teens, being taught by an experienced, knowledgeable teacher, should already have a good idea of which music college will suit his or her requirements. One college may be well known for the quality of its teaching staff, another for its excellent orchestral training. Yet another may have the best student campus and general atmosphere.

It is essential that the potential student should pay a visit to all of the institutions which are of interest. The student should talk to, and especially listen to, several of the current students. A clear picture will emerge from their casual comments to add to personal impressions. Colleges now compete strongly for the better students, so it is important to distinguish between salesmanship and quality.

The student must develop as exact a picture of the music profession as possible, whether locally to the college being considered, or in London, or in any other national centre. Even at this very early stage it is important that students look ahead to their eventual place of work.

Taking a Second Opinion

At the point when a student realistically feels that a professional career beckons, he or she should seek a high quality second opinion on their playing and career potential. Teachers also need this second opinion in order to check their own evaluation, and should be happy to arrange it. (CR Teaching) The opinions of another teacher or professional player will always give useful food for thought, even when they differ from those of the regular teacher.

Music College vs. University

For students with above-average academic ability, there is a very strong case for taking the route through university rather than music college. The standard college is primarily a conservatoire for performers, in which the emphasis is placed on the act of performing, and where other studies are seen as supporting, rather than of front-line interest.

When a school student has shown a taste and ability for academic work, it should not be dropped lightly. An academic degree develops a wider breadth of interest and expertise, which in turn gives valuable options further along the career track. Any fear of being sidelined and excluded from making a career in performance is quite mistaken. (CR Progress) Many master brass players, such as John Fletcher, John Miller and John Wallace, studied first at university, finding that their playing developed perfectly well alongside their academic studies. Post-graduate study is more and more commonly used to prepare for entry into professional music.

Which Teacher?

Do not automatically expect master players to be master teachers. The craft of teaching is a separate skill from that of playing. Many of my best students have come to me from 'unknown' sources, well-grounded and prepared. In some cases players will be taught in the family by someone with no professional qualifications or experience. This practice is not common now, due to increased separation between the generations. My first ten years' of playing were guided by occasional advice from my father.

In choosing a teacher, careful research is essential, enquiring and probing the suitability of potential instructors. For the young player from a non-musical family it is especially difficult to know what questions to ask. (CR Teaching and Being Taught) In the event of drawing a blank, contact a major music college, the Musicians' Union, or one of the Societies of Musicians and ask for advice.

Available Career Paths

After the choice of a teacher, the next major question which the young student must address is that of career paths. At the early stages of development it is not possible to have a detailed grasp of the various possibilities, as there are too many unknown factors. However, it is never too soon to start collecting and considering them. Gradually conflicting ideas will resolve themselves, and a pattern will begin to emerge among the possibilities.

The development of a good young musician into a good adult musician is by no means assured. A very high proportion of those who show early talent fail to mature, while the slow starter often comes through to succeed. The options open to players are constantly varying. New opportunities appear while others fade and disappear. The last few years especially have seen a bewildering number of changes, both in the performing and teaching worlds.

Options

The most obvious options, which I cover in detail in Careers 1 and 2, are as follows:

1. An orchestral career.

2. A freelance career.

3. A solo career.

4. A classroom teaching career.

5. An instrumental teaching career.

Expectations, Dreams and Realities

The development of a satisfying professional life depends on holding realistic expectations. In certain circumstances, and after a long hard look at where his or her career is likely to go, the student may need to find the courage to quit playing and seek a career elsewhere, whether in music or not.

In a section dedicated to careers in trumpet playing, it may seem bizarre to include paragraphs suggesting that there are circumstances in which the student player should consider giving it up. If, to be a fine trumpeter, the student simply turned up at classes, learned a body of knowledge, and then took a job filling in five days a week using that knowledge, then few problems would exist.

That description, however, is of a non-performance environment. To reach the level of professional performance requires that a player successfully passes through thousands of harshly judgmental performance situations, in which no personal allowances will be made for any musical failings.

It is curious how naturally ruthless we are in judging musical and sporting performance, in comparison to showing some consideration for other kinds of career failure. This is what makes music a very difficult career field to enter. To be attracted to it by its glamour, or to have some early promise, is not enough.

Harsh Realities

There are musicians who are in love with the trumpet, with music and its lifestyle, but who are never going to be more than moderate performers at best. To suggest that this type of player gives up any idea of professional playing may be thought dismissive and unfeeling. Experience has shown, however, that continuing failure over many years has a corrosive effect on an individual's personality. Long-term failure depresses the whole life.

It is far better to be realistic and face unpalatable advice bravely and honestly. I can name many now in rewarding positions and careers who began with dreams of becoming a professional musician. Some of them sensibly accepted the truth of their own lack of talent, others realised that their personalities needed a different stage on which to operate, while yet others could see that the rewards of a moderate career in music were not equal to those elsewhere.

It is a curious fact that many trumpet players of all standards have made the decision to leave playing to pursue other musical careers, often in administration. Almost all of them have proved remarkably successful in new or related fields.

Career Moves - Sooner or Later

It is true that many successful performers deliberately make a mid-career move into conducting, teaching or writing. These are performers who see that they have other capabilities, and having experienced success in the field of playing, wish to explore different challenges and horizons.

This is my own experience, which I have no hesitation in recommending to anyone. By the time I had reached my late thirties I was becoming bored with orchestral life. I saw that as a danger signal to be heeded. The result of making a change is that my interest in, and affection for, the trumpet and for music are stronger than ever.

Range of Interests

I would counsel any young player to cultivate a range of musical interests. A mind which is alert over a wide area will serve its owner better throughout a long career. In today's fast changing world, no one can imagine where opportunities will lie in twenty years' time. The world of the professional performer is changing ever more quickly, meaning that the future will belong to those who see and exploit opportunities as they arise.

As music becomes ever more present in people's lives there will be extra opportunities, but they will not be in the established orchestras or other institutions. At least the non-musician no longer asks the musician 'But what do you do during the day?'

Coda: *Exciting Realities and Career Satisfaction*

If these preceding paragraphs suggest that a life's work spent playing the trumpet is not to be recommended, let me say immediately that this is not my intention. The vast majority of professional trumpeters complete their careers with great satisfaction to themselves and the public.

The exciting reality is that there is nothing in my musical experience to match playing the trumpet well. For me it was a totally absorbing thrill, with a unique immediacy. If it also took place while playing great music or the trumpet showpieces, so much the better.

As a child I absolutely refused to listen to any advice suggesting other careers. All predictions of failure, all expressions of incredulity that I should want to make a living doing something as precarious and fancy as being a musician, were ignored! I could see the light at the end of tunnel and I was going to travel towards it as fast as I could!

CAREERS

2: ORCHESTRAL PERFORMANCE

The skills needed for a successful orchestral career are extra to, and distinct from, a general ability to play the trumpet.

The expertise demanded by different section positions also varies, and must be understood and mastered if the player is to achieve full professional success and satisfaction.

Awareness

The main ensemble skill for any musician is the ability to listen responsively to others while playing. This capability gives the performer the freedom to lead, to follow, or whatever is appropriate in any musical circumstance. It means that the player has the musical equivalent of wide vision. Mastery of this hidden skill is the reason why many a player has held an orchestral post with distinction while not being, on a technical level, the best player available for the position. (CR Awareness, Listening)

The Symphony Orchestra

This skill of awareness must be developed to work simultaneously at close and long range. The ensemble within the trumpet section is obviously the first priority, followed by the work of the whole of the brass section. The expert player is constantly re-assessing the sounds that are around him or her. This process goes on all the time as naturally as one looks where one is going.

The Brass as Part of the Orchestra

Beyond the brass section lies the orchestra. Listening and responding to the musical needs of the orchestra as a whole should be high on orchestral brass players' lists of priorities. Unnecessarily loud playing is perhaps the commonest fault among otherwise great players.

The Trumpet Section

The normal orchestral trumpet section consists of four positions, each with its own responsibilities.

1: The Principal Trumpet

This is the position which most obviously comes to mind when players think of a career of orchestral playing. It is also the one which they are least likely to fill.

The requirements for this position at the top level are obvious: total command of the instrument, a knowledge of what is appropriate stylistically to the music being played, and a commanding personality. The Principal Trumpet must be constantly aware of improving professional standards and must be ready to stay ahead of the field in order to have a long career. Above all the Principal Trumpet must be aware of what is going on musically in the orchestra, in order that his or her decision making is of the highest quality.

Adolph Herseth, with over forty years as Principal Trumpet at the Chicago Symphony Orchestra, presents an example of trumpet quality and longevity never likely to be equalled in any major post in orchestral history. His sound, his knowledge of how, when, and where to play, is peerless. I first heard him play on a 1960's Chicago Symphony Orchestra recording of Mussorgsky's 'Pictures at an Exhibition' conducted by Rafael Kubelik. That first impression is still as vivid to me now as if he had just played it. It is not volume or brilliance, it is the quality of sound that holds its place in one's mind.

2: The Second Trumpet

Musically this position has a wider scope than that of the Principal Trumpet. As a support role, this player must produce a sound which is sonorous, and which complements the Principal Trumpet's sound and does not compete with it for prominence. In the classical repertoire with its emphasis on octaves, the first player's brighter sound should float on the warmer sound of the second. (In octave playing, the second player should always be a fraction louder than the first because the extra resonance of lower sounds casts a glow on the higher ones.)

Above all, control of intonation and flexibility of ensemble are key virtues. To be instantly adaptable in knowing and matching the rhythmic and tuning habits of the Principal Trumpet is vital. Just playing well is not enough.

While the second player must occasionally venture into the highest ranges, particularly in twentieth century music and sometimes as a soloist, as in the last bars of Stravinsky's Petroushka, it is as a specialist in low range that he or she is most important. The ability to produce a fine sound, at all dynamics, with a wide range of articulation and technical flexibility, is a complete field of study in itself. I am constantly amazed at the attention which students give to high range repertoire in comparison to a lack of attention to low range work, where they are likely to find their first freelance work and their first permanent position.

The role of personal support to the Principal Trumpet from the second is also vital in the work of a top quality section. The overtly competitive section player is unprofessional and should be dispensed with as soon as possible. I say this not because of any threat to position, or uncomfortable comparison with regard to standard, but because co-operation is the prime basis for good music making.

Good rapport can make the variable life of an orchestral brass musician most enjoyable. My own second trumpet at the London Symphony Orchestra was George Reynolds who, in addition to being the ideal partner, spoiled me by counting my bars rest!

3: The Third Trumpet

This player usually fulfils the duties of Assistant or Co-Principal Trumpet, and is recognised as taking the responsibility for Principal Cornet parts, in addition to the works of lesser importance such as concerti accompaniments. Piccolo trumpet parts are usually written for, or assigned to, the third player. Assistant Principal Trumpet is the role from which many players naturally progress to becoming a full Principal.

4: The Fourth Trumpet.

This is a mobile position in the section, sweeping up loose ends and changing parts when necessary. Musically this player needs the qualities of the second trumpet as the role demands a good deal of intelligence, experience and a willingness to fit in and be useful. The good team player is extraordinarily valuable, and will often play as assistant to the Principal.

5: The Extra or Freelance Player

The extra player must match the section on all counts: intonation, rhythm, sound and style. The listening element is very marked in this role. In one sense the good extra is never noticed and never missed! It is the position in which the promising player will get a first chance.

6: The Assistant First

On occasion the Principal Trumpet will use an assistant. The requirement may be for only one or two notes at important moments, or, more rarely, it may be a heavy passage leading the whole brass section.

The main problem with this role is knowing when and how to step in and out with tact and judgement. It is also difficult to keep the lips primed ready for action through long spells of inactivity. The Principal will not want to have to explain what is wanted or needed. Apart from the slightest gesture from the Principal, the assistant will be expected to know what to do.

7: The Off-Stage Trumpet and Band

This role is fraught with difficulty. Humorous stories of disaster are many, concerning various works, players, and occasions. One tale recounts a player being shouted at to be quiet while playing the off-stage calls in the Beethoven Overture: Leonora 3. 'Don't you know there is a concert on?'

The very occasional performance of Mahler's Second Symphony have arrived at the Off-stage Band's music to be met by total silence, except for distant sounds of merriment from the bar, 'aus weiter ferne' as Mahler requests - in the furthest distance.

Musically the main points to remember are as follows:

1. Distance flattens pitch, and therefore the offstage player needs to sharpen the instrument relative to the distance from the stage.

2. There is the need to keep the embouchure primed. Many players find this particular musical spotlight extremely difficult to handle. Calmness and skill are needed to perform in these strange surroundings, shut away from the main performance.

A Word on 'Managements'

If you are entering an orchestra and have some leeway for negotiation, remember that after you have signed the contract, the terms only deteriorate. You are most desirable to the orchestra before you have signed. Very rarely will a contract be upgraded without conflict, even for the most brilliant player. If you have been positive and co-operative with the conductor and management maybe a re-negotiation will be easier. Maybe! (CR Professionalism)

CAREERS

3: THE SOLOIST

This career option is the most difficult of all. The decision to become a soloist must be made early in a player's career, as it will lead well away from the usual paths which professional trumpet players tread. Few attempt it, but my view is that it will gradually become more popular, hand in hand with teaching work at college and university.

Performance Quality

The quality of a soloist's performance must be superb. Anything less will be unacceptable, as standards are now set on a world-wide basis. Sound and television recordings allow everyone to hear the very best all the time. In solo performance no allowance is made for a brave try. In some areas of music performance, clever promotion of a glamorous non-musical image can sell a substantial volume of recordings. If however the playing quality is not of the highest standard, the brass public will be merciless in its judgements.

Second Opinions

The young player, having decided on a solo career, must then mark out a career path which avoids orchestral playing. Nothing short of total self-belief is sufficient, backed up by the encouragement and support of experienced musicians. To rely on self-belief alone is not wise because self-delusion always lurks close behind high levels of motivation; it is part of the thrill.

Is There a Market?

Having decided to be a soloist, the young player must decide which market to target. It is important to remember that for the right player, with personality and a high level of musicianship, there will always be room. The public always wants new heroes, but is extremely slow to accept a new soloist unless he or she is superior to, or different from, what has gone before. Almost without exception, solo careers have to be built slowly and steadily, concentrating on developing individuality.

The brass soloist today will struggle unless he or she has a speciality. The public likes to pigeon-hole performers, whether, for example, as a Baroque musician, or as a performer interested in the newest contemporary music. This latter path is a very useful one to follow, as it attracts the attention of critics and other opinion-formers.

Critical attention in the press and in the other media follows contemporary music out of all proportion to the public's interest. The public, however, takes note of the resultant publicity, and remembers the name. Becoming associated with the work of a particular composer or type of music is a familiar tactic among many present day musicians in the effort to achieve celebrity.

Every musician can develop his or her own interests as a backup to solo ambitions. It could be through the creation of an ensemble, or by the performance and exploitation of unusual or interesting repertoire in concert and recording. It is essential for the young soloist to catch the public's attention by whatever musical means are available. Promotion, whether by self promotion or by an agent, is a very high priority for the budding soloist.

Today it is quite possible for the fine young soloist to develop his or her own market. There are several organisations dedicated to helping new and aspiring soloists to create a career; details of these can be found in most music libraries. Not only can they occasionally provide concert appearances, but they will help with advice on the mechanics of brochure production and the best methods of entering the education circuit and approaching concert promoters, whether they be music clubs or the Artistic Directors of festivals.

This is not a way to make money, but an opportunity to build up performance skills out of the limelight. (The serious musician should always enter a field of work for musical reasons. Do what you enjoy and are good at, and financial rewards will follow you.) Manufacturers' sponsorships are also becoming important in assisting young soloists' careers. In return for using their instruments and providing masterclasses at music colleges, the more adventurous companies will give limited support, while being careful with their money and methods.

The Total Soloist

The single-minded soloist must seek to progress on that path alone. In order to establish an image in this role, and to add the maximum cutting edge to his or her own attitudes, the soloist should avoid all orchestral and ensemble work.

Once the public and the critics have pigeonholed a performer as an orchestral musician, they are reluctant to rethink, except after many years. The total soloist's career requires a tremendous will to persist, not only through possible financial difficulties, but also through musically lonely times. Hakon Hardenberger is a good example of a player who made that decision at the start of his career, did not deviate from it, and is now established as one of the world's leading soloists.

Music performance is essentially a social activity, and the necessary isolation which a potential soloist must endure can be highly disorientating.

The musical training to be undertaken for this career has to be very rigorous. The budding orchestral player will gain a substantial part of his or her practice and experience while rehearsing and performing with different kinds of ensembles. For the soloist, four hours' lonely practice per day is the minimum, undertaken in a precise and controlled way, seeking technical perfection and security to defy the most demanding occasion and repertoire. The public will want to be amazed, and not simply satisfied.

The Soloist who Graduates from the Orchestra

In spite of the problem of recreating an image this career progression is gradually becoming more frequent, as the world-wide interest in brass and its repertoire continues to expand. This player often has to be something of an entrepreneur, probably creating a speciality ensemble to give concerts, make recordings and undertake tours. He or she will certainly teach and possibly conduct, using a network of contacts to build an impressive round of activities.

The Occasional Soloist from the Orchestra

This category covers the vast majority of brass concerto performers. Sometimes a very occasional outing to play a concerto is part of the orchestra's policy of encouraging its more valued members. For orchestras of less than the highest rank, this is a reasonable practice. For orchestras of the first rank, the opportunities are often significantly less, because so much of its work is very high profile, and linked to recordings and concert series.

Leading orchestral players frequently receive invitations to appear with lesser ensembles, but the occasional change of musical profile from the back of the orchestra to the front, with the different musical style necessary, is not always a successful one.

The musical and presentational difficulties for the orchestral brass soloist stepping up to the concerto position lie in the difference in musical requirements between the two roles. Instead of providing what is mainly a strengthening voice to the orchestra, with only the occasional solo, the player is required to present a coherent picture of a complete work and to appear to the audience as a full personality. Fine playing is not enough. The performer must appear to be completely at ease in a role which he or she rarely undertakes, and must be able to engage and communicate with an audience in a positive way. (CR Performance)

COMPETITIONS

At the development stage of a player's career, all opportunities to measure progress should be taken. It is invaluable to play on the big occasion and to test oneself against the best of the same generation. The soloist of high potential will revel in the limelight.

Expert Opinions

Competitions and contests shine a very bright light on a player's work. For the finest performers, this will be just what they want. For others, it may not be a comfortable experience, even for the potential master player, but remember that professional opinion is just that: only an opinion. As I have mentioned elsewhere (CR Teaching), master players are often overly influenced by their own playing style, and are unable to judge with an open mind. Read any opinions in that context.

The Jury

It is sensible to spend some time considering the personnel of the jury. The best competitions will have an international panel. Where there is a strong national bias to the jury, do not expect a French panel to appreciate the Hindemith Sonata, or a German panel to enthuse over the works of Bozza. Consider national playing styles and tastes in music. It is a perfectly legitimate tactic to colour your performance to suit the situation.

Unfavourable and Favourable Criticism

The contestant should not dismiss negative opinions without considering them fully, uncomfortable though they may be. Constructive criticism is one of the most valuable gifts that can be offered to anyone. A player must use all information from whatever source to produce the most accurate reading possible as to the true state of his or her work. In response to unfavourable criticism, be honest.

Praise is of course very pleasant, but by itself is of little value. What is really helpful is well-judged encouragement, one of the surest signs of a good teacher and an intelligent, sensitive musician. (CR Aims and Goals, Critics and Criticism)

Jealousy

At some time or other, every player suffers unjust and spiteful criticism motivated by jealousy. Someone, somewhere, will hate you just for being alive! This is so much a natural part of human behaviour that all young players should regard it as nothing out of the ordinary. The sooner one accepts it as standard the better.

To behave towards others in this manner is to be avoided at all costs. It is wholly bad for the perpetrator, creating bitterness which corrodes from the inside.

However, it must be said that the most malicious comment almost always contains a grain of truth. Even though it is distasteful, extract the grain of truth, then discard the malice. The young talented player will have to get used to absorbing clever jealousy as a regular fact of professional life.

Types of Competition

Competitions come in all shapes and sizes. Each must be assessed on its own terms, particularly with regard to repertoire. Where entrants have a choice of repertoire, they should choose music which will show themselves to the best advantage. This may sound too obvious to need mentioning, but it is surprising how often contestants' choices are inappropriate, and aimed at entertaining the audience. While it is important to create an enjoyable experience for the audience as well as the jury, the prime concern must be to influence the jury.

Own Choice Works

When the contestant chooses the programme, certain points must be kept in mind which can make a difference to the result if the jury is faced with a close decision.

If only a single work is allowed, the player must ensure that technically it displays a wide variety of challenges. It must also present a strong musical personality to the jury. I have heard many fine performers go unrewarded because of poor repertoire choice.

Beware the boring middle-of-the-road modern repertoire! The presentation of the musician-as-a-personality to the listeners is not an extra element, but is an essential. Serious music today is as much of a business as popular music and must be treated accordingly.

Programme Shapes

For short programmes, three 'shapes' are possible for maximum effect.

- In the first, a bright start must be followed by a very contrasted second choice. A change of instruments would be a natural extra point to consider. The final work should renew the bright strong mood and bring the programme to as positive a finish as possible. If time permits a fourth piece of a lightweight or scherzando nature should be included, being placed second or third. Soft slow music must not be neglected; nothing is so tiring for the listener as constant brilliance and power

- In the second case, the programme as a whole can grow from a quiet start, and musically express a crescendo, through to a strong finish. This is a more difficult format with which to be successful. Care must be taken to have enough variety of texture and display as the performance progresses. If repertoire can be found which will achieve this shape and the quality of performance is good enough, the effect can be very strong.

- Hardest of all, and only an option for the finest musicians/performers, is the programme which finishes softly. The finish must be the emotional high point, brought off in the hushed atmosphere of total control. For example, in the right place, the Hindemith Sonata for Trumpet and Piano can achieve this effect.

- The quality of 'finishing' a programme, as opposed to just 'stopping', must be in the player's performance. Obvious? In fact it is often ignored, with a consequent weakening of effect. This quality is achieved by very few performers, but only because those few are aware of the need for it.

Choices

Be sure that there is variety in the keys of the pieces to be played. Key relationships are a study in themselves. In fact, as I write this I am listening to a recording which has just featured three consecutive pieces in the same key and the same style! The sameness of effect of the same key centres dulls the interest in what is otherwise good playing.

These thoughts on programme choices will seem very obvious and routine, yet it is extraordinary the number of times that indifferent programmes are chosen by good and very good players. Undoubtedly competitions have been won and lost on this matter of choice.

Puzzlement or dumb anger are often the result on the part of the performers and their advisors when the result does not go their way. A little applied intelligence avoids that particular reason for disappointment.

The Display Element

Brass performance is only occasionally about music quality in the sense in which the great composers established it. Brass performance is largely about individual performers, and the music played is mostly material to facilitate a display. Brass players and brass audiences are united on this, although it offends some purists whose whole interest is in music with compositional merit and little else.

Other points of interest include the need to show beauty of sound quality. Soft playing, which is always impressive in itself, gives the jury and the audience a different kind of performance enjoyment. These subtler points allow the listener to be refreshed not only by the absence of volume and noise, but also to be stimulated by effective contrast. Fast/slow, loud/soft, emotional/playful, warm/cool, these are all contrasts to be exploited by the player as musical actor. (CR Performance)

Competition Results

Results come in all shapes and sizes. There are some good, some poor, and a few ridiculously bad ones. These latter usually occur when there are muddled heads on a panel, who pick on random, inessential points in a player's work, which have only a cosmetic and no structural significance.

On occasion, winners have been picked on the basis of 'potential', as if that were somehow better than the best-on-the-the-day performers.

Winners have even been chosen on the basis of being-felt-sorry-for, it's-time-he/she-had-a-turn, and, on many occasions, as a compromise candidate between two better players on whom the jury cannot agree.

Good players who offer themselves for judgement at competitions and awards can be sure that, in the long run, they will achieve due recognition from the public, if only occasionally from the jury. Competitiors may not score in the events they most wish to win, but long-term, that is rarely important.

CONDUCTORS

Conductors are regular presences in the lives of most brass players.
It is sensible to use them positively when they are competent, but to be able to neutralise them when they are a hazard.

Relevance and Irrelevance

Many attributes of the conductor's craft given so much attention by critics and audiences are largely irrelevant to the player. Non-musicians have very little notion of the practical relationships between players and conductors.

Working with Good Conductors

Most orchestral musicians would leave a blank space under this heading! However, it is important to say that on the occasions when a fine conductor occupies the rostrum, making music becomes what it should ideally always be: enjoyable and life enhancing. When the orchestral performer works with a master conductor, the experience is beyond price.

It must also be said that it is impossible for the orchestral player who has no conducting experience to conceive of, and understand, the range of skills deployed by the master conductor. The immediacy of playing is quite at odds with much of the managerial thinking that goes into good conducting.

Working with Bad Conductors

Poor conductors are in the majority, and always will be, for reasons beyond the scope of this book to explain. Patience is a prime virtue for the orchestral player, and should be cultivated to the point of sainthood. I have always noticed that players who allow themselves to become seriously upset by bad conducting often play less well on the performance. The disturbance to concentration caused by 'having a go' at a poor conductor usually affects the player's own work. Deal with the inefficient conductor if you wish, but be careful to remain unaffected yourself.

The Player's Most Frequent Concerns

Some orchestral musicians develop a bunker mentality when faced with new ideas and personalities.

This mentality is much more damaging to the player than to anyone else, and suggests an unwillingness to be intelligently flexible. A fixed set of responses denotes laziness of attitude, especially where contemporary music is concerned.

Does the conductor mean what he beats?

The physical co-ordination of many conductors is very faulty, with the result that confusing signals lead to poor ensemble. Players must develop an awareness not only of their immediate section, but of the orchestra as a whole. This radar is composed primarily of listening skills, but additionally visual clues linked to breathing, or the giving of lead-in gestures by a section principal, can be important in many circumstances.

Can the conductor be relied upon to be clear at the awkward corners, especially when the music slows down or quickens up, at pauses and awkward breaks?

The stop-start opening of Beethoven's Fifth Symphony, for example, is a classic test for the conductor. Many fail, some spectacularly. The orchestral repertoire is full of moments like these. Again, heightened awareness is the best protection for the player.

Are there situations where the conductor panics? Are his performance speeds always faster or slower than the rehearsals?

In preparation for an orchestral performance containing significant technical passages, the player should prepare them at a very wide range of speeds. The principle is that the player must have spare capability ready to deal with conductors' excessive changes during performances. In the case of slow solos, these should be drawn out to great lengths. In quick passages, the fastest and slowest possible tempi should be prepared.

Particular attention should be given to crossing the articulation gaps between single and compound tonguings. Unrehearsed tempo differences can often lead to an expected tonguing speed or pattern becoming the wrong one. Cover all eventualities. Work out alternatives for different speeds. Two good examples of passages which can be technically very different in varying circumstances are the Trumpet Variation from Britten's Young Person's Guide to the Orchestra, and the trumpet solo near the start of Ravel's Piano Concerto.

Be prepared for unreasonable, and insensitive behaviour on the part of conductors with regard to frequent repetitions of heavy passages.

Often the uncertain conductor will be rehearsing for his or her own benefit, which is quite inexcusable, unless admitted. Therefore the section principal should be prepared to ask politely about the purpose of a passage being repeated many times. In the case of the bully-conductor, be prepared to defend yourself robustly while being aware that he (or she) may attempt to unsettle you later.

Some orchestral musicians develop a bunker mentality when faced with new personalities and ideas.

This mentality is much more damaging to the player than to anyone else, and suggests an unwillingness to be intelligently flexible. A fixed set of responses denotes laziness of attitude.

The player under contract and in a permanent position will have to take a more cautious view of both conductor and management.

Where a good Musical Director is seeking to develop the orchestra's style and technique in a certain direction, it is common sense to try to understand what his or her aims are and to attempt to fulfil them. Be prepared to go with the tough but good conductor who can recognise willingness to co-operate.

CRITICISM AND CRITICS

At some time all musicians receive criticism, favourable and unfavourable, just and unjust. Make use of it wherever it comes from, whatever the motive behind it.

Favourable and Unfavourable Criticism

Praise is always very pleasant, good for confidence, and should be accepted gracefully. Unless tempered by some qualifying comment, it is of no value as an aid to improvement. Whether fair or unfair, examine negative criticism for any grain of truth it might contain. Even the smallest amount of truth is useful, if you are serious about improving yourself, as opposed to flattering your ego. (CR Competitions)

Jealousy

At some point almost everyone experiences jealousy from others, and also feels jealousy towards others.

At the student stage, it almost always takes the form of verbal bullying. I have known jealousy severely retard the progress of at least two talented students, whose unconscious response has been to remain as part of the pack, and not be seen to excel.

Initially I could not understand why they did not make the progress which their talent suggested they should. In fact, they were unconscious of the fact that they were musically keeping their heads down to avoid harassment. Once I had uncovered their states of mind and revealed to them what they were doing, they instantly woke up and put the problem behind them. They are now extremely fine professional players. (CR Careers: 1, Aims and Goals)

Jealousy must be dealt with by students themselves, either by a water-off-the-duck's-back method, or by matching aggression with aggression. The entry of a senior third party into a situation simply delays the moment when the bullied person finally has to face the matter.

Equally those who feel jealous of the talents and achievements of others have a problem, which is best corrected by a re-examination of their aims, goals and professionalism. In a music college, comparisons are very sharp and immediate between players of the same instrument. One or two former students of mine were simply unable to swallow the fact that others were as, or more, talented, than they.

Public Criticism

Negative criticism in public from a conductor or other person happens to all musicians. An aggressive response is totally natural, but it may not be the only or best one. Watch how more experienced musicians handle it, and learn from their response.

Criticism in the press from critics is unlikely to occur in the initial stages of a career. When it does, ignore it totally unless it gives useful material for your publicity brochure.

As a musician you are master of your own destiny. If you play your instrument very well everyone knows it, and will credit you fully. The natural prominence of the trumpet makes this particularly so.

MASTERCLASSES

The masterclass is an activity which promises much, but rarely delivers more than curiosity value. Too often it is just a showcase for the master player.

The Value of Masterclasses for Students

The excitement of hearing and meeting a famous musician is always valuable. To listen to the advice and personal ideas of someone who has achieved much is fascinating for anyone, even for another master musician or teacher.

It is the nature of a masterclass to be superficial. It is a casual encounter where the master player is expected to dispense words of instant wisdom about someone previously unheard and unknown.

However, if the opportunity arises for a student to play to a master performer it should always be taken. The advice received may be interesting, not necessarily for its intrinsic value, but for the light it throws on the star's personality and priorities. Master performers, with their special blend of concentration and relaxation, are always worth observing closely.

By the very nature of the event, however, this can have only a superficial value, because the student will have played only briefly and perhaps not typically. The danger is that the master player will dispense an unrelated series of hints and tips in no special order. The best teachers need to hear a student for many, many hours before thoroughly understanding how their playing works.

The Preferred Formats

A well-prepared masterclass *can* be used to valuable effect, but only if the master player carefully controls the format of the class. The two possible formats outlined below both offer good value to students.

1. Each masterclass should have one specific subject. The student members of the class must be realistic in their expectations, and make the effort to understand the master player's progression of thought. It is always beneficial and highly revealing to observe different players' responses to the same point.

For this format to be successful, the master player must be able to give a comprehensive verbal account of the reasons behind the playing. This will opens up related topics, but in a natural, coherent and educational manner.

2. From each student's performance, one major element of the class's subject can be selected to be improved in the few minutes available. This will give the student a genuine lift and will equally impress the other student listeners as to the effectiveness of the advice given. The illustrations provided by several students should go together to make a series of points. The whole picture will be incomplete, but these inter-relations will give the listeners some food for thought.

The High Quality Student Performer

The very high quality student presents a different problem. If the master performer hears a highly successful performance by a mature student, it is much better to acknowledge the student's quality and restrict comment to knowledgeable encouragement, even if it is a very different kind of playing to his or her own. If the master player feels obliged to suggest different detail and interpretation when the student's interpretation has been very successful, inevitably the student and observers alike may well be puzzled and unconvinced, unless the master's is clearly so much better.

A professional level of achievement on the part of a student means that he or she is already a mature performer with a high level of interpretative skills. The type of teaching needed for this level of student is more a matter of stimulation and discussion between equals, rather than instruction.

MUSIC EDITIONS

It is important to work from the best editions of non-copyright music.

The Dividing Line: the Haydn and Hummel Concerti

Before the Haydn and Hummel Concerti, solo repertoire for the natural trumpet and its predecessors was reasonably varied and moderately plentiful. These Concerti were actually written for the keyed bugle, one of the many strange instruments spawned by the search for a chromatic trumpet. After these works, major composers virtually ceased writing for the trumpet in any solo role until the late nineteenth century.

Buying the Right Edition

Most editions of the Haydn and Hummel Concerti, together with repertoire from the eighteenth century and before, are corrupted by poor editing. By this I mean not only the editor's personal additions to the text, without acknowledgement, but the use of source material which may well be previously and similarly edited versions, etc. (See below, The Editor as Arranger)

It is all too easy for the unsuspecting young player to buy one of these editions straight off the retailer's shelf, assuming it to be of good quality. Once a player buys a copy of 'the Haydn' it is very rare that he or she buys another because of the editing. It is therefore important to buy well in the first instance.

The student player must take care at the start, through his or her own enquiries, or through guidance, to buy the best edition available of any work. Training the eye on good material will help to develop musical taste and discrimination, especially in the field of phrasing and ornamentation.

A few publishers and editors explain the quality level of their work on the title pages of each publication. All editors should do this, thus allowing the potential purchaser to judge the standard of text being presented. Beware of editions which do not offer this advice.

The Editor's Role

The title of editor should be restricted to those of scholastic intention and integrity, who have, in person, consulted the known originals and can verify the fact. The editor should present the composer's best existing manuscript. If he or she has chosen between contradictory 'original' versions it should be explained how, and why, the choices were made and musical examples offered for the readers to judge for themselves.

For example H.C. Robbins Landon, in Haydn: The Years of 'The Creation' 1796-1800 (pp 225-240) discusses bars 216-7 of the last movement of the Haydn Concerto. The upper line of the excerpt shows the solo part as originally written by the composer, before being crossed out. Compare it with the lower line, which gives the manuscript alternative as it is usually played today. Perhaps the original trumpeter, Anton Weidinger, complained about it! Musically there can be no doubt that the upper line is superior to the lower by some distance.

Example 1

Recommendations, such as slurring or tonguing, should be bracketed, or in some way identified as not being in the original. The player can then accept or reject the editor's ideas.

The Editor as Arranger

Some 'editors' include a mass of unexplained expression, dynamic markings and written-out ornamentation included as if it were the composer's. With this practice they have in fact become arrangers, and should announce their work as 'arranged'.

What certainly happens in most of these editions is that previously published versions have been used as the basis for their version. These will have been filleted, given a new coat of paint, and presented to the public as authoritative.

Pitch Variations

Some publishers produce editions transposed into easier keys, without any note to warn the buyer. The Purcell Trumpet Sonata in D and the Vivaldi Double Concerto in C are especially badly served in this respect, with a number of editions transposed into Bb concert pitch, without any acknowledgement of the fact. The Hummel Concerto is usually published in Eb Major with no note to say that the original is in E Major. To my knowledge this is currently registered clearly in only one edition.

Add to this the Haydn and Hummel Concerti editions published only with Bb solo parts, and it is immediately obvious that the unlucky innocent can easily make many expensive mistakes.

Pre-Classical Concerti, Sonati and Obligati.

These texts vary a great deal. A few enjoy enough popularity to have prompted several editions, e.g. the Purcell Sonata, the Telemann and Torelli Concerti, and Handel obligati such as 'The Trumpet Shall Sound' from the Messiah and 'Let the Bright Seraphim' from Samson. Some of these works in particular suffer from editions with a mass of misleading articulation, phrasing, notes, rhythms and implausible cadenzas.

Where only one edition is available for a minor work, it should not necessarily be taken as valid. It may be that a good text has simply not yet appeared in print.

The Haydn and Hummel Concerti

Undoubtedly the best critical editions currently available are published by Universal Edition. The overall editor is Robbins Landon, who, with the American trumpeter Edward Tarr, has produced the most reliable scores possible. Almost all other editions I have seen are corrupted by personal phrasings, articulations and dynamics.

An inexperienced young player may take these poor editions as the composer's gospel truth. While any edition has a certain interest, in seeing the variety of ways in which these works are approached, purchase of them should be avoided.

Repertoire after the Hummel Concerto

After the Haydn and Hummel concerti, there is an almost complete lack of nineteenth century works for trumpet. By the time concerto and solo works began to appear again with the rise of the modern trumpet, the whole process of publishing had changed. From this time forward properly copyrighted editions prepared by composers were issued; the question of which edition to buy becomes irrelevant.

Using Scholarly Editions

Editions such as Universal present the composer's manuscript bare of all the detail to which we are used. The performance habits of any period were understood at the time, and did not then need to be written down. They never thought of us! I would doubt whether any detailed description of how to perform the music of Count Basie or Duke Ellington exists. Of course we have the recordings. But to tell us about pre-nineteenth century music we have only a few books and that most unreliable of guides, tradition.

The original edition is therefore a skeleton on to which each player puts musical flesh. If the player has a sense of what is appropriate, this is by far the best way to proceed. When a player is unversed in the principles of ornamentation and phrasing, the result may be worse than simply reading a poor edition. The comment is often made that by the time these 'original' editions have been made ready to perform, they look just like a normal edited edition. However, the performer will have done his or her own homework, and will have a greatly improved understanding of the work

Research

It is open to serious students to do the research themselves. The first call should be to your music library where, without fail, the librarian will be pleased to help. (Librarians love their subject.) Thereafter a trail of contacts and information will lead eventually to the source material. The only requirement is the will to ask and ask again.

RECITAL PROGRAMME PLANNING

Programme content and shape have a crucial effect on the success of a recital performance.

The Main Questions for Consideration

1. What kind of audience is expected?

2. Is the repertoire appropriate for that audience?

3. Is the shape of the programme effective?

4. Is the programme stimulating, both for the soloist and the audience?

Exams and Diplomas

Students must present examination and diploma recitals regularly. Normally the format for examinations is set in advance, whereas diploma recitals are own-choice programmes.

In the case of the diploma recital, students will be judged partially on choice of repertoire, because it reveals their musical tastes and interests. Colleges are traditional institutions, and while many musicians progress into popular music, jazz and big band performance, the basic quality of the musical repertoire played in a conservatoire should be appropriate to its character.

The student must build up a wide-ranging repertoire list, not only of the obvious concerti, but of recital pieces.

The Public Recital

Choice of repertoire will be dictated by the kind of audience expected at the concert. Is it going to be a specialist brass audience, or from the general music public? Does it have special interests such as contemporary music? Will music for trumpet and tape, or other electronic media, be of interest to the audience? Will speaking to the audience be important? (Audiences enjoy the extra contact which speaking offers.) Is there an educational element to the event?

The venue and available accompaniment will also affect choices. Is the hall or room large or small? What is the ambience of the hall, and the quality of the piano? Is the pianist or organist one with whom the soloist is familiar? Is a rehearsal possible in the hall or church?

Repertoire should be developed to meet these potential situations. If a player starts to think about repertoire only when the offer of an engagement comes in at the last moment, not only will preparation be sketchy, but editions of music may be unavailable at short notice.

Programme Shape

Every programme should show contrasts of musical intensity, mood, humour and colour. Above all each one must have an appreciable shape, a beginning, a middle and an end. It takes a true artist to convey a sense of progression and then of resolution. Many unlikely possibilities can be made to work, but only if the skills of discernment and presentation are brought into play. This is the kind of programme which lifts a concert on to a higher plane, however good the playing has been.(CR Competitions for further discussion)

The performer must puzzle over hundreds of programmes before expertise and understanding can develop. A glance through the pages of the trumpet and brass press show a majority of ill-planned and ineffective concert and competition programmes. (CR Competitions)

The Playing Challenge

In a long programme most players need to consider the stamina factor. The sensible player remembers that playing through a programme in a carefree manner in the practice studio is not the same thing as a real concert-giving experience. (CR Practice and Performance) The supreme player can start anywhere on the difficulty scale, whereas the normal player should start sensibly and allow time to settle in to the programme. Even though the master performer can carry off a series of tough challenges without fail, all programmes should provide some relaxation from virtuosity in the course of the concert, for player and audience alike.

Instrument Choices

The sequence of instruments used is an important consideration, especially the juxtaposition of the piccolo Bb and the standard Bb trumpet. Players vary in their response to instrument changes, but most prefer to move from smaller to larger in the course of a recital programme.

Repertoire Selection

The solo repertoire is available in the usual catalogues and library lists. These are augmented regularly by recital programmes in brass and trumpet magazines. (CR Repertoire)

A senior student's repertoire list will look something like the list below by the time the student has reached soloist standard. Great care must be taken to have a variety of keys in the works chosen, especially in baroque music. For example, if a sequence of keys can be arranged in which the key of the first and last piece is the same, there will be an underlying sense of return and unity in the programme.

The list should contain the following:

- One hour or so of Baroque repertoire, both original and arranged.

- Six concerti, to include the Haydn and Hummel.

- At least 10 Sonatas and recital works of substance, with piano or organ.

- 15 or so shorter concert pieces.

- At least five pieces of contemporary repertoire, both solo and with tape.

REPERTOIRE

The serious trumpet player develops as wide a knowledge of repertoire as possible, even though he or she may be active in only a few areas of performance.

The Scope of Trumpet Repertoire

The music of the trumpet and its ancestors span the whole of written musical time. For ease of reference the periods can be listed as Renaissance, Baroque, Classical, Romantic, and Twentieth-Century. While the first three are relatively self-contained in their range of demands on the player, the romantic period, with its development of varying national styles of composition, saw a massive expansion of the possibilities of the instrument. In the twentieth century we have seen trumpet performance and repertoire explode into a very important position in musical life, particularly in popular music. This expansion has been fuelled by the growth in recorded performance in various media, and by the publishing industry. This growth is bound to continue.

The Renaissance

Mostly confined to small ensemble music, there is nevertheless a large quantity of original music apart from that which has been arranged. As much of the music of the time does not specify a particular instrumentation, there is always the possibility of expanding the repertoire with versions for brass. Publishers such as Musica Rara specialise in the Renaissance and the Baroque, but great care must be taken with the quality of some publishers' editions. (CR Music Editions) The cornett and the natural trumpet are the authentic instruments for this music, but effective performances on modern instruments are acceptable when performed with the appropriate style and sound.

The Baroque

In the Baroque period, the trumpet began to develop the sound we know today. Range and flexibility increased, and the musical use to which the instrument was put widened a great deal. One has only to look at the varied treatment afforded the instrument, by Bach in the Suites, the Masses, the Cantatas, in the still extraordinary Second Brandenburg Concerto, and by Georg Telemann in his Concerti and Suites, to see the prime position taken by the trumpet and the important roles occupied by leading players.

The Classical

For a very significant period the use of the trumpet became restricted. String and wind instruments were deemed by composers to be more appropriate to their musical thinking, and with the exceptions of the Concerti by Haydn and Hummel for the keyed bugle, the scope of writing for the trumpet shrank to an extraordinary degree.

The trumpet of the time diminished in musical importance and was used mainly to strengthen climaxes, point up the rhythmic background and provide fanfaronic colouring. The technical development of the trumpet proceeded along many paths in many different places. As the more bizarre efforts of inventors were discarded, the technological basis for the explosion of interest in the trumpet in the late nineteenth and early twentieth century was established.

The Romantic

Even after the trumpet and its players had developed substantial technical capability in the modern manner, composers remained relatively unambitious with their musical thinking for the instrument. For example, Liszt's solo trumpet, when he was the conductor at Weimar, was none other than Ernst Sachse, whose studies are still used today. Yet - strangely for a composer who was always in search of heightened musical effects -   Liszt's use of the trumpet remained tediously conservative.

The acceleration in the growth of brass performance and repertoire was happening outside the orchestras and the serious music world, in specialist bands and at a very different musical level. In England, France and America, substantial genres of band music were building up hand in hand with a new virtuosity. Russia and Eastern Europe were evolving their own unique styles which would give a special slant to their orchestral repertoire in the future.

During the latter part of the Romantic period the musical picture changed for good. With playing members made redundant by changes in policy by military and religious authorities, brass and wind bands prospered. The emergence of folk music from the back parlour, and the appearance of jazz and dance bands, were also factors helping to free brass instruments in general and the trumpet in particular. Tschaikovsky, Scriabin, Mahler and Richard Strauss (whose father, an eminent horn player, wrote band style bravura variations and sentimental melodies) are just a few of the composers who re-invigorated trumpet writing for the concert hall, the opera house and for the modern era of serious and popular music.

The Twentieth Century

This period, soon to close, has been truly astonishing for the trumpet in its variety and excitement. If the new modern solo trumpet can be said to have arrived, it was with Stravinsky's Petroushka and The Rite of Spring, together with Scriabin's Poem of Ecstasy. The trumpet joined the centre stage instruments in the orchestra.

Musical possibilities for the trumpet are increasing constantly. The imaginations of today's most talented players are taking flight into uncharted territories. However we still await the composers who can make full use of the instrument and its players; reheated cliches are offered far too often. It has to be said that, currently, the trumpet in popular music and jazz is being used more imaginatively than by serious composers.

The Sources of Information

Today there is access to almost all music through the network of music libraries, while the Internet increasingly offers information and contacts for the musician. If someone comes from an educational background which has not fitted them for research, or even a confident use of the normal library files and resources, the advice must be: 'Just ask!' If you don't ask, you don't deserve!

Orchestral music is the most widely available of all kinds of music, whether through published scores or compilations of excerpts. A basic list follows at the end of this section, supplied by Murray Greig, Principal Trumpet at English Opera North, a former student of mine. It is generally possible to see the complete trumpet parts for unusual works by ordering them from the publisher, through a music library, for a loan period.

Solo and Ensemble Material

The essential sources are the catalogues of specialist retailers such as June Emerson of Ampleforth, North Yorkshire, England. Comprehensive lists such as hers are a mine of information. Publishers' lists contain items of interest not shown elsewhere, while magazines such as Brass Bulletin and that of the International Trumpet Guild list unpublished material, but with points of contact for follow-up.

Here in Britain the newly formed CATS (Cornet and Trumpet Society) Magazine has begun to provide information on all aspects of repertoire. A great deal of interesting repertoire is to be found in the lists of works in the Appendices of composers' biographies. Whether for original works or for material to arrange, the sources are readily available.

Orchestral and Operatic Trumpet Repertoire

The following list is a representative selection.

Bach, J.S.	A Christmas Oratorio Brandenburg Concerto No 2 in F Cantata 51 Magnificat Mass in B Minor Suites Nos 3 & 4
Bartok	Concerto for Orchestra Dance Suite The Miraculous Mandarin Piano Concerti 1-3 Violin Concerti 1 & 2
Bax	Coronation March Overture to a Picaresque Comedy Symphonies 1-6 Tintagel
Berg	Lulu (opera) Kammerkonzert Three Orchestral Pieces Violin Concerto Wozzeck (opera)
Beethoven	Overture: Egmont Overtures: Leonora 2 & 3 Symphonies 1-9 Violin Concerto
Berlioz	Overture: Beatrice & Benedict Overture: Benvenuto Cellini Harold in Italy Overture: Le Corsair The Damnation of Faust Requiem Mass Overture Roman Carnival Romeo and Juliet Symphonie Fantastique
Bernstein	West Side Story: Dances Symphonies 1-3
Bizet	Carmen (opera) Symphony in C
Bliss	Checkmate Morning Heroes Things to Come
Borodin	Polotsvian Dances Symphony No 2

Brahms	Academic Festival Overture
	Symphonies 1-4
Britten	Prince of the Pagodas
	A Midsummer's Night Dream (opera)
	Sinfonia da Requiem
	A Spring Symphony
	A War Requiem
	A Young Person's Guide to the Orchestra
Bruckner	Symphonies 0-9 (10 in all)
Chabrier	Espana
Copland	An Appalachian Spring
	Billy the Kid
	El Salon Mexico
	Fanfare for the Common Man
	A Quiet City
	Rodeo
	Symphonies 1-3
Debussy	Iberia
	Images
	La Mer
	Printemps
	Nocturnes
Delius	Brigg Fair
	La Calinda
	Paris
	A Village Romeo and Juliet
Dukas	The Sorcerer's Apprentice
Dvorak	Carnival Overture
	Cello Concerto
	Symphonies 1-9
Elgar	Overture: Cockaigne
	The Dream of Gerontius
	Enigma Variations
	Overture: In the South
	Pomp & Circumstance Marches
	Symphonies 1 & 2
Franck	Symphony in D Minor
Gershwin	An American in Paris
	Piano Concerto in F
	Rhapsody in Blue
Handel	Coronation Anthem
	The Messiah
	The Royal Fireworks Music
	Samson (opera)
	The Water Music

Hindemith	Kammermusik (various)
	Konzertmusik for Strings & Brass
	Symphony: Mathis der Maler
	Symphonic Metamorphoses
Holst	A Perfect Fool
	The Planets
Humperdinck	Overture: Hansel & Gretel
Ives	Symphonies 1-4
	Three Places in New England
	The Unanswered Question
Janacek	Glagolithic Mass
	Katya Kabanova (opera)
	Sinfonietta
Kodaly	Hary Janos
	Symphony
Leoncavallo	Il Pagliacci (opera)
Liszt	Les Preludes
	Piano Concerti 1 & 2
	Tone Poems (various)
Mahler	Das Lied von der Erde
	Das Knaben Wunderhorn
	Symphonies 1-10
Mascagni	Cavalleria Rusticana (opera)
Mendelssohn	Overture: A Midsummer's Night Dream
	Symphonies 1-4
Messiaen	L'Ascension
	Turangalila Symphony
Milhaud	La Creation du Monde
	Le Boeuf sur le Toit
Monteverdi	Orfeo
	Vespers
Mussorgsky/Ravel	Pictures at an Exhibition
Mussorgsky	Boris Godunov (opera)
Nielsen	Symphonies 1-6
Orff	Carmina Burana
Poulenc	Les Biches
	L'Histoire de Babar
	Sinfonietta
	Suite Francaise

Prokofiev	Alexander Nevsky
	Lieutenant Kije
	Peter & the Wolf
	Piano Concerti 1-5
	Romeo and Juliet
	Scythian Suite
	Symphonies 1-7
Puccini	La Boheme (opera)
	Madame Butterfly (opera)
	Tosca (opera)
	Turandot (opera)
Purcell	The Fairy Queen (opera)
	Funeral Music for Queen Mary
Rachmaninov	Piano Concerti 1-4
	Symphonic Dances
	Symphonies 1-3
	Variations on a theme of Paganini
Ravel	Alborada del Grazioso
	Bolero
	Daphnis and Chloe (Suites 1 & 2)
	La Valse
	Piano Concerto in G
	Piano Concerto for the Left Hand
	Rhapsodie Espagnol
	Le Tombeau de Couperin
Respighi	The Fountains of Rome
	The Pines of Rome
	Roman Festivals
Rimsky-Korsakov	Capriccio Espagnol
	The Golden Cockerel (opera)
	Scheherezade
Roussel	Symphonies 1-4
Saint-Saens	Samson and Delilah (opera)
	Symphony No 3
Schoenberg	Chamber Symphony No 2
	Die Gurrelieder
	Piano Concerto
	Variations
Schubert	Symphony No 9
Shostakovitch	Concerto for Piano, Trumpet & Strings
	The Golden Age
	Symphonies 1-15
Sibelius	Karelia Suite
	Lemminkainen (Four Legends)
	Symphonies 1-7

Scriabin	The Poem of Ecstasy
	Prometheus
	Symphonies 1-3
Smetana	Ma Vlast (Symphonic Cycle)
Strauss, R.	An Alpine Symphony
	Also Sprach Zarathustra
	Le Bourgeois Gentilhomme
	Don Juan
	Don Quixote
	Ein Heldenleben
	Elektra (opera)
	Salome (opera)
	Sinfonia Domestica
	Till Eulenspiegel
Stravinsky	Agon
	Danses Concertantes
	The Fairy's Kiss
	The Firebird
	Fireworks
	Le Jeu de Cartes
	Octet
	Oedipus Rex
	Petroushka (1913 and 1948 versions)
	Pulcinella
	The Rake's Progress (opera)
	The Rite of Spring
	The Soldier's Tale
	The Song of the Nightingale
	Symphony in Three Movements
	Symphony in C
	Symphony of Psalms
	Suites 1 & 2
Tschaikovsky	Capriccio Italien
	Overture: 1812
	Francesca da Rimini
	Marche Slave
	The Nutcracker
	Romeo & Juliet
	The Sleeping Beauty
	Swan Lake
	Symphonies 1-6
Tippett	Byzantium
	A Child of Our Time
	King Priam (opera)
	Concerto for Orchestra
	The Mask of Time
	A Midsummer Marriage (opera)
	Symphonies 1-4
Vaughan Williams	Job
	Symphonies 1-9
	Overture: The Wasps

Verdi	Aida (opera)
	Falstaff (opera)
	Il Trovatore (opera)
	La Traviata (opera)
	Othello (opera)
	Requiem
	Rigoletto (opera)
Vivaldi	Gloria
Wagner	The Ring Cycle of Operas
	The Mastersingers (opera)
	The Flying Dutchman (opera)
	Lohengrin (opera)
	Parsifal (opera)
	Siegfried (opera)
	Tristan & Isolde (opera)
Walton	Belshazzar's Feast
	Crown Imperial March
	Facade
	Orb & Sceptre March
	Overture: Portsmouth Point
	Overture: Scapino
	Symphonies 1 & 2
Weber	Overture: Oberon

SELF-PUBLISHING

The self-publishing of compositions and arrangements by performers is a recent phenomenon made possible by new forms of technology. It is an activity which can be of great value, particularly to the freelance musician.

Who Needs This ?

A surprisingly large number of performers and teachers produce arrangements and compositions. Whether for their own use with professional brass groups or for teaching use in schools, a vast amount of high quality material exists for which there is a public. Once created, these bodies of work often lie unused for lack of specialist exploitation, but when publicised they can provide small but long-lasting annual incomes for their producers.

For Self-Publishing

The main points in favour of self-publishing for the performing musician are as follows:

1. Full ownership of all copyrights is retained.

2. Control of how they are exploited is retained.

3. The receipt of 100% of all income from music sales, recordings, radio, TV and all other forms of use is also retained. This is in contrast to percentages from commercial publishers varying from the norm of 10% for music sales, up to a standard 50% for broadcasts, TV, recordings etc. The basic sources of information on publishing are the Performing Rights Society, and the Mechanical Copyright Protection Society, both in London. They are important once a writer's work begins to be recorded and otherwise exploited.

Against Self-Publishing

The main point against self-publishing is the difficulty of effective marketing. Time, money, a development of specialised copyright knowledge and an ability to do business are all needed if the composer/arranger is to operate successfully as a self-publisher.

To Publish or Not to Publish

A performer who is also a talented composer/arranger must examine all the evidence before deciding whether to self-publish or not.

Take soundings from people in the field of publishing. These should include small business advisors, whose services are often provided free by the government. Enquire at government offices. For the musician who can create a business plan acceptable to business people, there may be government support available for a start-up enterprise.

The Background to a Decision

A high profile performer will create a demand for the material he or she uses. The star player may well be able to endorse the work of arrangers whose music he or she plays, and receive a royalty for doing just that.

For the writer the realistic options are as follows:

1. Do a deal with a top of the range publishing company and negotiate as high a percentage as possible.

2. Register the copyrights - see 'For Self-Publishing: 2' above - and do a percentage deal with a publisher for the exclusive retail rights. This latter option is likely to mean a lesser income from sales, but the writer retains all of the income from performances and recordings. If that strategy works well it will mean a continuing income for yourself, your family, and your heirs for up to seventy years after your death. It would mean that you would own a valuable catalogue of copyrights that will have an asset value should you wish to sell it later.

3. The final option is for the writer to set up the reproduction processes of his or her work, including advertising, promoting, distributing and selling the material. Unless the performer-writer can employ help for these operations, then his or her performing life will gradually be submerged in administration.

The low-profile performer, who may well be a fine composer/arranger, should not despair. My advice would be to build up a small, quality group of works which present you in a strong commercial light, secure informal recordings to underline their sales appeal, assign them to a publisher in the conventional way, and when your writing profile is strong enough, move at the appropriate moment to the second option outlined in the previous paragraph.

SECTION SIX

ATTITUDES, STRATEGY and TACTICS

INTRODUCTION

These chapters deal with the personal background against which playing and performing take place. In the widest sense everyone controls or is controlled by the subjects in this Section.

These chapters can be seen as dealing with life skills as applied to music performance.

AIMS and GOALS

Everyone has general aims in their life. Definite goals are more specific and need to be handled with care.

The Clear-Minded Musician

The player who has aims and goals clearly organised is easily able to chart progress, and make alterations when necessary. This player can focus on specific points of interest, or change the overall picture at will, a valuable position to be in, not only in music but in all aspects of living.

The Muddle-Headed Musician

This player has deliberately put off the matter of which direction and what career, and is just drifting with whatever happens. Fifty years ago, in a less organised world, this approach might have worked. Today this musician will remain at a very moderate level.

Aims and Careers

I refer to aims as general paths to be followed. As a young student I was absolutely set on becoming an orchestral player, come what may. I resisted all attempts to persuade me otherwise. That was my immovable aim.

Inside me was a certainty that, above all, a Principal Trumpet was what I wanted to be. This was my specific career goal. I was totally sure of it even though I admitted it to no-one. It shaped my attitude, work and ideas. The fact that I eventually followed my own teacher, George Eskdale, at several removes, into the position of Principal Trumpet in the London Symphony Orchestra was a fortunate end to that goal.

The Young Player

In the first instance almost all young players want to become professional players. If they have received the best quality advice they can begin to take either a realistic direction towards the profession, or away from it, according to what is appropriate. In my own teaching I constantly prompt the student to review his or her state of mind about their way forward, both as a musician and, if relevant, as a person.

The lucky student will have been taught by a first-class teacher, will have enjoyed high quality experience in a well supervised youth orchestra and will have picked up knowledge of what it is like to be a working musician.

The unlucky student will have had moderate-to-poor teaching and little experience of ensemble playing. His or her idea of the music profession will be totally unclear, but somehow it will seem desirable because it will allow them to do what they enjoy most: play the trumpet. Four years at music college, then straight into the music profession, so they've been told.

Both the lucky and unlucky students may be equally talented, but they will begin their college careers from two very different starting points. The lucky student will get away fast and will be likely to be up with the front-running students. Contact with good teaching, experience and know-how will have provided enough information for him or her to know the map of the musical world.

For example, would post-graduate study be beneficial, some occasional lessons with other teachers be useful, or a spell in another country both studying and playing be the way forward? Aims and goals must be fine tuned. (CR Careers)

The unlucky student will take time to re-adjust and catch up. Time will have been lost while the gaps in essential know-how are filled in. Some students can take two years to recover lost ground. For performers, the opportunity to study can never be replaced once it has been lost. Never again does society so actively help students to devote themselves to full-time learning.

More importantly, the student's biological clock has ticked on and the prime learning and development years for the musician's physical skills have gone.

Verbal Bullying among Students

Over the years many examples have come to my attention. When I uncovered the first one I could hardly believe it. It turned out to be true, and appears to be a regular factor in present day hothouse college conditions. It has little or no effect on the mentally stronger students, but on others it can be damaging.

In discussing his career with a particularly talented but under-achieving student, I was puzzled about his vagueness concerning his future. He had come to study with me three-quarters of the way through his time at college, so I was putting together my picture of him as quickly as possible.

After some time getting nowhere, I was reduced to the question of 'What do you actually want to be?' I was asking this in the light of his being capable of exceptionally brilliant playing. The best answer I got was to the effect that he didn't really know what he wanted to do. In the subsequent conversation I gradually found out that, yes, he wanted to be a professional player, but because there was so much verbal bitchiness among his peers, it seemed that not only was he hiding his musical aim from them, he was also hiding it from himself, with the subsequent poor playing and loss of direction. (CR Critics and Criticism)

As soon as we had identified the problem he realised the nonsense of his position. He is now a successful, consistent, and brave professional player, working upfront in an exposed musical situation with a strong personal character to his playing. He is fortunately still a mild person, but now has no inhibitions about moving upwards and onwards.

Conclusion

I have found this situation duplicated many times since then, and while most are naturally strong enough to deal with it, some fine players can be affected if they don't realise what is happening to them. I have found that revealing the problem to them almost always immediately cures it. The student's sense of direction then re-asserts itself.

ANXIETY CONTROL

For many players, the control of anxiety seems virtually impossible. As they see it, anxiety represents an impenetrable barrier to achieving full realisation of their talent. In most cases the use of straightforward routines will comfortably control anxiety.

Anticipation

Anticipation of a coming performance is experienced by everyone, whether the performance is musical, sporting, or of any other kind, private or public. It is a natural and desirable response in the sense that it alerts and sharpens our faculties. Anxiety, however, can be defined as anticipation which has got out of control.

For a musician not to feel some anticipation of a performance suggests a seriously negative attitude. It signals the need for the player to conduct a thorough re-evaluation of being a musician at all. A life spent without a sense of excitement is no platform from which to be a musician. Personal enjoyment, satisfaction and excitement in music are the necessary bases from which one communicates to others through performance.

The danger in regular, as opposed to occasional, high risk anticipation is that it can easily develop into a habit of anxiety, unless controlled by sensible attitudes and habits. Uncontrolled anticipation accelerates and tightens the breathing, which interferes with all human functions, not just playing. The most obvious symptom of this is that the breathing takes place high in the chest. This condition, which is called hyper-ventilation, is one of intense discomfort, and is accompanied by a sense of impending disaster and a complete lack of control.

Total Response

Effective control of anxiety means that the player's total response is working in a healthy manner. This total response exists when the various parallel strands of knowledge needed to play the instrument, and realise the music, are woven into a single strand of attention. The player has a sense of doing something simple and natural, not complex and awkward. The whole purpose of study and practice is to achieve this state in performing. Exactly the same is true particularly of sportspeople but equally of many others in occupations where high risk anticipation is a daily experience.

Common Misconceptions

When anxiety is an habitual problem for a player, it is futile to say that more effort, discipline and hard work are needed. While these attitudes are essential to building quality playing, **anxiety needs to be dissolved rather than confronted**. Habitual anxiety points to imbalances within the player's overall approach. Realism, mental balance, patience, persistence and awareness are the key attitudes.

Students and young players often ask themselves 'Have I got enough talent to fulfil my aims and goals?' This additional cause for anxiety also acts as a poison to the system. (CR Talent and Personality)

Types of anticipation

The commonest patterns of anticipation are as follows:

- Anticipation builds to a pre-performance high, subsiding a little as soon as playing starts. There remains an unreliable edge to the work, especially in the repetition of regularly practised skills, such as slurring or articulation.

- Anticipation builds to a pre-performance high, transforming into extreme anxiety, and perhaps panic. This state can remain throughout the whole performance. Typically the performer will feel good habits buckle, break and the whole structure of playing crumple in ruins.

- The performer will experience no significant pre-performance anxiety, but will suddenly, without reason, be hit by an explosion of panic during the performance, with shattering loss of control.

Anticipation builds to a pre-performance high, and then relaxes as soon as playing starts. This transformed and confident expectation gives a definite lift to the playing. This is the truly expert player with his or her total response operating with freedom and enjoyment

Short Term Controls of Anxiety

The most effective control for anxiety is good breathing. Breathing affects everything. It is the best measure of our inner state of mind, and it is the most immediate route by which we can influence that inner state.

Here are three exercises for daily use (1-3) and a general suggestion (4) to help with the control of anxiety, and the long term development of an effective total response. Do not expect these exercises to work if you adopt them as a last minute pick-me-up for a fast-approaching performance. On the other hand, everyday use of them will give you a reliable defence when anxiety threatens. Practical experience with students has shown that these skills maintain players' stability, and prevent the onset of anxiety without damping down the positive side of their anticipation.

Anxiety Control Exercises

Exercise 1. Wall breathing

- Posture: stand with your back to a wall. The head should also lean back against the wall. Shoulders should be moved as far back and down as possible and then relaxed. The bottom should be against the wall, but feet can be a couple of inches away.

- Exercise: relaxing the front of the torso, top to bottom, breathe slowly and deeply. For most people this action produces a definite sense of relief, a sense of well-being and the lifting of anxiety. In order for this free breathing to become constant, a one minute spell every hour will create the habit very quickly. I only have to think of doing it to feel the relief! (CR Posture, Breathing and Sound)

Exercise 2. Field of vision eye exercise

- Stare hard at the detail of an object two or three feet away. Note your breath pattern. After a few moments let your field of vision go peripheral, that is, with no focal point, passively aware of the whole circle of your sight. Note your breath pattern again. In the vast majority of cases the breath will be high in the chest or stopped altogether when the vision is focused and staring. This hyper-ventilation both causes, and is caused by, anxiety, and is an invaluable two way road into our inner mind. When vision is peripheral, our breathing appears to drop low down in our lungs, to a position of relaxation and comfort, for normal living as well as for playing. (CR Sound Quality) I also use this exercise as a prelude to resting, before a ten minute siesta, for example.

Exercise 3: Calming movement

- Stand with feet slightly apart, hands held in front of you at collarbone level, as if lightly holding a pair of reins, the fingers loose, the tips an inch apart. With vision unfocused, move the hands apart, extremely slowly and smoothly, at no more than half an inch every five seconds.

This will slow your body's system down, reducing tension and easing breathing. Use regularly, for no more than minute, perhaps during changes in practice. In the right circumstance it can send you to sleep.

Exercise 4: Personal Tempo

- On the day of a playing session or concert when there is a high degree of tension in your work, adopt a tempo for yourself which is a definite step slower than normal. Drive slowly, eat slowly, change slowly, warm up slowly, in fact, do everything more slowly. When you arrive at the moment of playing your total response will almost certainly be steady and unflustered. This is not an approach which I consciously invented; during my playing days, I simply noticed that this is what I did on those kind of occasions, with highly consistent results. Anticipation is made more enjoyable, and best of all, the performance can also be savoured and is not over in a frantic flash.

Breathing and Seeing

As a footnote to this paragraph, and a direct reference to the entry on posture, I would say that another symptom of anxiety is in the sense of physical discomfort, particularly in the neck, shoulders and upper body. This symptom is created during those thousands of hours of poor quality practice, when bad posture is complicated by bad habits of seeing, and by uncontrolled peering at music. (CR Reading /Practice).

One calculation suggests that a typical musician, from the start of musical activity to entry on a professional career, spends at least ten thousand hours in practice and performing experience. The potential for bad habits to become ingrained during this length of time is unlimited, aside from damage caused in the schoolroom and at home.

Control Your Body Tempo

It will be obvious that control of body tempo is at the root of all these exercises, through the way we breathe. While it would not be accurate to highlight vision at the expense of the other senses, it is the main route by which we take in information. The musician gives out sound, which is monitored mainly by another sense, hearing, but also by physical feeling. (CR Sound) This linkage between seeing, breathing, and feeling is total. Good habits in both breathing and seeing are essential. If one has those good habits it is easy to say 'What's the problem?' For someone with bad habits anxiety is a maze enveloped in fog.

N.B: Staring hard, with resultant breath tension, is the natural animal response to danger. It heightens our readiness to attack or defend as fast as possible, or to complete a task requiring intense attention (concentration), like threading a small needle. It is the normal response to an extreme situation. To be at that level of arousal permanently, which many people are, is the main source of anxiety and aggression.

Long Term Control of Anxiety

In the long term, *the most important control of anxiety is the player's acceptance of his or her own fallibility,* which is why so many successful players say 'Just play! Don't think about it!' Of course you can't play without 'thinking', but worrying is the wrong kind of thinking.

The process is simple. Do your best, think over what you did, extract any lessons you can, then forget it, throw it away, even to the point of imagining crumpling it up like a piece of paper and throwing it in the bin!

Start each day fresh, and while incorporating into your practice the lessons of yesterday, do it without guilt at having played badly, or undue satisfaction at having played well. Accept your errors, but don't resent them. They are as much part of you as your virtues. Even the master brass player makes mistakes, but knows how to hide them.

This process requires courage, because competition among musicians is quite pitiless. Only in sport and high-profile business are performers discarded more ruthlessly. Ill-conceived aims and ambitions tend to rush young players onward too fast, with negative results. There are also too many people who use young players to fill roles for which they are not yet mature enough. The process of development needs patience, persistence and realism.

The habit of drowning in angry self pity over the shame of not playing well is pure self-indulgence, from the same stable of behaviour as shyness. We cannot place orders for good performances. Accept yourself as you are. The comfort which that gives will ensure that your total response is balanced and increasingly reliable in the way it operates. Improvement will then come as quickly as is possible, though it may not be as fast as you wish. (CR Learning, Teaching)

Some players who have become chronically anxious give the impression of being reluctant to let their anxiety go, as if it was a friend they didn't want to leave. It is as if they would be totally naked and exposed without anxiety! This is a state of mind which can only go on for so long before resolution. It should be faced as soon as possible.

Drugs

Since the late nineteen seventies drugs such as beta-blockers have been available on prescription. These suppress the flow of adrenalin created by anticipation. The physical symptoms of extreme anxiety, such as sickness, diarrhoea, trembling and the scrambled mental process usually called panic are the result of an excess of adrenalin in the body. The well known 'fight or flight' response is buried very deep in the primal parts of the brain. The normal use of beta blockers is in the control of heart disease, although there are others, such as the control of glaucoma in the eyes.

The Use of Drugs under Supervision

It is routine to condemn the practice of using beta-blockers to ease performance anxiety. However, prescribed under medical supervision it would appear to be physically harmless, certainly in comparison to the amounts of alcohol, food, smoke and inactivity with which most people assault their bodies.

A Positive Case

One string instrumentalist of my acquaintance used beta-blockers to counteract a bow trembling symptom, until one day, half way through a concert, he realised that he had forgotten to take the drug. He had not been nervous, obviously expecting the drug defence to be in place. The result was that the player was permanently released from the trembling symptom, and gave up using beta-blockers. This is a good illustration of a player's total response being improved by the removal of uncontrolled anticipation, albeit in this case by an exterior factor i.e. the drug.

The Negative Case

I believe that there is a musically negative side to beta-blocker use. The performance of a drug-user will have an expressive flatness, which is the price that the player (and therefore the listener) pays for the player's sense of comfort. Additionally, the drug-user is fractionally slower to respond to errors or emergencies. Expert performers can often sense a rough moment about to happen. This sense is not there in a drug user. The error occurs but is followed by an almost lazy recovery. Alertness, edge and sensitivity are dulled, as a trade off with the feeling (if not the fact) of security. The comfort zone, as it is called, is a dull place to be.

AWARENESS, ATTENTION and CONCENTRATION

All performers must be aware of the whole musical space in which a performance is given, alert to everything, whether in a small ensemble or a full orchestra. Equally they must be able to pay attention to their own performance. To concentrate is the ability to apply intense attention.

The Meaning of Awareness

It is easy to be aware of what is happening around us while we are doing nothing ourselves, but while playing it is harder to keep the whole picture in view. Master musicians are constantly aware of what is going on everywhere around them even while they are playing.

Hearing and seeing are the senses through which musicians' awareness works. It is essential to pick up all information relevant to the performance as it happens. Lack of awareness is a main characteristic of moderate and poor players. They listen only to themselves and have no ability to listen to others at the same time.

'Fletcher's Radar'

John Fletcher, the uniquely gifted tuba soloist of the London Symphony Orchestra during the late sixties and seventies, called awareness his 'radar'. This radar guides the player in when and how to play, and picks up musical sensations from the whole orchestra. All the best musicians have it. They are the best because they have it. Yet it is incredibly easy to acquire; just think of it and you've got it!

The Meaning of Attention

Attention is the focus we put on to a subject of our own choice. In the case of the musician, the specific focus of attention is our personal performance.

The Meaning of Concentration

The most positive kind of attention is called concentration. However, if it becomes too intense, it blots out everything else. In order not to go too far with the effort of concentration, master performers are always careful to stay at about 80% to 90% during performance. This is the point at which the finest performances occur.

With 100% effort, performance quality tails off, as can be seen when sportspeople try too hard. Effort crushes skill. There is agreement about this in all types of human performance activity. Descriptions of peak performances are always described as having happened easily, in a flowing manner, almost without effort.

Awareness in Practice and Performance

All of our senses can be directed at precise targets. Focusing the sight upon a specific object is the easiest example to imagine. Our sense of hearing works in the same way. When a player practises alone, he or she tends to focus the senses inwardly on self-improvement. Playing in public can feel so different, strange and threatening because it is necessary for the performer to focus outwards for a once only effort.

Being in a much larger space than the practice room introduces sensations of strangeness and unease which everyone feels in new places among strangers. This fear, which is a natural animal response to unknown situations, accelerates our mind's responses as we sort out all the signals. (CR Practice, Visualisation)

The degree to which the player is aware constantly varies according to the musical demands of the score. This ability to remain sensitive to the changing picture of a performance is one major sign of a master performer. Without this kind of situation-intelligence it is impossible for the player to respond and link up with fellow performers.

The musical side of awareness is the ability to listen while playing, which is a vital element in musicianship. The very act of listening automatically triggers musical rapport.(CR Listening)

Problems with Awareness?

Why should someone who has chosen to be a musician have a problem with awareness? Why should awareness flag and attention wander? Lack of awareness suggests boredom and disinterest, which is a sure pointer to poor work. The player who regularly arrives late at rehearsals or lessons, yawning and unprepared, is certainly not going to make progress.

The indifferent musician who is bored during practice will suddenly become alarmed and anxious during a performance. The fact is that attention and awareness must be practiced every day. It is easy to be interested in new situations, which is when they are at their most exciting. The player with the professional attitude works well in all situations, not just the 'interesting' ones.

Interest and Method are the Keys

Awareness is always alive and present when someone is interested in what he or she is doing. The hungry animal stalking its prey is very aware. The prey is even more aware! The indifferent musician referred to in the previous paragraph is not aware that he or she is a prey! (Number one rule of survival: never be the weakest member of an ensemble. You will not last long. If you are the second weakest you may have a little time. Jungle rules apply!)

Awareness is the Heart of Professionalism

The student must cultivate professional awareness as the foundation to playing. The empty headed are bored, and it is the bored who are unaware. The key is to have a plan of work, rest and relaxation in good proportions, with constant variation. Enjoyment then flourishes. The cultivation of regular good habits, plus clear aims and goals, will make sure that attention and awareness are in full control. (CR Aims and Goals)

Awareness: the Musician's Best Friend

On many occasions, orchestras can and do perform brilliantly without significant guidance from the conductor. Leaving aside any roll-call of famous conductors who, over the years, have been rescued by orchestras from getting their just desserts when hopelessly lost, one story about the height of musical awareness concerns Otto Klemperer and the Philharmonia Orchestra, during that conductor's last years. He was certainly a great conductor, in spite of suffering crippling illness towards the end of his life. He managed to continue working, achieving some magnificent performances by sheer strength of will and personality.

At one particular recording session of a late Bruckner Symphony the slow movement was greeted by the producer as being wonderful beyond belief. In fact an extremely ill Klemperer had fallen asleep just after the start of the twenty minute movement. The orchestra completed the movement perfectly on their own, their awareness and musicianship needing only minimal visual contact between the leader, the principals and the rest of the orchestra.

CONSISTENCY

All players value consistency, but it cannot be pursued as an end in itself. It is the by-product of a mature network of skills.

What is Consistency?

We all search for consistency in our physical actions. A baby tries to walk, falls over, tries again and again, until it learns the actions reliably. We go through the same process time and time again, learning at amazing speed during very early childhood, steadily building up habits and skills.

Sportspeople and musicians use an advanced version of the same process in order to learn their special skills and build up capability. We refine specific actions until we can reproduce them every time, not identically, but within reasonable limits. For example, we practise slurring and articulations to be able to rely on them when required. We also practise skills of judgement, like listening when playing in ensemble, or in practising.

How is Consistency Achieved?

Combining these actions into a secure network ensures consistency. If any major part of the network is unreliable, for example articulation, then playing involving that element will obviously be unsatisfactory and may well affect other parts. In short, consistency will be absent.

Reliable physical skills are created by the habits of good methodical practise, sensibly conceived, and executed regularly. These habits lead to the creation of master-level skills in the areas of articulation, range, slurring, and sound. Players must equip themselves with these playing skills in order to realise their musical ideas on their instrument. What is very curious is the great number of players who practise as if they **want** to become inconsistent, using completely unmanaged, random practice routines. (CR Practice)

The key to consistency is the patient and intelligent build-up of good habits over a period of time. These twin concepts of good habits and patience are the foundation for all reliable work.

Personal Maturity

The young person today often finds it difficult to accept the idea that humans mature gradually, both physically and mentally. We proceed at nature's pace and not by our demand. For most players elements, such as high range and stamina develop, naturally as the body matures. They can be encouraged but not hurried. The process can be helped, but not rushed.

The foundation of personal maturity also must be encouraged, especially in developing patience. The foundations for this critical quality of patience must be laid down in early childhood by disciplined work. The fact that disciplined work and study in music are now seen as painful and unnecessary by many educationalists is tragically misguided; no practical musician thinks that way. Its absence almost always leads to a waste of talent later.

Personal maturity enables the student to organise sensible practice routines and develop realistic aims. The talented young performer whose immature approach to practice, and whose self-indulgent leisure activities interfere with quality work, will find progress slow. At worst it may stop completely.

Talent must be cultivated constantly or it decays. It will not wait indefinitely to be exploited. If a student's normal behaviour includes many alcoholic late nights, then progress will be delayed. In this situation, the player must realise that he or she cannot have it all ways. Mature attitudes and skills will not flourish in certain soils. Both are needed before consistency will appear.

Experience

Consistency also comes through experience.

- Experience teaches what to do and what not to do in certain situations.

- Experience warns against dangerous music-traffic situations, by recognising the signs that lead to them.

- Experience teaches that on days when you don't feel so good, a thoroughgoing pretence of feeling confident and positive is as good as the real thing. (It *is* the same thing!)

The Nature of Consistency

It should be clear that consistency cannot be a goal in itself. It is there when the basics are right. It is dependant on our primary physical actions for its existence and level of effectiveness. As I mentioned earlier, a universally common skill such as walking is learned by a process consisting of hundreds of trials and errors. This in itself is a process of strengthening and maturing.

The vast majority of us walk without having to go through a daily re-learning process. Or do we? It is not in the least a simple activity. It involves the whole body musculature, all the joints and an overall command system that is far too complex to programme. For most people a few days' illness in bed means slightly insecure walking. After several weeks we struggle. The muscles have weakened and are in disarray until exercise revives them and their co-ordinations. Playing is a much more specialised activity, but the principle of consistency through repetitive action is the same.

The Search for Consistency

The search for consistency therefore lies, not in the hunt for a formula, not in the magic mouthpiece, or in that total trumpet with three lead pipes and a gold bell, but in unhurried progress towards the imagined goal of your playing. If you adopt sensible attitudes and routines, consistency will become your reliable friend.

LOSS OF FORM

Almost all players are subject to temporary loss of form and the occasional problem. The solution usually lies in a quick check of the basics of playing.

Two Warnings

1. Most players instantly blame their embouchure for any loss of form, when other factors almost always cause the difficulty. The reason why players find it easy to blame the embouchure is that it is very visible, sensitive, and the critical contact point with the body. Apart from the fingers, it is the only principal part of the playing system which can be seen. (CR Embouchure)

2. The fact that master players can be ready to play after a few brief moments of warm-up must not be misunderstood. They are not being casual or slipshod. They do what they need and no more. The master player is so efficient, that a few seconds is all that is needed to assess the day's set-up. The majority of the finest players do an orthodox warm-up. In the parallel situation, some athletes vary the amount of warming-up they do, but most stay with a set routine. (CR Practice, the section on warming-up)

The Order of Checking

Players whose form is variable are prone to be undisciplined with their warming-up routine. The very first casualty of inadequate warming-up is the quality of breathing and consequently sound quality. It is quite normal to wake up and think that the basics can be skipped 'just this once', but more than once and the thread starts go.

The player who listens to the sound finds there a mirror image of the state of his or her breathing. As soon as the sound begins to lose its best quality it means that something has changed in the breathing process to cause the deterioration.

• Do pre-warm-up breathing work in conjunction with a check on basic posture, first of all without the instrument, and then with it. Over-tiredness or over-anxiety lead to tension and heaviness. The inevitable result of these will be undue mouthpiece pressure on the lips. Occasionally, because of stiffness or tiredness, the arms will lean the trumpet on the lips, and/or at slightly the wrong angle.

- The top to bottom lip angle changes slightly all the time in response to changes in range. Therefore sensitivity to instrument angle is important. If posture is stiff for any reason, the trumpet may be gripped in such a way as to prevent these fine adjustments happening naturally. (CR Fingering, Posture and Anxiety Control)

- Next, work on mid-range long notes, aiming at fullness of sound. This is an absolute priority, because it puts the spotlight back where it belongs: on the sound. When sound (and breathing) deteriorate, it is often the player's attention which has wandered onto other playing matters, such as loud volume, stamina, technique and range.

- The player who experiences serious long term problems should take early advice from the best source available. I have known many fine players who, as professionals, have continued to take the occasional lesson. Even if the advice produces no immediate gain, the contact and discussion give a new view of the problem. Developing other perspectives often produces solutions, albeit gradually. Long term problems generally build up slowly because of mistaken directions taken earlier. Dissolving these problems means a change of direction followed by an equally gradual return to form.

Experience of Problems

The cause of a loss of form will become evident during the process of checking out the system. It is then easy to forget problem patches when everything has returned to normal and is going well. The sensible player files it in the memory for future reference, building up experience of dealing with problems quickly. By the time a student's days are over, he or she should have collected sufficient know-how to provide fast solutions. The wise professional develops this know-how into an early warning awareness which largely avoids the onset of problems.

Every player has periods of concern, even though they may not be audible to anyone else. One element of a good professional is the player who solves problems before anyone else notices. It is my experience that the large majority of occurrences of loss of form can be solved within a few hours by the application of these simple reviews.

PROFESSIONALISM

Professionalism is the combination of qualities both musical and personal which enables the player to deliver a proficient service. The expert professional can instantly call up the skills necessary for whatever task is in hand and focus on it without interference.

The Qualities of Professionalism

In order to be called 'professional' it is not enough to be just a fine player. Good professionals develop a comprehensive knowledge of the many different situations in which they may find themselves, and base their behaviour on the good models they see around them.

The good professional solves a problem before anyone else notices that there is one. This creates a sense in other people that he or she has no problems, which is an enviable reputation to have. The ability to pick up the early danger signs which lead to a loss of form is also a vital skill. (CR Loss of Form)

The Purpose of Professionalism

Professionalism underlines the musical quality of a player, and smoothes working relationships with other musicians. It ensures that not only will the player be well respected, but also that he or she will gain musical opportunities when personal reliability is added to good playing. Contrary to former years there is now very strong competition among musicians for playing positions, whether in orchestras or freelance. The inefficient, difficult or badly behaved player is increasingly excluded and redundant.

The Professional and His or Her Peers

The first relationships which young players build are with teachers and peers. Later, as they develop, they make contact with fully professional players, and further on, acquaintance with master performers. Working in a small profession where the same faces come round again and again means that people's characters and personalities become well known. This opens or shuts doors to opportunities according to how they are perceived by others.

The leading professional in each group will accept someone who adds quality to the section, but will instantly discard a player, however promising, who lacks professionalism. One player's lack of professionalism reflects badly on the whole section. Lateness for engagements, or any other behaviour which attracts undue negative attention, whether in rehearsal, concert or backstage will immediately be noted. The need for a group to be a united team is paramount. (CR Careers)

A very strong bond develops between good professionals who work well together. This bond guarantees a helping hand when it is needed. Everyone will need that hand at some point in their career. A player who has been unsympathetic or antagonistic to his or her peers or juniors will not be helped out in his or her own moment of crisis.

The Professional and Employers

The second type of relationship is with employers, both permanent and occasional. The lines here are more formal and obvious. The finest players have a negotiating position with regard to terms and conditions, but even they will have only a few occasions when they can use their standing to gain an advantage. Remember that the best situation you will ever have in a negotiation is just before the contract is signed. After that point, unless you are very special, all contracts and agreements tend to deteriorate!

The Professional and Conductors

Professionalism in relation to conductors and directors of music will always be on the agenda, whether for the orchestral and ensemble player, or the soloist. Most player/conductor relationships contain a hint of conflict, because of the very nature of the roles being filled. The best professional handles this element positively, genuinely seeking to give a service that will be appreciated, but knowing also how to repel erratic and ignorant behaviour from the podium. (CR Conductors)

The Professional's Musicianship

The well trained student will have been taken through all aspects of musical history which apply to their special fields of interest. For professional players whose academic education has been inadequate, an alertness to what is appropriate will see them through most stylistic situations. My own musical education was wholly inadequate in regard to specific preparation for orchestral playing, but a keen appetite to pick up anything that was relevant saw me through my early days at the professional level.

Even the wide variations of style between different periods of music and composers reveal themselves by attention to common-sense factors. This is quite apart from that which can be heard, and how the music looks on the page. Musical awareness and determination are all that is necessary in order to match the challenges of the job. (CR Musicianship)

PROGRESS

Progress comes in fits and starts. We would like it to happen tidily to order, but it doesn't. The student must view progress, or sometimes the lack of it, in a detached calm manner.

The Nature of Progress

We check our progress against our hopes and against what has happened to us previously. Then we try to work out why progress has occurred, and whether it is as a result of planned practice or not.

Progress is made in two ways. The first, planned route runs via sensible steady work, without haste or anxiety. The second, chance route includes any factor which we do not clearly understand. Just getting older is a major method of improvement! That is clearly not subject to understanding or control; a young person achieves physical maturity when nature says so and not before. Added to that are the many influences of a person's background.

The Plateau Effect

My experience is that progress occurs in jumps from one level to the next, and not in a steady upwards line. It is best to look back over a lengthy period of time when progress can be seen more clearly. A player can often be depressed by remaining on a plateau for too long with no appreciable progress. Be patient and vary the practice work. (CR Practice)

With my own students I emphasise the value of Routine 1 in the chapter Practice 2. When used thoroughly it purifies the playing and sets it up for further improvement. It seems strange to call it a cleansing effect, but the improvement is of course to the listening ability, which then feeds directly into the playing.

Realistic Expectation is the Key

Expectation creates the environment in which a player works. It is always an error for a player to demand progress from himself or herself, especially in specific areas of technique. The result of specific targets being adopted is that it creates undue pressure and expectation, exactly the attitude which prevents progress. (CR Aims and Goals)

Failure to Make Progress in Specific Areas

When a player decides to highlight a certain part of his or her playing in order to improve it - for example, tonguing or high range - it usually means that he or she will devote a great deal of extra time and attention to that area. What normally follows is two or three weeks of intense work - binge practising - on this one element. The inevitable result is that in spite of all these efforts the player's work deteriorates, with depression following on close behind. After this experience a player will often conclude that 'practice is bad for you!' The conclusion of course should be that *bad* practice is bad for you.

Success in Making Progress in Specific Areas

How far and fast a player may want to progress is irrelevant to what is possible. A patient practice plan supported by consistent work will eventually achieve the ends required.

Reference to the chapter on Practice is essential. When looking at one area of playing, the player first must see the problem clearly. Different parts of any player's technical capability will be in variable order and must be assessed separately. Analyse in order to isolate the relevant points from the irrelevant. Then devise a practice plan for solving (or rather dissolving) the problem.

Very short but frequent practice periods interspersed into the player's normal work is the best method for achieving progress. For example, if working on speed of single tonguing, ten periods of one minute will be very valuable, whereas one period of ten minutes will not. (CR Practice)

The reasoning behind this procedure is threefold.

1. The player avoids excess highlighting of one particular area of playing.

2. The wholeness of the person's playing is not being disturbed; every player has a general picture of their own capability on which they can rely. Any undue emphasis on one part of the whole will cause an imbalance in other places in the playing system. I have known players permanently damage parts of their playing by obsessive focusing on one element. 'Little and often' is the rule.

3. The brain is given time and space to absorb the extra attention being applied to one particular subject. Different brains work at different speeds. If that factor is ignored, the brain will gradually seize up and provide you with poor thinking and poor results. (CR Learning)

Progress in Pieces of Music

As noted above with regard to technical problems, when learning a difficult piece of music, work hard on it for a period, then put it away completely for several weeks or months. Know when to stop and have the confidence to do it. Giving a piece a rest allows the brain a chance to absorb and sort out what it is learning *in its own time and way*, without interference from the conscious mind. Taking the pressure off for a brief spell allows the mind to freshen up and come alive again. When the piece is next taken out it will have matured in the mind by itself and be ready for more work. It is the rest period which allows the mind to absorb problems, to get on without nannying, worried interference.

Judging Progress

Keeping a check on progress is best done by looking backwards over a substantial period of time. It is a mistake to make comparisons day-by-day, because form varies slightly all the time, and is therefore difficult to judge. A player should work for a month or more before making a considered comparison with the point from which he or she started. This will give a clear impression of the progress made. Inevitably a sense of achievement will follow, together with a feeling that control actually can be exercised, if applied in the right way.

VISUALISATION

Visualising a playing situation is very valuable preparation for every kind of performance, especially those in public. Performance, being very different to practice and rehearsal, must be mastered as a skill separate to playing.

What is Visualisation?

Visualisation is seeing in your mind: a visual-mental rehearsal. In sports science it has long been established that the regular practice of visualisation is invaluable as part of techniques for the realisation of potential.

All serious athletes use visualisation routines, thinking through skills and situations to make them automatic and familiar. Research has shown that intense visualisation as a learning process is only fractionally (approximately 1 in 30) less efficient than actually doing the thing itself. (CR Auralisation)

The Practice of Visualisation

Once the player feels comfortable with an orchestra, an ensemble, or a hall, then performing becomes easier. Visualisation mimics this experience in advance, helping to take the strangeness out of it. Are there any other ways to avoid insecurity, so as to be able to perform at the top level, whatever the situation?

The regular experience of playing in a particular place, or ensemble, gradually makes the experience more familiar and therefore more comfortable. It is a natural animal response for anyone to feel uncertain in new situations. For example, walk into a room containing total strangers, noting your response.

The clues by which we orientate ourselves have to be collected and weighed up. The mind goes into a superfast assessment of the situation: the place, the people, the atmosphere. All have to be taken in and synthesised into a single picture. A sense of insecurity is perfectly natural. Advance visualisations of situations help to make them 'ordinary'.

In my teaching I use visualisation in the following ways:

1. Imagine as exactly as possible the hall in which you are to play. Look out from the platform into the hall from your playing position, whether standing or sitting. Visualise the audience. Include as much detail as possible. Imagine playing into the space, and holding the audience's attention with your eyes and your presence.

2. Feel the ambience of the place, the atmosphere and the acoustic, so that the sense of it is as realistic as possible. The more completely and often the experience is thought through, the more comfortable and normal it will seem.

3. For a solo performance, I outline preparation for different situations. This includes a complete visualisation of every move to be made in a diploma recital, for example. (CR Performance)

4. In orchestral or ensemble rehearsal, visualise and sense the feelings of excitement which a performance brings, so their effect becomes commonplace. Practise being nervous and the controls which you use to combat it. (CR Anxiety)

These methods normalise the player's response to the unknown. Expert performers never lose the heightened anticipation which precedes a concert, but they learn to harness it. (CR Performance/Anxiety)

The Value of Visualisation

We all anticipate. Anticipation of an event, person or situation to be experienced, is common to all people. This expectancy, an assessment in advance of the reality, may be pleasurable or fearful according to our preconception of what is going to happen. As we can all also visualise, the practising of visualisation harnesses this faculty of anticipation in such a way as to use it beneficially.

Visualisation and auralisation are simply the practice of forms of thinking. All thinking processes can be experienced as random (uncontrolled) sensation, or organised (controlled) sensation. Both have their appropriate places.

The Experienced Player

The experienced performer has gone through thousands of professional situations and can match any approaching ones with something from the past. Any up-coming engagement can be matched with a previous one. The player automatically sees it ahead and knows how to respond.

Whether playing a solo recital in a small room, leading a brass section at a symphony concert, giving a masterclass, or recording a concerto, the master performer will have seen something like it before. Repeated visualisation can supply this 'experience' factor to those whose actual experience is limited.

The Inexperienced Player

For the young performer, everything is novel and full of unknowns. At best, this player, with a thorough knowledge of repertoire and a strong confidence and capability, will cope with all eventualities. This is the way in which many new talents make their mark, taking unexpected opportunities with relish. Their thought processes work smoothly and effectively, while the calmness and confidence of their practice preparation and technical skills hold up under stress, allowing them to enjoy the occasion.

In past years it was easier for top talents to come through early. The lack of systematic college training, particularly lack of knowledge of the orchestral repertoire, allowed the more naturally gifted players to shine. The middle ground was not so crowded with well-trained young professionals as it is now. The challenge created the response. Thrown in at the deep end, you sank or swam.

Today each player must take every advantage possible, in order to gain that extra percentage point which may take them clear of the pack, and which may earn that contract. The practice of visualisation is one of several techniques which may just help to do it.

SECTION SEVEN

RECAPITULATION

INTRODUCTION

This section presents a unified view of music performance, practice and teaching, as I see them. How they fit together in a coherent overall picture has long been a concern to me.

In this I have been helped by many personalities who have made indelible impressions on me during a long life inside and outside music. These have been people from a very wide range of backgrounds.

Luckiest of all have been my meetings in my youth with musicians, who were not only encouraging, but who were able to teach me some of the harder lessons which we all must learn if we are to be of any real use to our fellows.

My Approach

I have based my overall approach firstly on my judgement of what the finest players do when they play, from observing them at work over forty years, as a professional player, conductor and teacher. Secondly I have tried to look afresh at how students best absorb guidance and help.

Most players develop in a stop-go manner, coming to a halt when confused, and having to rediscover afresh a simplicity of approach in order to proceed. The end result is a confused journey through the study years. A fortunate few never lose this initial simplicity of approach to playing. They seem to develop from their beginning to their achievement of mastery without any serious hold-ups. At the other extreme there are some who remain permanently confused, and who never achieve their potential.

I have concentrated on achieving consistency across the broad range of the subject. I have followed many interests outside music which seem to me to be relevant, in order to compare and match up my musical ideas relative to those operating in other fields. In addition, it is my view that a knowledge of the craft of teaching is essential as a quite separate skill from the actual subject being taught. It needs to be consciously developed, after which it can be used across a range of related activities.

We play music. We play instruments. The word 'play' is not an accident, but reflects the character of musical activity. Within the general theme of play, sports and games share a great deal of territory with the arts. In spite of the obvious differences there are so many things in all these fields which match music performance in a way which I have always found fruitful. The sense of play is a basic factor in the way we function; the various manifestations of playfulness and the sets of rules we devise to control it are superficial differences. I have found it very valuable to make use of parallels outside the arts because of the vague and self-indulgent nonsense which surrounds so much artistic activity. In comparison, sports are models of precision. Performance in music, while not about winning, losing or the scoring of points or goals, takes place within limited time-spans, and thrives on comparisons.

No musician reaches mastery without the sense of play being constantly present in his or her performance; the improvised and the unexpected are valued in all fields as the bringers of revelation. Similarly in sport, for full satisfaction the sense of play must be at the front of the picture. Without the play element I see sport as containing little value. It reduces the participants and onlookers to crude tribalism, the debased practice of winning-at-all-costs, and a meaningless triumphalism.

Play is a process in which the players trust themselves to produce new solutions to new situations out of nothing, out of the unconscious mind. The performer of value respects good play wherever it is found, in music as well as sport. If performance is not play, it is nothing. (The unconscious areas of the mind are not directly open to our attention, but are thought to be much the largest part of the brain.)

Words and their slippery meanings always present a problem for the writer. We all have our own personal and unique meaning for any one word or phrase, so it is not surprising that a sentence rarely means exactly the same thing to two people. In this book, as in my teaching, I have tried to maintain consistency in the use of key words, such as rhythm, time, attention, awareness and so on. While my overall choice of words is intended not to get in the way, they regularly require the reader to attend carefully, and, occasionally, concentrate hard. My aim is to help players find their own talent. It may be that only one page out of the whole book helps to do it, and that the others are redundant, but if that one page opens the door, that is enough.

In every area of skill performance there are the master performers. There are also good performers who are not quite masters. And so on to the lower levels. The question is: what makes the difference in final achievement between two student players who start with similar potential and talent?

Any person undertaking a physical action such as playing has to string together a series of thoughts to make it happen. Repetition and experience give us the capability to do this faster and faster till the thought and the action appear to be the same thing, and the thought 'disappears'. Most people do not regard this process as thinking, but it surely is. Sequences of thoughts (algorithms) which are efficient and well put together will give actions which can be repeated time and time again, efficiently and reliably. The opposite is also true, which is where the difference lies in producing reliable or unreliable actions. These algorithms are unceasingly built up during childhood for use in daily living. When a special activity is undertaken which has not been developed by evolution, such as playing a brass instrument or driving a car, algorithms must be learned which deliver those skills. As the responses and skills of the racing driver are at a higher level than the normal motorist, so is the performance of the master player compared to the enthusiastic amateur.

Therefore the difference in final achievement between the two students will be controlled by the quality of their thinking, conscious and/or unconscious. On the one hand intelligence, aided by patience and boldness, is the general prescription for the realisation of talent. On the other, musicality and a healthy physique must be exploited by good teaching and experience. The two students may both become master players by different routes!

Watching and listening to a master brass player, as with any other elite performer, is to observe someone using a very complex range of skills and knowledge, which flow along in an apparently single stream of effort. That somewhat contradictory impression is correct.

> 'To the eye the actions of a skilled athlete seem simple and effortless, embodying such characteristics as co-ordination, control and efficiency. In contrast, the actions of many novices in sport may be described as 'skeletomuscular anarchy'. Learners appear to have inadequate time to carry out actions and are, seemingly, burdened with too many awkward body parts, which tend to impede rather than aid performance.'

This quotation from an article in the Journal of Sports Sciences (Keith Davids, Craig Handford and Mark Williams, 1994, 12, 495-528) runs completely in line with comparisons from musical performance. Good playing looks simple because it is simple. Good players do the essentials and no more because the learning process has stripped away the unnecessary. If it is unnecessary it gets in the way and is a burden to carry.

The control which successful performers exert is not a clever conscious control, but the whole mind, the conscious and the unconscious, working together to organise the body's stream of action as a whole. The working complexity of our mind as it activates us is totally beyond conscious knowing, whether in a normal action like walking for which natural selection has (partially) prepared us, or an uncommon one like playing a trumpet, for which natural selection has definitely not prepared us! Our systems handle an inconceivable quantity of biological traffic. Master performers in all spheres of action are those who are sensitive to variations in the demands of their action environment, and can meet those demands, however diverse, by varying their responses. Most players play well on occasion; the good ones do it all the time.

As I outline in the section on Awareness, Attention and Concentration, I define awareness as unfocused alertness to the whole field of an activity. Events happening at the same time are received equally, without special focus on one thing rather than another. Attention, however, focuses on a single area of interest or action and follows it consciously. Concentration is the most intense kind of attention. If over-intense it is very likely to block out other information being made available by awareness. In everyday parlance, trying too hard unbalances us and blinkers us to the big picture. The master performer holds these three states in balance, ready and able to move between them and to zoom in and out as needs dictate.

Reference to the sections on Breathing and Anxiety Control will reveal the effect that sight has over breathing, and also how sight functions. It follows on that I emphasise the value of playing from memory, because, apart from other values it may have, it allows the eyes to be freed from the anxious highly focused reading of music under performance stress. With practice, the eyes and the mind can be released from the working memory state of reading 'known' music, into an entirely superior state where the music to be played has been totally absorbed and is ready for performance. To achieve this state requires patience and persistence to learn, and boldness to take the chance. Once achieved, an extraordinary sense of freedom and confidence ensues. Making the transition happens quickly for some, while for others it is a long dark tunnel.

We all suffer divided attention at various times. As soon as attention is divided between different points of interest, its method is to zigzag frantically between them. Attention is like vision and hearing, it moves in fast, mostly short, jumps. (CR Reading Music) Any sense of wholeness in a 'picture' is arrived at by the mind synthesising these separate flashes of information. If divided too much, the attention rapidly becomes inefficient as competing points of interest multiply. Hence 'scatterbrain'. This state is usually the precursor of panic. (CR Anxiety Control)

In music performance, the faculty which balances, blends and manages all the musician's parallel functions into a single strand of performance is the playful imagination. This imagination is situated in the deepest area of our responses, the emotions. Its materials are the elements of music, pitch deployed in time. Sports take place in time also, and seem to be concerned with the achievement of set objectives and the manipulation of space. As in music, the numbers of people involved can vary from singles to very large numbers.

Imagination operates at its best through an open awareness, judgement through attention and a limited amount of taking care. In both sport and music performance, peak performances are almost always spoken of as just happening, flowing smoothly, and without any struggle. They occur in music when attention and awareness are in harmony. In sport the exercise of judgement and imagination is also the key control. The ability to move effortlessly between focused and unfocused action is the hallmark of a master performer. The musical imagination uses and manipulates this ability.

In the section on Vocalisation I make the point that, when asked, the majority of trumpet students sing or vocalise music better than they play it. This is because the instrument is absent and is no longer the barrier, the enemy. The student's imagination can roam freely without hindrance. The pleasure is without the potential pain. Imagination is generally agreed to be a faculty beyond reasoning, logic, or control. It utilises everything in our minds, most of which we can never know, and should be encouraged to run wild if only to see what it brings back. An individual's sense of fantasy must be exercised in order to become powerful; the more it is, the finer the playing.

The section on Anxiety Control is derived from practical personal observation and experience. In it I have condensed my observations into 'read-and-do' suggestions. These suggestions act with no conscious thought being necessary. While some have only limited usefulness if the player is already seriously anxious, they are not primarily for fire-fighting an already raging problem. Their value is revealed when a player has recognised the need to set new habits (thought sequences), and then incorporates them together with the routines set out in the section on Practice. Thus new habits can be developed to replace the old.

Learning and Teaching

My practical experience has been derived from two sources: first, noticing what I do naturally myself, to produce a state of mind which allows me to perform to my highest ability in any circumstance. Second, noticing other performers, from master players to students, in their successful and unsuccessful strategies, in rehearsal, performance and teaching situations.

Everyone 'thinks', without interruption, from birth to death, across the whole landscape of their consciousness and unconsciousness. Everything we see or know is inside the mind and not outside it. The types and quality of the thinking that we do in different circumstances ultimately determine our successes and failures. We can exercise the conscious mind to improve its function and scope, but we can only influence the unconscious mind in roundabout ways. We can influence but not control.

We learn in a number of ways (1) by personal study and practice, (2) by competitive experience, such as in an audition (3) by non-competitive experience in a supervised forum, such as an orchestra, and (4) by being taught, one-to-one,

This last process (4) is a formal one and follows an understood pattern.

- Firstly, the student performs.

- Secondly, the teacher mentally reviews one of several responses which will influence the student's performance to improve. This review will judge the student's ability (a) to accept verbal stimulus, whether as image or information, or (b) to benefit from copying an example of performance, or (c) if he or she will be best served by a course of practice routines. The active teacher makes these reviews hundreds of thousands of times over many years, until, in the finest teachers, the response reaches the level of instantaneous and effective reaction.

- Thirdly, the teacher delivers the chosen response.

The act of teaching operates most responsibly if students learn to teach themselves as soon as possible. In the Section on Teaching, I detail my personal approach, and my wish to develop a player's own natural self-organisation.

Boldness creates sureness and flexibility of response from the player, which most people call technique, as if it were a fixed quantity. I prefer to call it capability.

My first move is always to find the musical result being sought by the player, the sound and the feeling. When the student's mind is fully on the expression of the music, the result will be positive and progress results. The strength of the musical image blends the player's actions into co-operation. Technical talk should be kept to a minimum, and used to support, but not to confuse. It is better for the teacher to be silent than to risk confusion.

My emphasis on feeling and boldness means that the short term result of the student's work may not be polished or finished in the sense of being a complete, tidy and rounded object. I am more concerned with the student's final development and destination in several years' time. There is often a conflict between the needs of an immediate priority performance and the direction to be taken towards a distant aim or goal. Almost always I favour the latter.

Practice routines such as flexibilities or scales are abstracts of musical situations. There is a very important place for these in the practice room. These routines not only present nearly all the patterns commonly found in music, but also act as a form of circuit training, developing thinking and support skills well beyond what is likely to be demanded in the concert hall. Skill to spare always shows up as poise. These patterning routines create habits which the student hopes will withstand the most severe examination with poise.

In the section on those most traditional of all patterning exercises, scales and arpeggios, I suggest ways of varying them in order to promote problem solving ability on-the-hoof. The ability to deliver patterns under flexible performance circumstances is a key skill, as no music performance is ever the same twice. Flexible response is only possible on the back of secure patterning. In the Section on scales and arpeggios I show variations which will severely test the quickest mind and add to its flexible response. Other aspects of performance practice are outlined elsewhere.

Most players at some time have to face problem patches, usually the malfunction of one of the primary areas of playing. A methodical check of the basics of breathing is the first option, with undue mouthpiece pressure on the lips the likely cause. (CR Breathing)

The musical image can be released most effectively by vocalisation and gesture. (CR Vocalisation) Vocalisation taps into the deepest and most natural response to expression. I restate many times that the musical image constrains and co-ordinates the body's efforts to play. I use the word constraint in the sense that a seed is constrained by soil, moisture, temperature and competition from other plants. The seed's success or failure depends on its response to these constraints.

I mention the concept of 'constraint' again, because it is the guiding principle behind all of the exercises I have devised over the years to improve the technical efficiency of student players. These exercises, routines and loops have threefold aims:

1. To improve the physical basics, such as articulation.

2. To solve immediate problems in specific pieces of music.

3. To develop understanding by the internal activities of auralisation, visualisation and memorisation. In short, the exercises and algorithms (exercises that work in a set sequence) that I have devised focus the concentration so as to ensure as far as possible that the player plays correctly, both physically and musically. In a related field I have developed similar exercises and algorithms in what is now my principal performing work as a conductor.

In one sense all types of learning are constrained by the stage on which they are set.

1. Unsupervised, or loosely supervised, experience has a low value to students. They pick up chance hints from a situation which has only a small interest in them as individuals. Random orchestral engagements come into this category.

2. Supervised experience, such as lessons, masterclasses, and conducted performance, has value according to the quality of the supervision.

3. Generalised study and composed material, such as studies, scales and arpeggios, concert repertoire, and orchestral excerpts, can be used to match actual against required performance.

4. Exercises, and algorithms designed to constrain the player into functioning well just by playing them, as previously described, are relatively rare, but of enormous value in self-teaching.

5. Direct competition offers a very sharp education. The audition is the standard illustration of this kind of situation. (CR Auditions) The expectation of winning or losing is an excellent, if harsh, stimulus.

Coda

My approach to practising, learning and teaching is based on what I perceive to be required to achieve performance of the finest quality. The balance, flexibility and different forms of intelligence needed to enable musicians to move around in their mental landscapes will always be one of the major whole-person challenges. In performance, both conceptual and manual skills are exercised, in isolation and in harness together. Research has shown that to achieve this linkage, many diverse areas of the brain must co-operate to create the necessary connections required by successful musical activity.

Today and in the foreseeable future, music is and will be the foremost of the arts, present everywhere in a profusion of forms. The universal appetite for musical sound is generally unexploited by educators as a tool for general mental development. Music as novelty is the strategy being increasingly followed by school educators, with no effort being made to create the ear-eye connections so essential for musical competence and creativity. Music is used largely as a temporary (and therefore time-wasting) stimulus. As I have written earlier, the eye must learn to hear and the ear must learn to see. The eyes of the majority future generations of performers may well be deaf and their ears blind.

The arts and educational establishments (at school level) now show little interest in, or recognition of, the civilising values of formally taught music. The inevitable assumption must be that, in the main, they do not understand either education or the arts, but merely indulge in them, or follow careers in them. They have been signally unable to present a coherent case for the arts in general and music in particular, and have depended on merely asserting that the arts are 'a good thing,' without offering a credible justification, expecting to be believed without further ado. Very few, if any, of those who are not already convinced of the overwhelming value of the arts, have been persuaded.

My view is that formal musical education should, for at least a period, be a part of every child's education, as important as number, language and physical activity. Research into the workings of the brain shows that the connections which music learning makes in the mind are uniquely wide-ranging. When adequately taught by the traditional methods of linking the ear to the eye to the body, music fosters general intelligence to a unique degree. The continual creation of neural circuitry in the brain which the practice of music requires, is the development process of intelligence at its most efficient. What makes this process so educationally effective is our shared common feeling for musical sound, in spite of its many different forms. The vocabulary of music touches more people more effectively than any vocabulary of words.